ETERNAL AND TRANSIENT ELEMENTS IN HUMAN LIFE

The Cosmic Past of Humanity and the Mystery of Evil

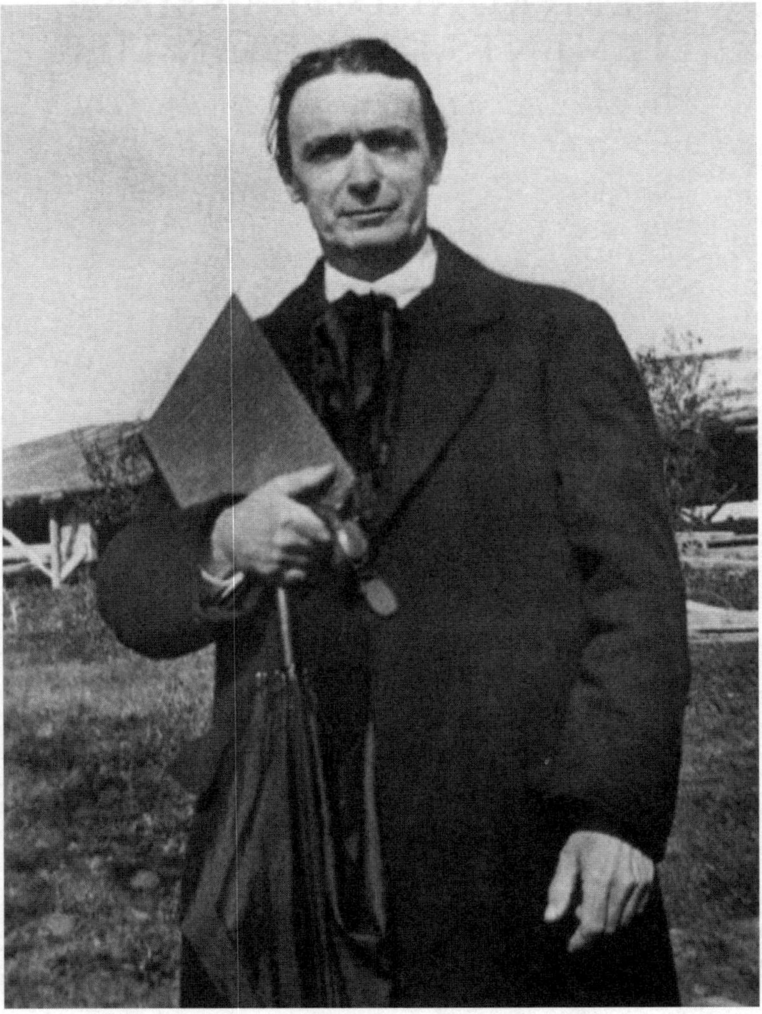

ETERNAL AND TRANSIENT ELEMENTS IN HUMAN LIFE

The Cosmic Past of Humanity and the Mystery of Evil

Fifteen lectures given at Dornach, Switzerland, from 6 September to 13 October 1918

ENGLISH BY ANNA MEUSS

INTRODUCTION BY ANNA MEUSS

RUDOLF STEINER

RUDOLF STEINER PRESS

CW 184

The publishers gratefully acknowledge the generous funding of this publication by the estate of Dr Eva Frommer MD (1927–2004) and the Anthroposophical Society in Great Britain

Rudolf Steiner Press
Hillside House, The Square
Forest Row, RH18 5ES

www.rudolfsteinerpress.com

Published by Rudolf Steiner Press 2015

Originally published in German under the title *Die Polarität von Dauer und Entwickelung im Menschenleben* (volume 184 in the *Rudolf Steiner Gesamtausgabe* or Collected Works) by Rudolf Steiner Verlag, Dornach. Based on Helen Finkh's transcript of her shorthand records, which were not reviewed by the speaker. This authorized translation is based on latest available (third) edition (2002), edited by Johann Waeger and Robert Friedenthal

Sketches within the text are by Hedwig Frey, based on Rudolf Steiner's blackboard drawings

Published by permission of the Rudolf Steiner Nachlassverwaltung, Dornach

© Rudolf Steiner Nachlassverwaltung, Dornach, Rudolf Steiner Verlag 2002

This translation © Rudolf Steiner Press 2015

All rights reserved. No part of this publication may be reproduced, stored in a retrieval system, or transmitted, in any form or by any means, electronic, mechanical, photocopying or otherwise, without the prior permission of the publishers

The right of Anna R. Meuss to be identified as the author of this translation has been asserted by her in accordance with the Copyright, Designs and Patent Act 1988

A catalogue record for this book is available from the British Library

ISBN 978 1 85584 523 7

Cover by Mary Giddens
Typeset by DP Photosetting, Neath, West Glamorgan
Printed and bound by Gutenberg Press Ltd., Malta

CONTENTS

Introduction, by Anna Meuss ...... *xiii*

LECTURE 1
6 SEPTEMBER 1918

Dualism and fatalism. The connection between birth and death in the macrocosm. Riddle of old Moon. The sun as creator of conscious life. Historical prospects. Characteristic figures in history. Augustine and Saint-Simon, demonology, metaphysics, positivist science. (The soldier, the civil servant, the industrialist.) Auguste Comte—Roman Catholic Church without Christianity. Schelling—Christianity without a church.

pages 1–19

LECTURE 2
7 SEPTEMBER 1918

The nature of sleep: interaction between I and higher hierarchies. Delusion about life and delusions of the mind. The history of the concept of truth. The ideals of the present will be the natural world of the future. Inner relationships: world of the gods and theocratic order; metaphysical concepts and civil service order; philosophy and industrialism. Bentham and utilitarianism. German Goetheanism.

pages 20–36

LECTURE 3
8 SEPTEMBER 1918

Man in the fourth development, the mineral world. Plant world, animal world, human world are the fifth, sixth and seventh developments; before that the three elemental worlds existed. Man extending into the divine world or the eighth development. Time a delusion. Use of the term 'time' in historical evolution.

Newton, Leibniz, Marx. Humanity must work its way through, initially in the historical field, from the sham history of sequence in time to the real events that are behind the reality perceived through the senses.

pages 37–61

Lecture 4
13 September 1918

Dualism in present philosophies of life and fatalism of pre-Christian times. Radical change in the state of the human soul in the course of time. The hallucinatory nature of the intellect and the illusory quality of the natural order. Dreamlike idea of the spirit, prophetic vision and taking the apocalyptic view. Cosmic hatred and cosmic common sense, e.g. in language and in thinking; luciferic and ahrimanic influence. Thinking is seed of the future. Acting out of the will bears within it awareness of infinitely far distant past. Acting out of the will we are basing ourselves on the past; thinking we base ourselves on the future.

pages 62–81

Lecture 5
14 September 1918

How man relates to the cosmos. Relationship of the different periods of human life to one another. Understanding life as a task. Life truths that are not in accord with one's wishes. Relationship between human being acting out of the will and thinking human being. Grasping what has been thought before in the second half of life. Intellectuality tinging modern people's state of mind of soul. The horizons of modern man do not extend to far distant spaces in time; other levels of insight need to be gained if we are to investigate the origins of the world. The concept of time—evolution and perspectives. Spiritual science takes one from duality to trinity. Wisdom for life based on thinking that is in accord with reality.

pages 82–98

Lecture 6
15 September 1918

Human life in spirit and soul as thinking, feeling and doing. Man's cosmic orientation. The world scale beam. Relationship of temporal to eternal. The region of eternity—the upper. The region of transience—the lower. Elements side by side in the spirit. Mingling of things that take place in time and in eternity; keeping them apart needs initiate knowledge. Emanationist and creationist philosophy. We grasp reality when the two flow together in a living way, the one for the region of spirit and soul, the other for the region of body and soul, and in this way escape the dualism.

pages 99–117

LECTURE 7
20 SEPTEMBER 1918

Tripartite space as image of tripartite Godhead. Concrete experience of space and of time in earlier times and the abstract way in which the three dimensions are seen today. Divine cosmic intelligence, cosmic feeling and cosmic will interwoven with space. Threefold space as image of the divine trinity, time as image of the one god. Monotheism is based on the old experience of time; sentience of the trinity goes back to the old experience of space. Duality of above and below, order in spirit and order of nature.

pages 118–129

LECTURE 8
21 SEPTEMBER 1918

The two streams of reality which are behind our life. The development in time of the human being in body and soul, the experience of space for the human spirit and soul in the realm of eternity. The battles of the one against the other in cosmic realms. Our relationship to the world appears to us only in form of an image. The contradistinction between ahrimanic and luciferic aims; human beings must find their way through this spiritual battle. Initiation science teaches them to develop cosmic sentience. We do not understand this life unless we see it in dualistic terms; but we must learn to establish balance in natural and in social life between growing rigid, frozen and growing volatile, between straight line and irregular line. Life is made up of a precipitate and a retrograde movement and the state of equilibrium must be found. The law of the pendulum swing applies. Our building in Dornach represents the state of balance in the universe; this takes it out of Ahriman's and Lucifer's realms—oneness in manifoldness, manifoldness in oneness. The secret of the state of balance must show itself in place of the old feeling for space and time.

pages 130–144

Lecture 9
22 September 1918

Maya reality—two worlds coming together which are at loggerheads with one another. The lower nature of man, bearer of unconscious inner life, grows more and more spiritual with the materialistic way of life but is exposed to the influences of luciferic spirits because higher nature is not having an influence. Conversely purely ecclesiastical and idealistic ideas encourage the material aspect of lower nature which is then exposed not to the influences of head nature but to ahrimanic influences. The science of human social life and historical life needs to be penetrated by a spiritual science which builds the real bridge between natural and spiritual order.

In the human microcosm the I corresponds to the macrocosmic mineral world. The polar opposite to the crystallizing tendencies of minerals is the dissolving tendency inherent in the human form; it is reflected in the human corpse, i.e. in the power of form in dead human bodies which dissolves the crystallizing tendency of the earth. Again a bridge is built between two streams in the world. Natural science does not do so. And the bridge from natural science to human science also comes from here. The law of polar opposites is accepted as the basic law not only for gaining insight into the natural order but also in the human order and the order of the spirit.

Cancers developing in modern civilization. The materialism of our time was encouraged by the increasing rigidity of the Roman Catholic Church and also by occult Freemasonry in Anglo-American countries with its luciferic character.

pages 145–163

Lecture 10
4 October 1918

The relationship between the lower levels of human existence and the spiritual powers of the hierarchies. Subconscious and conscious elements. In the evolutional stream given directly by the Spirits of Form, the power of coming upright, which influences the human form, influences our I; at the same time the lateral streams of the luciferic and ahrimanic spirits intervene in course of time. Considered in the light of human life, the influence of the luciferic powers causes hyperconsciousness to enter into the conscious mind. Luciferic fantasies in human beings and the degree of their justification; the extreme leads to evil. Ahriman's influence extends into everything which comes up from the subconscious in human beings. Spirits of Form govern the earth; they influence us through the spirits that serve them, especially the Archai. Higher spirits that lag behind disguise themselves. Realization of non-space in space through configuration, and also of spatial elements in space through those disguises as an ahrimanic counter-image. How we relate to the realm of eternity. The special position of the Spirits of Form as the only ones among the timeless hierarchies to be in time. Luciferic spirits assume disguise to enter into time. Death as balancing power, as counterweight in their moral impulses to inherited similarity of form. Reading life in the three great letters.

pages 164–182

LECTURE 11
5 OCTOBER 1918

Historical development in the fifth age. Lucifer active in this, Ahriman in the subconscious powers of the soul. The balance between them is never perfect. Polar opposition of Semitic and Greek civilizations. Ancient knowledge of man in the mysteries was wholly bound up with the state of balance between the luciferic and ahrimanic powers. At the time of the Mystery on Golgotha the ahrimanic powers were slightly stronger, as also from the sixteenth century onwards. Human inner life was consequently pushed towards abstraction. Human beings would no longer have been able to be sentient of their individual nature, gaining wisdom not concerning themselves but concerning nature. The Christ impulse made it possible for human beings to use their inner powers to grasp themselves as individuals. The ability to see oneself as an individual made one into a ghost, also losing understanding for the individual nature of others. The Christ impulse brought a different stream into earth evolution, addressing the most profound depths of the inner human being. Man would only develop these powers from inherent resources during the Venus metamorphosis. The enlightened among the dead can inspire human beings with Venus wisdom. That is how the Gospels were given by inspiration in the second century.

pages 183–194

LECTURE 12
6 OCTOBER 1918

The inspired Gospels could present the truth because the powers of understanding for the Mystery on Golgotha only developed fully in life after death. Three things said by Tertullian. Death and heredity are the two phenomena in the life of humanity which cast light on the Mystery on Golgotha. They are not part of human nature in so far as human beings belong to the world perceived through the senses. Human life proceeds in equilibrium between opposites. Because heredity was ranked among natural phenomena, original sin shifted to the moral field, a disparagement of the human will. Human thinking was then also ruined; intellectual rabbinical and social interpretations took the place of vision in the spirit. The same applies for death. The origin and end of man must not be grasped with the kind of rational thinking that is suitable for the natural world. If it had not been for the Mystery on Golgotha, a philosophy of life which had gradually grown corrupt could no longer have overcome man's identification with his nature in the sensible sphere. There would have been more and more mistaken views of heredity and death and the gates to the supersensible world would finally have closed completely. The Mystery on Golgotha provided the counter-thrust—resurrection, meaning metamorphosis of death, and birth as supersensible fact. Humanity is challenged to gain supersensible insight and so grasp the things which the rational mind, being a pupil of sensuality, is unable to grasp.

pages 195–216

Lecture 13
11 October 1918

Development of spiritual soul with natural-scientific way of thinking. Our ancestors' belief in ghosts and the ghostly nature of natural science. Limits of insight into nature. Richard Wahle as exponent of present-day humanity; his intuitive perception of the way ghosts are thought up for facts of nature. Task of spiritual soul is to recognize that our natural-scientific spectres are not real but merely pointers to realities which we must look for; otherwise we will not gain enlightenment about the human being and become spectres to ourselves. The year 666 is an important nodal point in human evolution where three streams come together, the normal linear stream and two lateral streams; the chaos in our world hides this from us. Sorat (the beast) and its projected aim to flood humanity with spiritual soul knowledge gained not in inner development but through ahrimanic revelation. This was prevented by the Mystery on Golgotha, which established equilibrium and limited the emancipation of drives.

pages 217–232

Lecture 14
12 October 1918

It will be the task for our present age that we gain independent individual nature by self-education. This was predestined for humanity by the divine spirit of their origin. The luciferic and ahrimanic powers work against it. The true ranking value of events and their spiritual background. Justinian banishing the Greek schools of philosophy in 529. The schools driven out of Edessa by Leo the Isaurian. Establishment of Gondishapur Academy. Aristotle translated from Greek to Syrian and from this to Arabic, which 'saved' his works. Tremendous but dangerous gnostic, ahrimanic wisdom flowed out from Gondishapur, though its effect was reduced (blunted) by the coming of Muhammad. This blunting of Gondishapur wisdom, though its intentions were taken along, reached European monasteries and became the natural-scientific way of thinking. Scholastics of the West fighting against Arab scholars. Our knowledge of the natural world will have to be ghostly unless we penetrate through to the spirit. There one first comes across Ahriman, then Lucifer. Human beings must gain wisdom by their own efforts, under the guidance of Christ Jesus. They will then find three things:

1) Supersensible insight into birth and death; they then know that our self was not allowed through the gate of birth, only our image.

2) Knowledge of the life of a person—only the form remains, the substance consumes itself—and about the powers of growth and renewal that give health. The rainbow as an example of the spectral, ghostly character of the natural phenomena. If we see through the ghostly aspect we find rhythmical natural orders everywhere. Penetration of the rhythms of nature will lead to a true science of nature, knowledge of the harmony of those rhythms will lead to new technology. The precondition is that we strive with real purpose to develop a completely selfless social order. For the rhythmical technology is identical with the healing power which calls for absolute conscientiousness also for things that are not remarkable.

3) To be able to face up consciously to Ahriman and Lucifer.

pages 233–252

Lecture 15
13 October 1918

Historical preparation for spiritual soul development. The year 333 as central point in post-Atlantean age, and important pivotal point in the new equilibrium established at that time. What were things like in Rome at the time of the Mystery on Golgotha? Augustus wanted to force civilization back to a stage where the things human beings can gain through the rational soul would be obscured; they were to have the ancient glories of Persian and Egyptian times again. Sentience was to be cultivated of the ancient rites of those times and people were to revive awareness of the divine world and harmony with it in a semi-hypnotic state. The aim was to leave intelligence aside. What, then, becomes of the part of the soul that seeks to develop spiritual soul? Rhetoric. The Roman Catholic Church has preserved this Augustinian impulse. The sacred quality of the great ancient rites must be given new life through the science of the spirit with anthroposophical orientation. The desire for sacramentalism which showed itself even in the nineteenth century must be encouraged with a new perception of the Christ. The concept of our building in Dornach is to create forms that show what is intended out of the great demands of our age. We must bring sacramentalism into our study of nature and let the power of the Christ enter into it. We must then also let this be present in the things we do in the social sphere.

pages 253–271

Notes 272

Rudolf Steiner's Collected Works 279

Significant Events in the Life of Rudolf Steiner 293

Index 307

INTRODUCTION

Background to this volume
1918 seems to have been a year of summing up and preparation. From 1910 to 1917 Rudolf Steiner had published at least one book a year. No new work appeared in 1918 but a remarkably large number of earlier works were revised or partly re-written—*Philosophy of Spiritual Activity, Goethe's Philosophy of Life (world view), Theosophy, Knowledge of the Higher Worlds, Goethe's Conception, Road to Self Knowledge, Threshold of the Spiritual World,* and *Riddles of Philosophy.* By the time the war ended almost all the works Steiner had written so far were available in print.

Rudolf Steiner lectured in Dornach and Berlin and in a relatively large number of other places. He gave twelve lectures in Munich, eight in Stuttgart, six in Vienna, and also spoke in Hamburg, Nuremberg, Leipzig, Prague, Heidenheim and Ulm. This established a basis for the work after the war.

The arts were also encouraged. Eurythmy was developed to the point where it would be possible to give a relatively large number of public performances the next year. The smaller eurythmy performances given in Stuttgart, Munich, Berlin, Leipzig, Vienna and Hamburg in 1918 may have been in preparation for these. Numerous internal eurythmy performances were given in Dornach in the autumn and winter. Painting the right dome of the Goetheanum and work on the Group Sculpture also continued.

Rudolf Steiner returned to Dornach on or around 12 August and stayed there until April 1919.

On 17 August Steiner thanked the members and staff in Dornach for their devoted work during his absence and reported briefly on the work and his experiences in Germany (see CW 183, *Human Evolution,*

A Spiritual-Scientific Quest). The following day he gave the first of the Dornach autumn lectures, speaking of the idea of the threefold nature of the human being, the polarity of space and time, the difference between ahrimanic and luciferic principles in relation to history and the study of man from many different points of view (CWs 183 and 184).

At the eurythmy performance of *Twelve Moods* on the 5th anniversary of laying the foundation stone for the Goetheanum, on 20 September, Rudolf Steiner again spoke of the obligation to stand up for the cause of anthroposophy.

On 27, 28 and 29 September, he discussed Goethe's approach to nature and his philosophy of life and *Faust II*, esp. the Classical Walpurgis Night (CW 273). There followed a eurythmic and dramatic performance of the Classical Walpurgis Night from *Faust II* (29 September).

On 8–10 and 15–17 October, Rudolf Steiner went to Zurich. As in the previous autumn, he gave four public lectures, speaking about anthroposophical research methods and about insight into inner life, social and historical life. He prepared thoroughly for these lectures. He also gave two lectures for members on the work of the angel in the astral body and on finding the Christ (CW 182).

Reading the lectures in CWs 183 and 184, it is evident that in spite of all positivity, Rudolf Steiner was deeply troubled by the state of the Anthroposophical Society and was concerned for its future. Members clearly had no idea of what that future might be and what needed to be done to bring it to realization. He warned against making compromises and said that what was needed was not mere intelligence to understand the things of the spirit but above all, and most urgently, that people met them with enthusiasm, fire and warmth of heart. 'We need people who stand up for them with all their hearts and minds' (CW 183).

A style that is difficult to read
Rudolf Steiner's heaviness of heart can be sensed in the lectures in this volume. There is sometimes a hesitancy, as if he had inwardly to

overcome a reluctance to speak, evident in the often tremendous length and complexity of sentences. The lectures are not easy to read. I have divided many of the long sentences but not all, for it is also my duty as a translator to give readers the 'feel' of the original. The text is based on the shorthand record taken down by professional stenographer Helene Finkh, which means that the German original is very close to Rudolf Steiner's actual words.

The volume has been said to be 'the most advanced course in anthroposophy', and readers will no doubt find it a challenge. It may need several readings of a sentence or paragraph to get a grasp of what they convey, and it may sometimes be helpful to sleep on them and read them again the next day.

Acknowledgement
I am greatly indebted to David E. Jones who has patiently read through every lecture for me, picking up any typing errors I had failed to see. We also discussed some aspects of terminology, which I have found most helpful.

Anna R. Meuss, September 2015

Bibliography
Christoph Lindenberg, *Rudolf Steiner, eine Chronik*
Peter Selg, *Rudolf Steiner 1861–1925, Lebens- und Wirkgeschichte*, vol. 2

Lecture 1

6 September 1918

I'd like to go more deeply into some of the things we have been considering here this summer,[1] and we'll add some historical details and also some factual things in the next few days. Today I intend to draw your attention to some historical facts and then present you with some conclusions drawn from a deeper study of these, and particularly from the revelations of some historical figures.

Initiates of the mysteries have through the ages always said one thing, rightly so. It is that if one does not know how to judge the two streams in philosophical life properly, two streams we have been considering—idealism and materialism—one will be in danger of either falling through a trap door into a poky little cellar hole, or coming to a dead end in the search for a philosophy of life. The cellar has been considered by initiates of all times to be dualism, where one does not find the bridge from ideas, spiritual thinking tinged with theory, to the sphere of matter, of material things. And the dead end one may reach in following different ways of looking at the world, when one does not manage to balance idealism against materialism, is what initiates call fatalism. In more recent times there has been a definite tendency to take a dualistic view and on the other hand to be fatalistic, though there are things which those taking the present-day views fail to admit or do not even realize.

To begin with I would like to take one individual who lived in the evening twilight of the fourth post-Atlantean era—just in general outline—with reference to the philosophy of life, and then look at others who are more characteristic of our present-day philosophy of life, of the fifth post-Atlantean era.

One highly characteristic figure with regard to western philosophy of life was Augustine of Hippo[2] who lived from 354 to 430 of the Christian era. Let us recall some of Augustine's thoughts, for, as you can see from the dates, he lived in the evening twilight of the fourth post-Atlantean era which came to a conclusion in the fifteenth century. It is clearly evident that this conclusion was approaching, starting from the third, fourth, fifth and sixth post-Christian centuries. Augustine gained impressions of many different philosophies of life. We have spoken of this before. Above all Augustine came to know Manichaeism and scepticism. His soul took in all the impulses which one gains when on the one hand one sees all that is ideal, beautiful and good, everything that is filled with wisdom, and then also everything which is bad, evil. And we know that in Manichaeism people sought to manage—putting it crudely, but it can also be put in this way—with these two streams in the philosophies of life, so that in a way they accepted eternal polarity, opposition persisting for ever between light and darkness, good and bad, wisdom-filled and evil.

In Manichaeism, people only managed with this dualism by connecting certain ancient, pre-Christian concepts with this acceptance of the polarity of phenomena in the world, and above all connected certain ideas which can only be understood if one knows that in earlier times people used an atavistic clairvoyance to see into the spiritual world, ideas that those visions were similar in content to the impressions gained through sensory perception. Having taken in such ideas, I'd say, of the supersensible as seemingly sensible, Manichaeism gave the impression for many people of making the spiritual material, of envisaging the spiritual in forms that are sense-perceptible. This is a common mistake made also in more recent philosophies, including more recent theosophy, as I've been telling you the other day.[3] Augustine gave up Manichaeism for the very reason that he could no longer bear the way things were made sensible, material. That was one of the reasons why he gave it up.

Augustine then also went through scepticism, which is a justifiable philosophy of life in so far as it makes people aware that merely considering anything which is to be gained from the sense-perceptible world and the experiences and events in the sense-perceptible world will not tell them anything about the supersensible. And if one then also holds the view that one cannot gain the supersensible as such, one will doubt if truth is to be found at all. Augustine also went through this doubt about knowing the truth. He gained the most powerful impulses from this.

Now in order to make you understand what really gave Augustine the position he had in western philosophy, I have to refer to the main element in his point of view, a point from which all the light shone out that lived in Augustine, and was indeed the main point in his later, his last, philosophy of life. It is the point which we may characterize as follows. Augustine realized that human beings can only be certain, truly certain, with a certainty free from all delusion, if they refer to their own inner experience. Everything else can be uncertain. It is impossible to know if the things we see with our eyes, hear with our ears, things that make an impression on any of our senses truly are constituted the way our senses make us assume. We cannot even know what this world actually looks like if we close our eyes and ears and other senses to it. That is how people think who think in the Augustinian way about the outside world, which they can experience. They think that this outside world, which they can experience as it presents itself to human beings, could not provide true certainty, that nothing can be gained from it on which one might base oneself as a fixed point in a philosophy of life. But with regard to the things which people experience inwardly—irrespective of how they do so—being with them directly, it is the individual himself who lives in the ideas, the feelings inside him; one knows that one is right within one's inner life. For a thinker like Augustine the fact, inwardly experienced, is that with regard to anything human beings inwardly experience as truth they can be under no delusion. You may think that everything else which the world says may be deceptive, but there can be absolutely no doubt that the ideas, the feelings that live in us are really and truly experienced by us in our inner life.

This solid basis for accepting one truth about which there can be no doubt was one of the starting points in Augustine's philosophy of life.

In the fifth post-Atlantean era this point was taken up in a most striking way by Descartes,[4] who lived from 1596 to 1650, already in the dawn, therefore, of the fifth post-Atlantean era. For Descartes, too, saw this element which remains when all else is in doubt as the starting point, and he put it in the well-known words 'I think, therefore I am'. And he was really wholly in accord with Augustine in taking this view.

Now the situation is that when it comes to one's philosophy of life one always has to say: 'Someone who is in the stream of human evolution at some point in time will have certain views. There will be certain aspects of his views of which he is not aware. People who come later will see them.' We might say that those who come later are privileged to see something in a fuller and truer sense than someone who has to say certain things at a particular time in human evolution. This is a fact that cannot be denied. And it is good, as I have mentioned on previous occasions, if people who are taking our anthroposophical point of view will consciously and thoroughly realize the following. The knowledge of spiritual things one is able to gain at the present time, however distinctive it may be, must not be taken as a sum of absolute dogmas. It has to be clearly understood that there will be others at a later time who will see a greater truth in such things as we are able to present today than we are able to see for ourselves. This is indeed the basis for humanity's cultural evolution. And any obstacle to, all inhibition of cultural advance ultimately depends on people not being prepared to admit that they would really like to be given truths that are not the truths of a particular era but are absolute, timeless dogmas.

Today in particular we are able to look back from our point of view on Augustine, and we'll have to say to ourselves: 'If one takes the Augustinian point of view, one will have to be very clear in one's mind that he assumed uncertainty as to the truth in all external revelations, but genuine truth in experiencing the things that live in our soul.' It calls for a degree of courage for someone to take this point of view. Perhaps one would not need to speak of this in the decided fashion in which I have to do it, if it were not the case that exactly in our time courage would characteristically be lacking when it comes to philosophies of life. This courage to which I am referring shows itself in two directions. One is that like Augustine, you boldly admit: 'You will have genuine certainty only with regard to anything you experience inwardly.' Then there has to be the other pole of this courage, and at the present time this is indeed lacking. One must then also have the courage to admit to oneself: 'The revelation of external things through the senses does not have this genuine certainty of their being real.' It does need inner courage in our thinking to say that there is no genuine certainty about external reality, which is considered to be absolutely certain in modern materialism. On the other hand it needs a degree of courage to say to oneself: 'Genuine certainty comes only if one is really aware of one's inner experiences.'

Yes, even in our day this has been said again and there are people who ask others—people who want to develop a philosophy of life—to have this courage which shows itself in two ways. Yet we have to think differently about this today if we really want to get to the bottom of things, and there we see the whole historical position held by Augustine for the people of today, and that our thinking about the matter has to be somewhat different. For today we have to know something which Augustine or Descartes did not consider—I have discussed this in the part of my book *The Riddle of Man*[5] where I was referring to Descartes—today we have to say: 'The idea that one might arrive at a satisfactory philosophy of life by grasping the direct inner life of man, the way people experience it today, this idea is refuted every time we go to sleep.' Every time someone falls back into the unconscious state of sleep in our day he or she will be deprived not of the absolute, true certainty of inner experience of which Augustine spoke, but of the reality of this inner experience. The reality of this genuine experience is always lost from going to sleep to waking up again. Today human beings experience the inner life in a slightly different way from the way people did as late as the fourth post-Atlantic era, and even in the evening twilight of Augustine's day. Today they have to say: 'However clearly, however exactly a certainty may be inwardly experienced, it still offers no certainty for life after death for the simple reason that we see reality sink down into the unconscious sphere every time we sleep, and the people of today do not know if it does not also sink down into unreality.' So today we may no longer conclude that things inwardly experienced in seemingly absolute certainty cannot be called in question. In theory none of it can be called in question, but the fact of sleep goes against this.

Turning our attention to what has just been said we will immediately see how Augustine was able to arrive at this view and did so with much greater justification than Descartes later on who really was more or less only repeating Augustine's statement. Some late echoes of the old, atavistic clairvoyance still existed for the whole fourth post-Atlantean era, including the time when Augustine lived. Sadly, far too little of this is taken note of in history today, and little is known of it. But throughout the whole of the fourth post-Atlantean era very many people knew from personal experience that there is a spiritual life, for they saw it in their visions. But during that fourth era they mostly saw it because it entered into their sleep life, and that was different from the way it was in the second and third eras. We may therefore say that in the fourth post-Atlantean era it was different from the way it is now in the fifth era when sleep means being wholly unconscious. In the fourth post-Atlantean era people still knew that from going to sleep until waking up was a time when the ideas and feelings they had in their waking hours acted in other forms. The waking life of truth went down, as it were, into the dim conscious awareness of sleep life. And they knew that the inner truth they experienced held not only truth but also reality. For they knew moments in the life of sleep when the things one learns in the inner life were present as real and not merely abstract life. It is immaterial if someone may be able to demonstrate even today that Augustine would have been able to say from personal experience: 'I know that the things we experience inwardly as true but unreal exist for the time from going to sleep to waking up.' But it was certainly possible in Augustine's day to gain such a view and base oneself on it.

If you now extend what I have been saying with regard to the subjective human principle and generalize it for the whole macrocosm, this will take you to something different. You then discover the element from which this subjective principle actually arose in earlier times, namely in the fourth post-Atlantean era, and what has made it possible. In pre-Christian times—the Mystery on Golgotha marks the boundary between the ancient atavistic views and later new ones which are still evolving today—people were still able to adhere to certain living mystery truths. The truths from the mysteries which I mean here are truths relating to the great secret of birth and death. Some initiates considered the secret of birth and of death to be a secret which should not be made known to the world because the world was not yet ripe for it. But within the mysteries, some view was also held in pre-Christian times on the connection between birth and death in the macrocosm, man being part of this in the whole of his essential nature. During that time before Christ, it was through the mysteries that attention was above all directed towards birth, towards all that was being born in the world. Anyone familiar with the old philosophies of life will know that the emphasis was on being born, on coming into existence, shooting and sprouting. And I have, of course, made it clear on several occasions that the opposite came with the Mystery on Golgotha. I used the following words: 'Consider that about six hundred years before Golgotha Buddha, who in human evolution represents something like the ending of the pre-Christian philosophy of life, did among other things develop his views on seeing a corpse. Death is suffering—and it was like an axiom for Buddha that suffering must be overcome; the means had to be found to enable one to turn away from death. It was the corpse from which the Buddha turned away to arrive at something which, albeit spiritualized, was to him nevertheless something in which one can get a sense of shooting, sprouting life.

Looking at life in other regions six hundred years after the Mystery on Golgotha we see that seeing the dead body of the Christ on the cross was not something people would turn away from but something they would turn towards, something they would look upon with all their heart as the symbol that would solve the riddle of the macrocosm in so far as it related to the human being and his growth and development.

This is a very special relationship within those twelve centuries: six hundred years before the Mystery on Golgotha turning away from a corpse led to something that was to be an elevating principle in the philosophy of life; six hundred years after the Mystery on Golgotha the symbol of the cross had evolved, a turning towards death, towards the dead body to find there the strength to arrive at a philosophy of life that would cast a light also on the progress of man. Among the many things which characterize the tremendous change that came with the Mystery on Golgotha is this Buddha symbol of turning away from the dead body, and the Christ symbol of turning towards the dead body which is seen as the dead body of the most sublime spirit ever to have appeared on earth.

It truly was the case that in a certain respect the old mysteries placed the riddle of births at the centre of philosophies of life. In doing so the mysteries, which sought to convey mystery knowledge and not just superficial views, did at the same time present the human soul with a profound cosmological secret. They directed attention to the principle connected with the life of births in world evolution. And you will not be able to understand the life of births in world evolution unless you go back to the ancient riddle of the Moon. We know, of course, that before the earth came to be earth it was embodied as the old Moon. Various phenomena connected with our present moon, the late descendant of the old Moon—you can read it up in my *Occult Science, an Outline*[6]—have to be seen as late echoes of events that happened in the time of the old Moon, a time which preceded Earth evolution.

There would be no births, none in all the realms of nature in Earth evolution if the laws of the old Moon did not apply, or rather those of its late descendant which is the earth's satellite. Every birthing in all the realms of nature and in humanity is connected with the moon's activities. And it was in connection with this that the ancient Hebrew initiates considered Yahweh to be a moon god, Yahweh as the god who controls all bringing forth. It was understood that cosmologically the laws of the moon governed all bringing-forth processes in all realms of nature. They were thus able to speak of a profound secret in cosmology, symbolically as it were, saying: 'As the light of the moon shines on the earth, all shooting, sprouting life, all births, come from the principle represented by the moonlight.' In the highest mysteries of pre-Christian times people did not turn to the light of the sun but to the sun's life as it was reflected by the moon when speaking of the secret of births. The particular nuance given to pre-Christian philosophies of life in their depths had arisen because in the old mysteries people knew the secret of the moon.

The light of the sun was considered to be something veiled, something not very good for people unless they were well prepared, for it was known that it is delusion, maya, to think that the sunray coming to earth called forth the shooting, sprouting life forms in the different realms of nature. It was known that getting born did not depend on the life of the sun but rather the other way round, being scorched, the diminishing of life did so. The mystery secret was that the moon lets life forms be born and the sun lets them die. However much people were venerating the life of the sun for other reasons in the pre-Christian mysteries of old, they venerated it as the ground and origin of death. The fact that life forms must die cannot be ascribed to the Sun which we know from *Occult Science* to have been the second embodiment of the Earth, but we can ascribe it to the present sun which we see on the horizon in all its glory.

Well now, the end of life, which is the opposite of those births, is connected with the life of the sun. But there is also something else, something that was not so important in pre-Christian times but has become particularly important in post-Christian times: all conscious life is connected with the life of the sun. And the conscious life which human beings go through in a life on earth, that conscious awareness which shines out particularly in the fifth post-Atlantean era, which is our own, is intensively connected with the life of the sun. We merely need to consider this life of the sun from the spiritual point of view, just as we have been doing in the lectures given earlier this summer.[7] Yes, the sun is the creator of death, the scorching life in the cosmos and also for human beings, but it is at the same time also the creator of conscious life. This conscious life was not so important in pre-Christian times because they still had the atavistic life in clairvoyance inherited from the old Moon. Conscious awareness has become important in post-Christian times, more important than life itself. For the goal of Earth evolution can only be achieved if this conscious awareness is gained in an appropriate way. Human beings have to accept this conscious awareness from the one who gives us not only this but also the life of death, not the life of births.

It is with this that through the Mystery on Golgotha the Son of the Sun, the Christ entered into Earth evolution, going through the living body of Jesus of Nazareth, the power as it were, which has become the most important principle in Earth evolution. This is connected with profound cosmic secrets. 'From your sleep life,' the initiates at the old mysteries would say to their disciples, 'a sleep life into which the powers of the moon enter even when you are awake—we know, of course, that human beings are partly asleep even in their waking hours. The life of the moon tinges this life of sleep just as the silver sickle of the moon tinges the darkness of night.' Christian initiates have to say to their disciples: 'Seek to understand that conscious awareness shines out from waking life because the powers of the sun enter into it just as the sun shines on all life on earth from morning to night.'

The change came with the Mystery on Golgotha. In pre-Christian times it was most important to perceive the origin of life. Now it has become most important to perceive the source and origin of conscious awareness. It is only by knowing how to connect the cosmological truth to which I have been referring with the true certainty that lives in our souls—that is, only by grasping spiritual science inwardly—that we will be assured of the reality of the spirit within the principle which otherwise does not assure reality in this inner life.

We cannot get far with the means available to Augustine, the means available to those who base themselves on Augustinian principles. Every sleep confutes the genuine certainty of our inner experiences. It will only be when in addition to these inner experiences we come to experience their reality that we can gain a genuine, firm foothold on the soil of these inner experiences.

Anything we think, anything we feel in our present life on earth is not real in this present life on earth—even today there are some scientific thinkers who acknowledge this. It is unreal for the present time. The strange thing is that our most intimate experience, where the truth shines out for us beyond all doubt, is not real in the present time, but it is the actual perpetuating seed for our next life on earth. We may speak of this principle, of which Augustine spoke and for which in his case there was no guarantee, as the seed for our next life on earth. We may say: 'It is definitely true that the truth shines out within us but does so as something which is not real. Today it is still unreal, but in our next life on earth this unreal principle which is seed in its unreality will be fruit, a fruit which will bring the next life to life, just as this year's seed in a plant will bring the visible plant to life next year.' We have to overcome time; only then will we find reality in the things we are able to experience inwardly. We would never be the human beings we are meant to be if at the present time the inwardly experienced truth did have the same reality as the outside world. We would never be able to be free. Freedom would be completely out of the question. Nor would we be individuals. We'd be part of the natural order. Anything happening within us would happen of necessity. We only are individuals, and indeed free individuals, because on the billows of necessary developments there arises, like a miracle, the unreality of our inner experiences, something which will only be outward reality of the kind we see in the world around us in our next life on earth.

That is the deceptive quality of time—something which still lives in people's fantasies today—people do not consider that anything which inwardly shines out as unreal in one life on earth will be real in the next. Well, this is something we'll be considering further tomorrow and the day after.

We see how from the point of view we are able to gain today we can survey Augustine's point of view and see something in his way of looking at things, as it were, which he himself was not yet able to see. Thus Augustine is perhaps especially significant for us as someone in the evening twilight of the fourth post-Atlantean era because he was with particular precision pointing to the ideal, conceptual stream in world events, seeking to find a fixed point in that ideal stream in world events. That is what Augustine tried to do. All we want to do today is to state this historical fact.

In his time people had not yet understood that a tremendous change had come with regard to the Mystery on Golgotha and to death. For it is only from this Mystery of Death that the true consolidation of the absolute certainty of the truths experienced within the human soul can then well forth.

We'll now take a big leap and characterize another individual, just as we have been talking about the characteristics of Augustine during the evening twilight of the fourth post-Atlantean era. We are going to consider characteristic individuals of the fifth post-Atlantean era in a particular respect. I'll select two of them. One of them, and beginning with him we can characterize what emerged for humanity in the fifth post-Atlantean era in one particular respect, was Henri de Saint-Simon,[8] who lived from 1760 to 1825. The other, a follower of Saint-Simon, was Auguste Comte,[9] who lived from 1798 to 1857. Augustine was someone who made every effort, using all means his insights had provided, to consolidate Christianity. Both Saint-Simon and Auguste Comte had grown utterly confused about Christianity. It will be easiest for us to get an idea of the thinking of Auguste Comte, and in a sense also of Saint-Simon, by considering some of Auguste Comte's main ideas, at least in a schematic way.

Auguste Comte was very much a representative for a particular kind of philosophy of life, and it was only because people were not much concerned about the way in which the different philosophies fit into people's way of life that someone like Auguste Comte was studied as a rarity in history. What people don't know is that basically, though perhaps not everywhere, people have been influenced by, in a way been pupils of Auguste Comte, though this is not what matters. Deep down in their thinking they are of the same mind as Auguste Comte. So we are able to say that Auguste Comte is representative of a major part of people's approach to life in the present time.

Auguste Comte said: 'Humanity has evolved. It has evolved in three stages and has now reached the third stage. If we observe people's inner lives through these three stages we find that at the first stage people's ideas inclined mainly towards demonology.' This means that the first stage of evolution in the Comptian sense would be demonological. 'People imagined that spirits were active, taking effect, behind the natural phenomena which are perceived through the senses.' You'd have to think of them the way people always imagine spirits to be in ordinary life. Demons are suspected to be everywhere—big ones and small ones. That was the first stage.

Then, having developed a bit further, people began to move from the demonological view to a metaphysical one. Where they had originally imagined demons, elemental spirits or the like behind all phenomena, they now thought of understandable reasons put in abstract terms. People turned metaphysical when they did no longer want to believe in demons. The second stage was therefore metaphysics. Certain concepts were thought up and connected with one's own life, and people thought that they would get to the ground and origin of things with such concepts.

Humanity has now also gone beyond this stage and entered into the third stage. Auguste Comte assumed, and this was very much in line with the thinking of his teacher Saint-Simon, that wanting to learn about the ground and origin of the world people no longer look to the demons, nor to metaphysical concepts, but merely to the sense-perceptible reality provided by positivist science. The third age is thus one of positivist science. People are meant to consider the things revealed to them in external scientific discoveries as enlightening and leading to a philosophy of life. They were to seek enlightenment about themselves in the same way in which mathematical enlightenment casts light on dimensions in space, physics on systems of forces, chemistry on the structure of matter, biology on the systems of life. In his great work on positive philosophy Auguste Comte sought to give a complete picture of the harmony of everything which the different sciences can tell us, saying that this alone was worthy of man in his third stage of development. He did consider Christianity, saying it was the most sublime development, but nevertheless only as the final phase in demonology. Metaphysics followed. They provided a sum of abstract concepts. But according to Auguste Comte, only positive science arrives at something that is truly real, also offering an existence worthy of humanity. He therefore wanted to establish a Church based on positivist science, to organize people in social systems which were based on that positivist science.

Auguste Comte did in the end arrive at some very strange ideas. I'll just take some characteristic elements today. He spoke a lot about establishing a positivist Church. This positivist Church—if you study this you will get to know the man's thinking—was also meant to introduce a kind of calendar. There were to be a great number of anniversaries dedicated to such figures as Newton or Galileo as representatives of positivist sciences. Those days of the year were to be devoted to the veneration of the individuals concerned. Other days were to be given to calumniating individuals such as Julius the Apostate or Napoleon. This, too, was to be regulated. Life in general was to be largely regulated according to the principles of positivist science.

If you know life you'll know that not many people want to put the ideals of Auguste Comte into practice. But that is sheer cowardice, for in truth people do think the way Auguste Comte did. If you study the image presented by his positivist Church you will certainly gain the impression that the structure of that Church is exactly the same as that of the Roman Catholic Church, although Auguste Comte's positivist Church lacks the Christ. And this is what is so strange. We have to consider it utterly characteristic that Auguste Comte was looking for a Roman Catholic Church without Christianity. He arrived at this by letting the three stages—demonic, metaphysical and positivist—enter into his soul. We might say that he considered all the trappings of Christianity that evolved in the course of history up to his time as something that was very good. But he wanted to remove the Christ himself from that Church of his. Basically that is the essence of Auguste Comte—a Roman Catholic Church without the Christ.

This is highly characteristic for the dawn of the fifth post-Atlantean era. Someone who had taken up Romanism, was thinking in a Romanist way, and at the same time was entirely thinking in the way of the fifth post-Atlantean era with its anti-spiritual character had to think the way Auguste Comte did. Auguste Comte and his teacher Saint-Simon are therefore absolutely characteristic of the dawn of the fifth post-Atlantean age. But much would be decided in this fifth post-Atlantean era. And therefore the other nuances which are also possible also came up. As I said, I want to give you some glimpses of history today. We'll then develop things on that basis.

Schelling,[10] who lived from 1775 to 1854, is in remarkable contrast to Auguste Comte. He is equally characteristic, as it were, of the dawn of the fifth post-Atlantean era. Today I cannot even schematically go into Schelling's philosophy, highly differentiated in itself of course, but I'd like to refer to a few things that are characteristic.

I said that in the evening twilight of the fourth post-Atlantean era Augustine's position was to consider the one stream, the ideal one, in such a way that a fixed point might arise from it where he might take his position. We now enter into the fifth post-Atlantean era. In its dawn we have figures like Saint-Simon and Auguste Comte who were looking for the firm base in the other, the purely natural, material order of positivist sciences. This gives us the two directions—Augustine on the one hand, Auguste Comte on the other. Schelling used the means available in the fifth post-Atlantean era to look behind the things one is able to see in the world for a bridge between the ideal and the real, the ideal and the material. You'll find the main points in my book *The Riddle of Man*. He showed tremendous energy in looking for a way of reconciling these opposites. Initially he only developed abstract ideas. By starting from the same base as Johann Gottlieb Fichte,[11] he made some progress and tried to come to something in the world that was ideal and real at one and the same time. There followed a time in Schelling's life when he felt it was impossible to arrive at such a bridge using the means of abstraction which had evolved in the course of time in that era. It seemed to him that this was impossible. One day he said to himself: 'People really have only gained these concepts for understanding the natural order outside on the basis of modern scholarship. But we have no concepts for anything which is behind this outer natural order, the sphere where a bridge can be built between the ideal and the real.' And it is most interesting that one day Schelling admitted that it seemed to him that the academics of recent centuries had come to a secret agreement that they would exclude anything deeper from their philosophy of life, anything that would lead to true and genuine life. One would therefore have to go to the non-academic people. This was also the time[12] when Schelling considered the works of Jakob Boehme.[13] There he found the spiritual deepening which led to the last, the theosophical period in his life from which has come the beautiful work on human freedom, the beautiful work on the gods of Samothrace, on the Cabeiri, then his *Philosophy of Mythologies* and *Philosophy of Revelation*.

Schelling was seeking, especially during this last part of his life, to understand what influence the Mystery on Golgotha had had on human history. This was what he wanted to know above all else. And he came to realize that the concepts available to the scholars of his day would not enable people to understand the life where the Mystery on Golgotha was flowing, and therefore also not the true life of man. Schelling—and that is the trait which I want to draw special attention to, we'll make this the basis for further study in the days ahead—arrived at a view that was the absolute opposite of the view held by his contemporary Auguste Comte. And this is the strange thing—we are able to say that Auguste Comte was looking for a Catholicism, or rather a Roman Catholic Church that was without Christianity; Schelling was looking from his point of view for a Christianity without a Church. A Christianity without a Church—Schelling was, as it were, seeking to Christianize the whole of modern life, make it wholly Christian so that everything human beings are able to think, feel and do would have the Christ impulse pulsing through it. What he was not looking for was a separate religious life for Christianity, especially not on the pattern that already existed in historical evolution, though he did take a careful look at this life. We thus have the two extremes—Auguste Comte's idea of a Church without the Christ and Schelling's idea of the Christ without a Church.

I wanted to speak to you about these two historical views so that we may make this our basis. We see one individual, Augustine, seeking a firm base in idealism, another individual, Auguste Comte, who was looking for this in realism, and Schelling who wanted to build a bridge. All these were tendencies that preceded the evolution in which we now find ourselves.

What we can say is that one can survey what happened through many centuries, what went on where philosophies of life are concerned, and one can then turn one's attention to the way in which people's ideas evolved in a wider context. Study of Auguste Comte yields a most important aperçu, but Auguste Comte was not able to grasp it in its pure form, being wholly caught up in his prejudices. However, we get something that will be an important starting point for us in the next few days if we consider the whole situation—I'd say Augustine, Auguste Comte, Schelling. I want to come to this aperçu when we conclude today's reflections for I would wish you to have it in mind. In the next few days we'll then speak of something which is connected with this aperçu in a most significant way. As it has arisen from the subject matter I have been presenting I will give it to you in aphoristic form without being able to go into reasons why this aperçu has come up not with Auguste Comte but with others when one takes the standpoint of a later time, as I put it today, and takes a point of view which is much later, the standpoint of someone who at the beginning of the twentieth century thinks about someone who was a thinker at the end of the eighteenth and beginning of the nineteenth century. But it really is important—I have stressed this many times over and also brought out clearly this time—that today we look at philosophies of life not just in abstract terms and on their own but in the way in which they are part of the whole life of humanity. This is the only way of coming to a standpoint of reality; we have to consider how it fits into the whole life of humanity.

Saint-Simon and Auguste Comte clearly understood that they were only able to arrive at their positivism in modern times, that positivism would have been impossible at an earlier time. Auguste Comte in particular was very much aware: 'The way I am thinking,' he more or less said to himself, 'is a way which is only possible in our time.' This is tremendously important in the modern movement and is indeed connected with the aperçu to which I was referring. If one makes the point which Auguste Comte considered to be the starting point for his threefold system, one can say, in his sense, that this threesome is theology, metaphysics and positivist science as he called it (rightly or wrongly so, that does not matter).

The strange thing is that we are able to ask: 'Who is most liable to be a believer where one of these directions is concerned?' Please do not misunderstand me with regard to what I am now going to say with reference to the aperçu, and do not take it as a one-sided dogma, nor to take it as if it might be crudely observed with absolute certainty. No, we have to consider the whole course of human evolution if we want to turn our attention to the words I am now going to say. But in that case we cannot ask 'Who'll be the believer?' but 'Who'll be most likely to be a believer in one of these directions?' Careful observation will then show, however much the facts would seem to contradict this, that the one most likely to be a believer in theology, not a representative of theology but a believer—I am not talking about religion but about theology—is the soldier. Civil servants, especially in the legal field, are most likely to believe in metaphysics, and industrialists will most easily come to believe in positivist sciences.

When one wants to judge life, it is most important not to be abstract but to look at life in a truly unbiased way. But one then has to raise questions like these.

Coming to a conclusion today I want you to treat this as an aperçu, something which comes to mind when one enters more intimately into Auguste Comte's thinking. He was aware that he could only be fully understood by industrialists and could really only come up with his views in an industrial age. This is connected with the fact that an industrialist will most easily believe in positivist science, a soldier in not just the Christian but any theology, and the civil servant in metaphysics.

Lecture 2

7 September 1918

Full insight into the situations we are currently considering will not be possible unless we take a closer look at the nature of the human being between going to sleep and waking up again, that is, in the sleep state. You are all familiar with this sleep state in theory. The principle which we call I and astral body if names are to be used separates from the physical body and the ether body. Yet if we want to take a closer look at the nature of sleep we have to be aware that it is actually in the sleep state that human beings experience the reality of which we spoke yesterday. I said that Augustine sought to grasp true and real certainty about the world in inner experience. But human beings do not fully grasp their inner life when they are in the waking state. It has to be understood that the principle known as I and as astral body does not really come to conscious awareness in the waking state. Only an image, a mirror image of I and astral body comes to conscious awareness in this waking state. If human beings were aware of themselves when in the sleep state, that is from going to sleep to waking up—or we might also say if they grew aware of themselves by doing the exercises which are described in my published works—they would in being aware of their experiences during sleep gain living experience of the true form, as it were, of I and astral body and not of the mirror image they have in the waking state. It has to be understood that this true form of I and astral body appears before the human soul, before conscious awareness, in images in such a way that in their sleep human beings truly experience inwardly, in their inner life, within their I and their astral body, something which we call the third hierarchy, the hierarchy of angels, archangels and archai.

In their waking state, human beings are not aware of this intimate connection with the spirits called angels, archangels and archai, a connection which continues for the whole of their lives. This is the delusion under which they are in their waking state, that their experience is limited to the abstract I and the shadowy ideas and thoughts that fill the human soul—for they are indeed shadowy—or indeed the dreamlike sense of wanting to do things. The whole point is that in their waking life human beings have to remain limited to this shadow nature of their I and their astral body, and that they cannot be conscious of the fact that the spirits of the third hierarchy are having an influence on their I. At the very moment when human beings were actually waking up in sleep, if I may put it like this, they would not have an outside natural world around them but would have an inner sense of those spirits—angels, archangels and the spirits of the age. It is because of this that we have something in the state of our soul which we would not otherwise have. If the hierarchy of the angels did not influence our astral body we would not be able to see ourselves as individuals. It is because the hierarchy of the angels influences our spirit and soul that we feel ourselves to be independent individuals.

Thanks to the influence of the hierarchy of the archangels we feel ourselves to be part of the whole of humanity. We may also say that we feel ourselves to be human because the archangels shine into our existence in spirit and soul, inspiring it. And because the Archai, the spirits of the age, send their pulses into our true nature, intuiting it, we feel ourselves to be creatures on earth, that is, not just part of present-day humanity but part of the whole of earthly humanity from the beginnings of Earth evolution to its end. So this is why we feel ourselves to be part of the whole of Earth evolution. We sense it only dimly, for we only have a dim inner sense of the spirits of the age.

We cannot say that we see ourselves as an individual. This we can only do when we achieve awareness in images. This awareness in images continues to be a kind of mirror image for as long as we only experience our thoughts in such a way that we feel ourselves to be individuals through our independent life of thought. Let us be clear once more as to what makes us feel that we are individuals. We do so in that we are able to join one thought arbitrarily to another. You would immediately cease to see yourself as an individual if you were forced to add one thought to another the way one natural phenomenon follows another. The experience of inner freedom—in taking our thoughts forward we feel ourselves to be individuals—is something which does come most clearly to conscious awareness when we are awake. It does so because from going to sleep to waking up human beings are fully imbued with their angel, and this angelic spirit belongs to our I. It is with much greater indifference, much less strength and intensity that we feel ourselves to be part of the whole of humanity, for we are naturally less close to the archangelic spirit which makes us feel that we are human than we are to our angel. And the principle which places us as individuals in the whole stream of human evolution does remain really, really shadowy. We try, of course, in working with spiritual science, to bring this feeling ourselves as part of the whole of earthly humanity awake, realizing that in the fifth post-Atlantean era human beings experience things in this way, in the fourth post-Atlantean era they did so in another way, in the third post-Atlantean era in yet another way. Through the science of the spirit we now gain awareness of the way in which the state of the soul changes through the ages under the influence of the different spirits of the age, the spirits from the hierarchy of the Archai. And this awareness really makes it possible for human beings to see themselves in history, realizing: 'I am an individual living in the twentieth century.' Most people do not realize at all that their individual nature is only thinkable, can only be real because it exists within a particular period of time.

Our mind and spirit is wholly imbued with the spirits of the third hierarchy. This is something people would come to realize if they sought to develop insight in images in a more intensive way.

As you will realize, this insight in images is not there in the ordinary run of human development. From going to sleep to waking up the reality of I and astral body is dampened down. When awake, human beings lose the connection with the spirits of the third hierarchy. This is because particularly in the present cycle of time they are under an illusion even when awake. As we have just seen, they are under the illusion in their sleep that their I and astral body are inactive. They are not inactive; they are in lively interaction with the spirits of the third hierarchy. In the waking state the situation is that in the present cycle of time our physical body and our ether body are, in a way, wrongfully absorbing our soul and spirit nature; they imbue themselves with it. The normal situation would be very different for human beings. It would be that in the waking state human beings would feel themselves to be I and astral body, with the physical body and the ether body like a kind of peel or shell which they slip into, like something they carry about with them. But that is not how human beings feel themselves to be. They feel as if physical body and ether body were them. But they are not. We are indeed this entity in soul and spirit which uses the physical and ether body like a tool. We are, however, unable to rise above this delusion; it is part of the influences which our cycle in time has. So we have to feel identical with our physical body and ether body, though in the normal state of conscious awareness this would be like a hammer we hold and use to strike. We have to give ourselves up to the delusion that it is we who move through space in the flesh. But it is not us; it is merely so because the conscious awareness is unlawfully absorbed by our physical body and our ether body. The reason for this is that the ahrimanic powers are more powerful in the present cycle of time than they would have been if human evolution had taken its normal course. They draw the I and the astral body to the physical and ether body, as it were, creating the delusion for human beings that this head they have is them, that these hands and the whole body is them themselves. The physical body does unlawfully gain the conscious awareness which makes it seem as if our physical body brought about our individual nature. Someone who thinks that his physical body brings about his individual nature is under the same delusion as someone who stands in front of a mirror and thinks that the mirror is producing him since it is reflecting his image to him. To say that a form made of flesh which we carry about with us is us is no better than if someone holds out his hand in front of a mirror and thinks that the mirror is producing his hand for him. The whole of modern science makes people believe that the individual nature we experience inwardly has something to do with the physical body and the ether body, and not that the physical body and the ether body reflect this I and astral nature, creating the illusory image which from waking up to going to sleep we say is our I and our thoughts, that is, our astral body.

This, as it were, is the fundamental truth which we must perceive in the first place. With regard to this fundamental truth people today are, out of the forces in our present cycle of time, giving themselves up to a delusion in the conscious mind which is exactly what I have just been saying. We think that the thoughts or also feelings we experience inwardly come from our living body. But human beings are subject to this delusion by nature; in their present state of conscious awareness they cannot escape this delusion. Just as the sun seems larger when it appears on the horizon than it does when it is up above—we know this to be an illusion but that is how it appears—so it has to seem to us that it is in flesh and blood, as it were, that we see ourselves as individuals. The conscious mind is deceived.

Human beings have not always been subject to this delusion. Essentially it is a character trait of post-Christian times, after the Mystery on Golgotha. Before the Mystery on Golgotha it was a different kind of illusion. People did then not think that their conscious awareness was bound up with the physical body. History does not refer to this, but it is so nevertheless. It would be nonsense to suggest that someone who lived in the second or third millennium before the Christian era thought his soul was somehow produced by the physical body. In earlier times no one felt that his soul and spiritual nature was bound to the living body the way people do today.

The people of those earlier times did, however, have a lively awareness of the spirits of the third hierarchy. This they did have. They knew: 'My soul is not identical with my body.' This gave them a distinct awareness that this soul is not bound to the blood or to the muscles and so on, but that the soul is connected with the spirits of the third hierarchy.

A different kind of illusion existed for them not in the conscious mind but with regard to life. They considered this soul with the spirits of the third hierarchy to be bound to the natural world outside just as modern man believes his soul to be bound to his physical body. Modern man is under the delusion in his conscious mind that his soul is bound to his physical body and therefore does not see angels, archangels and archai; his physical body obscures them for him. The human being of old—in spite of being distinctly aware of the presence of the spirits of the third hierarchy, of their being bound up with his soul—would see the sense-perceptible natural world only dimly, indirectly. Modern man thinks his soul depends on his body; the earlier human beings thought that the spirits of the third hierarchy were bound up with the natural world outside, a world they perceived only dimly. They would confuse divine spirits, the spirits of the third hierarchy, with natural phenomena, seeing them reflected in those natural phenomena. Modern man places his soul in flesh and blood; the people of those early times placed the spirits of the third hierarchy in the natural world outside. They did not have the natural science we have today but believed natural phenomena to be brought about by one demon or another, by more or less divine spirits about which they were under a life-delusion. They were under that delusion because in their view those spirits were active in the natural phenomena in an almost physical form. It is important to know that in human evolution there was this earlier, pre-Christian time when human beings were under the life-illusion which I have characterized. After the Mystery on Golgotha people were under an illusion in the conscious mind. The influence of Christ Jesus—we'll speak of this tomorrow—should be to remove this mental delusion at least in people's conscious minds in a way similar to the way it was done for the life-delusion in the ancient mysteries. With the 'Christ in me' people should feel that the principle which is I and astral body lives in spiritual freedom and is not bound up with flesh and blood. They will, of course, only be able to perceive it through vision gained in spiritual science; but thanks to Paul's 'not I but the Christ in me' they can feel it.

The things I have been saying will give you the reasons why human beings must, in a way, experience the duality of the natural order on the one hand. This has no ideals, linking one event with the next from sheer necessity, merely connecting cause with effect and effect with cause, so that it is never possible to think that moral or other kinds of ideals are connected with whatever happens in the natural world. On the other hand one comes to realize that our existence would not be truly human without ideals, if we did not have something else to live with as human beings, something other than mere natural order. However, with the existing conscious awareness we would not be able to see that our ideals can be as effective as electricity or magnetism or the power of heat, so that our ideals would actually influence the natural order. Because of this, the natural order and the ideal order are side by side for us, and we cannot bridge the gap between them. In our waking hours the ahrimanic-free thinking is: 'As an individual person I am not any more bound to my physical body and to my ether body than I am bound when I stand before a mirror and the mirror reflects my image for me.' If people's awareness of their I and astral body were like this and if they would realize that this I and this astral body are something very real and not a mere mirror image, then they would also acknowledge on the basis of their ideals: 'Those are real powers, like electricity and magnetism, but they do not have an influence in the present time but will gain effectiveness as we go from this present incarnation to the next, from this life on earth to the next.'

If human beings were to realize when in their waking state that their I and their astral body are bound up with the spirits of the third hierarchy, or in other words if they were able to know themselves fully as earthly human beings, not just feeling themselves to be an independent individual, if they could sense how they are wrong in feeling that they are human beings of flesh and blood, then they also would not think that the natural order which presents itself to their senses out there was indeed powerful enough to resist the power of their ideals. They would know that all matter disintegrates in the natural order of today, that there is no such thing as the conservation of matter but that everything which is natural destroys itself. When today's nature does no longer exist, something else—outward, sense-perceptible and real—will have taken its place. The ideals of today will be the natural world of times to come. We are therefore able to say: 'We experience natural order today [red in Fig. 1] and ideal order [yellow].' Physicists think that there is conservation of energy and of matter, that the natural order persists, with the same atoms and the same forces taking effect in future. If they are honest all they can say is: 'The ideal order has been a dream; it must drop away and

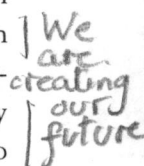

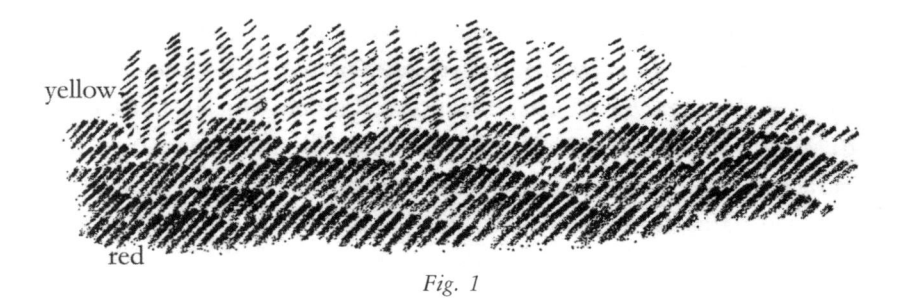

We are creating our future

yellow

red

Fig. 1

red

yellow

Fig. 2

vanish like the dream itself, so that in the earth's end state the ideal dream will no longer be there, will have been buried.'

Through spiritual science we see that this is an untruth, an illusion. We do have the natural order, but there is no conservation of energy and of matter. The natural order comes to an end at a certain point and today's ideal order will then be the continuation of it. None of the things that are around our eyes today, around our ears, around all our senses will exist when the earth has reached the Venus state. I have spoken of this before. Within that nothingness the possibility will arise for the ideals of present-day humanity to be outer reality. No philosophy of life which fails to recognize that the sense-perceptible world will perish can have any hope whatsoever that the ideal principle has the power to come to realization. If the sense-perceptible world were eternal, if there were such a thing as conservation of energy and of matter, the ideal world would be nothing but a dream. It is of tremendous importance that humanity needs to be enlightened in our day and know that the ideas of the present time will be the natural world of the future, and that it is a tremendous illusion to think that atoms and physical forces go on for ever. They are not eternal; they are temporal. It is a fatal aspect of spiritual science that one has to contradict a view which is considered to be the most certain of all in the established science of today when in fact it is nothing but an ahrimanic deception.

Let us consider once more what I have just been saying. Before the Mystery on Golgotha human illusion was an illusion in life. After the Mystery on Golgotha it became what we may call an illusion in the conscious mind. If we know this we understand many things in human evolution. Above all we understand why human beings who before the Mystery on Golgotha had atavistic clairvoyance nevertheless did not see the things which they did see in their true form but saw the spirits of the higher hierarchies as demons. This is why the old mythologies are largely demonologies. All the gods in the ancient mythologies are demons. This was so because there was this illusion in life and human beings did in a way have to think of a kind of false natural order as the divine order, just as today they have to think of a false bodily order as humanity's order.

There followed the Mystery on Golgotha. Human beings had to take their state of soul to the point, as it were, where they perceived what had resulted from the Mystery on Golgotha. The human soul related more directly in its waking state to the spirits of the higher hierarchies than it does today when the conscious mind is deceived. People would see the spirits of the higher hierarchies, merely recasting them, because of the life-delusion, into Zeus, Apollo and so on. Those were spirits of the third hierarchy but they had been recast, seen under the influence of the life-delusion just as today we see everything relating to man under the influence of the conscious mind's delusion. Yet with all this a divine world order extended into humanity. Just consider how close people of past ages knew their human world to be to the divine world order! There you'd have the human hierarchy, and then there would be the divine hierarchy. People did not feel as closed off above as we do today. Their world ran on towards that of the gods. Think how close a Greek would feel his world of gods to be to the human world, the human hierarchy!

There followed the Mystery on Golgotha. There it was no longer the case. It was not the Mystery on Golgotha—which was to provide a replacement for what had been lost—but it was time which brought it about that human beings were cut off in their evolution from that conscious connection with the divine and spiritual world of the third hierarchy. A memory remained, however, a historical memory. Then came the time after the Mystery on Golgotha. People had to think in a somewhat different way than they had done before the Mystery on Golgotha, but some of the immediate past still had an influence. In the immediate past human beings knew that the divine spirits had influenced events on earth, putting human activities on earth in order. Because of this people of old were convinced when they established states—the term 'state' does not quite meet the case but people are used to putting it this way—when the people of old created social structures, founded them, I'd say, they would know that these social structures were being established under the influence of the third hierarchy. People felt that their institutions on earth were institutions of the gods. You need only study the history of ancient Egypt, with no need for clairvoyance, and you'll find that the Egyptians were wholly convinced that everything human beings did in their social situations on earth was instituted by the spirits of the third hierarchy. This is how it was before the Mystery on Golgotha. Only a memory of this remained after the Mystery on Golgotha.

What was the consequence of this? Well, you know that the Church gradually established itself after the Mystery on Golgotha. The Church established a particular ranking order—deacons, archdeacons, bishops, archbishops and so on. There was a quite specific idea behind this which is still quite evident in the works of the early Church writers. Read Dionysius the Areopagite,[14] and you'll see it quite clearly. The administration of the Church was to reflect the divine order. The way a deacon related to the archdeacon was to reflect the relationship of angel to archangel. And then again the relationship of archdeacon to bishop—a reflection of archangel to archai. The social structure of the Church was intended to reflect the theocracy. Up in the spiritual world were the ranks of the hierarchies; below, reflecting the spiritual hierarchies, the ranks of Church dignitaries. The thinking behind this was not of the legal kind in the early days after the Mystery on Golgotha; it was theocratic. The Church's hierarchy was seen as a reflection of the divine and spiritual hierarchies. This was the thinking in the early Christian centuries on earth, intending to cultivate institutions on earth where the relative positions of human beings reflected the image of the hierarchies up above in the spiritual world.

People then gradually lost the awareness that had remained as a memory, a historical memory from the times of the old theocracy when they had still known that earthly institutions were in fact a consequence of things done by the gods. Abstract concepts took the place of the living world of gods which people had seen in the past and later on remembered. Instead of knowing that there is a world of divine individual spirits up there, people then had abstract metaphysical concepts. There followed centuries when abstract ideas, metaphysics, took the place of the individual gods—Christians would call them angels. The divine order which was to be reflected in the human order had provided a theocratic element; the application of mere concepts to the order of human society provided something which, well, could only serve to maintain order in human social relationships. Where before thought was given to creating an image of the divine world in the way human society was structured, the only aim in the metaphysical age was to maintain order, punish evildoers, neither punish nor reward the good, establishing the kind of order needed to maintain the social order. When abstract metaphysical concepts had replaced the living gods it was merely a matter of creating a human order in which people were labelled, making one the superior of the other not because being superior was meant to reflect the relationship of an archangel to an angel but because order was only considered possible if one person commanded and the other obeyed. Abstraction took the place of a social order that had been full of life.

Essentially this was the time of real metaphysics throughout the Middle Ages. It was the Roman mentality which essentially provided the elements for this metaphysical order which then spread everywhere. The German word *Fürst*[*] remains to remind us of the theocratic order, the first because someone has to be the first, just as one is the first also in the divine hierarchy. A reminder of the merely metaphysical kind of order, the order of officialdom, administrators, is the German word *Graf*[†] which is connected with *grapho*, to write. The metaphysical order involves registration, maintaining order, producing documents, making contracts.

Then came the more recent times. They brought disbelief in those abstract concepts, disbelief in metaphysics. People were only able to believe in anything evident to the senses, even in human life.

---

[*] Prince; pronounced 'first' and deriving from 'first, foremost'. Translator.
[†] In English a 'count'; originally a village elder appointed to remind villagers of taxes that were due. Translator.

Awareness of the traditions which had still persisted in earlier times, when traditions were living awareness of the fact that something or other was at work in social structures—originally people thought of gods, later of metaphysical concepts—such living awareness no longer existed in more recent times. It has to be regained in the ways indicated through spiritual science. But the industrial age brought the total eradication of all awareness of the spiritual background to the social structure. This is why Auguste Comte and Saint-Simon felt particularly connected with the industrial age, seeing that they were prepared only to accept positivist science, i.e. anything connected with external, sense-perceptible natural order of causal necessity.

The concept of truth has changed completely as a result. Modern people are not yet truly sentient of the fact that the concept of truth has a history; people have no real idea of this today. People who still knew themselves to be in a theocratic order did not see truth the way people do today on the authority of natural science. It is extraordinarily difficult to speak about these things. Today one thinks that with regard to the world order truth means that an idea is in accord with an external reality. This is because of natural science. They did not see truth like this in the early Christian centuries. Their idea of truth was different and this other meaning of 'truth' was largely connected with the theocratic social order. They truly did not have the idea of truth which lives in all human souls today. People fail to realize this extraordinarily important fact. It will be much easier for us to grasp the idea of truth which people then had if we connect it with the idea of the ordeal.* When two people enter into single combat—we need not concern ourselves with the view taken of a duel today, I'm merely giving it as an example—it cannot be decided beforehand if A will win or B; otherwise they'd hardly start their duel. No, the truth only emerges as the event proceeds. We still have this idea of truth today when a war is fought. People would not

---

* Historically an ancient test of guilt or innocence by subjecting the accused to severe pain, survival of which was taken as divine proof of innocence. The German term for this translates as 'divine judgement'. Translator.

go to war if everything was known beforehand, as it is when an experiment is done in a laboratory where every aspect has been considered beforehand and one knows what the result will be. People would hardly go to war if they knew the outcome in advance, as one does with a laboratory experiment. There we still have the old idea of truth which was that the truth will only be apparent in the process and all one can do is watch and see what the result of the ordeal will be. That was the old idea of truth.

People like Auguste Comte or today's socialists who have completely abandoned this idea of truth—other people have not, they only think they have—only acknowledge the kind of truth where developments can be foreseen. 'Gaining insight in order to foresee' was Auguste Comte's motto, and that is a radical reversal of the idea of truth in our time. But we can only grasp nature with this idea of truth. And people are under a colossal illusion in this respect. They think, for instance, that they are able to grasp historical life with Auguste Comte's notion of truth. But one cannot do this. Nor can one do so with the old ordeal notion of truth, but that was influenced by the life-illusion; our present-day idea of truth is under the influence of the mind being deceived. There will have to be the idea of truth developed out of anthroposophy, a concept of truth that is gained in a much more comprehensive way than the way in which Augustine, for example, arrived as his idea of truth. As I have shown, this was subject to a delusion.

This is connected with many things and very much depends on it. It is not enough to speak of an evolution of the idea of truth in abstract terms. We have to know in detail how the idea of truth takes the human soul in different directions depending on the nature of this idea of truth. It is an anachronism to speak of nationality the way it could be done in pre-Christian times. Then it was not just that people were thinking that the divine order extended into the human order. It truly was so. Now it no longer extends into it. So where people today cling to natural orders, to things merely brought about by birth following birth, the national principle, for instance, we are in an anachronism. People are forced today to look for different structures for their social order in post-Christian times, structures that are not determined from outside. People of earlier times were able to consider their nationality because they saw this as an institution of the divine order and saw life on earth as a reflection of the divine order. Modern man cannot venerate the nation itself as something special in the same way without falling into anachronism. We must endeavour to find different social structures. To venerate the nation as something special would lead to the ahrimanic deception of today. Nations are left-overs from pre-Christian times, and modern humanity must get beyond that by developing in the way which I have mentioned. We have to realize how much people are seeking a special form of the truth concept. This is important, even if it is awkward at the present time. If we are unbiased in taking the standpoint of truly grasping reality we will have to accept many an uncomfortable truth.

People are today literally moving towards the true aim of anthroposophy. The philosophy of life which had Auguste Comte as its particular representative is limited to the natural order outside. There is need to advance again into the spiritual world, and a bridge must be built between reality and ideality. This is indeed what I want to refer to particularly in these lectures. It will not happen, however, if we merely talk of these things but only if we grasp the concrete impulses in the world. For this we must look wholly without bias at certain facts. Strange facts are connected with the things we are now considering. Just think, yesterday I spoke to you about Saint-Simon and Auguste Comte. Both were only considering positivist science to matter, that is, anything relating to sense-perceptible life, to the causal natural order. And yet there is the strange fact that Auguste Comte turned away from Saint-Simon, his teacher and guide, because Saint-Simon had become too much of a mystic in old age. The strange fact is that Saint-Simon as well as Auguste Comte were on the one hand basing themselves firmly on the ground of ahrimanic science, consciously basing themselves on ahrimanic science in the industrial age, and then to turn mystic! Strange—it is a strange fact.

We have to enquire into the Why of such a fact. The Why of such a fact will, however, only show itself if we take an unbiased view of the way in which human beings are seeking spirituality. Many people who like Auguste Comte and Saint-Simon intended to go only by the natural order are moving towards spirituality.

Now there is something most peculiar in the human life of more recent times. Take another fact, looking at it wholly without bias, without any kind of national chauvinism, which does not become us. In the views that arise as the flower of more recent national characteristics, something is characteristic in a way which is to be found down below in these national characters. Starting from this, I'd refer you to another fact, to Bentham,[15] very much a trend-setting English philosopher who lived from 1748 to 1832. Bentham may be said to have been characteristic of his people's way of thinking. In a sense Bentham's way of thinking has been called utilitarian, also utilitarian in a deeper sense. There is a particular principle behind his thinking that relates to the ideal world order. This principle is usually also referred to as 'the greatest happiness principle'. This human happiness is, according to Bentham, that the good, i.e. the ideal to aim for, consisted in the greatest happiness of the greatest number of people on earth. Let us really look at this. The good is the greatest happiness for the greatest number of people on earth. This is indeed a key element in utilitarian philosophy.

We have to consider that those words have been called absolutely ahrimanic, not by Bentham and his followers but by people who take the spiritual point of view. Occultists in his own country[16] have said that Bentham produced this 'utterly devilish' statement. They called it devilish for, according to those occultists, if it were the case that the good consists in the greatest happiness for the greatest number of people, then evil would consist in the greatest happiness for the smallest number of people.

This is not something which I myself want to present as a definition or explication; it is what people say. So on the one hand the English philosophy of Bentham: greatest happiness. On the other hand English spiritualists saying: Bentham's thesis is absolutely devilish, for in that case evil would mean the greatest happiness for the smallest number of people. The conclusion would be that evil and happiness could exist together, and a spiritualist cannot accept that under any circumstances. I am merely presenting a fact in cultural life which is most eminently significant for the most tremendous opposition existing between spiritualists and the outward philosophy of life in a particular area on earth.

Having said that in tomorrow's talk these oppositions will be resolved, I am ending today's talk with a succinct statement. You can take three things—Goetheanism, Comteanism and Benthamism. These relate in three different ways to humanity's spiritual striving for the future. German Goetheanism as such has the potential to develop into spiritualism. French Comteanism is such that spiritualism can develop alongside it, like the strange mysticism alongside the positivist philosophy of Auguste Comte and Saint-Simon. With the English utilitarianism, Benthamism, the only thing that can arise is the most severe opposition of spiritualists to the popular view. This is a fundamental part of evolution itself. French nature has to evolve in such a way that idealism and realism, mysticism and positivism can run side by side. In England, within essential British nature, things will more and more go in a direction where the people who become spiritualists there will gradually have to fight more and more against their own national characteristics, that is, against the flowers of the philosophies of their nation.

As to Auguste Comte—I am not presenting theories but also giving you the facts, or at least some of them—when he had turned to positivism he abandoned his teacher Saint-Simon, but there was such a distinct inclination towards mysticism that at the end of his life he clearly accepted a trinity. He venerated three things—the Great Fetish, the Great Medium and the Great Spirit. And he said that the Great Fetish was the womb of humanity in space. Space was the medium from which humanity arose as from the womb. The Great Spirit is humanity spread out over the earth in abstract terms. Auguste Comte acknowledged this trinity. A strange combination of positivism and mysticism! We'll say more of this tomorrow.

LECTURE 3

8 SEPTEMBER 1918

First of all I must remind you of what we were saying yesterday, and we can then take this further. Essentially what I said yesterday was that it is not possible to gain insight into the relationship between the ideal or also the spiritual on the one hand and the material in the world on the other, the purely causal natural order, unless one takes the real nature of human sleep into account.

We started by considering Augustine's thinking, the way he wanted to gain true certainty about the world in his inner experience. Today we can no longer think like that, I said, for the simple reason that today we must know that human sleep always refutes this idea. We could never stay with the idea in some way that the inner experiences of human beings persist after death, that these inner experiences are truly eternal, if we had to look at the time from going to sleep to waking up the way we do in our ordinary conscious awareness today. In the ordinary conscious mind of today we see the inner experiences grow dim in sleep. We did say, however, that as soon as someone achieves the first stage of looking into the spiritual world they find that the human I and astral body—i.e. the actual human soul and spirit—are as much connected from within with the world of the angels, archangels and archai as human beings are connected with the animal world, plant world and mineral world in their waking hours. In sleep the world's adversary powers dim down human awareness and we are therefore unable to realize that in our sleep we are connected with the hierarchy of angels, archangels and archai. These imbue the human I and astral body with their own essential nature, holding and sustaining the human astral body and I. And we told how three things have come from this connection between human beings and the hierarchic spirits. The first is that even in our ordinary state of mind we have a more or less definite feeling of being an individual person. We know ourselves to be an I. We would never do so if we had only the powers we have in our waking hours. It is like an after-effect of our experiences in sleep that during the day, in our waking hours, we do all the time feel ourselves to be an independent individual. This is because the angelic spirit from the spiritual world of which we are part is connected with us from going to sleep to waking up. But the archangelic spirit or rather a number of archangelic spirits are also connected with our soul and spirit. The after-effect of this in our waking hours is that we know ourselves to be members of the whole of humanity, knowing altogether that we are human beings here on earth.

Every human being really has awareness of his or her independent individual nature, even if it is not entirely distinct. Awareness that we are human is less clear-cut; we have it at the back of our mind. Some philosophers—Feuerbach,[17] for instance, or indeed Auguste Comte—held the view that it is indeed an important discovery for human beings when they come to see themselves as human in general, as members of the whole of humanity. And we heard yesterday that Auguste Comte would speak of the Great Spirit, meaning the human being. He was, however, speaking from the point of view of ordinary materialistic science, not knowing the spiritual basis of being aware of our humanity in the background of our inner life. We would not be able to have the least idea of being human if the part of us which in sleep is separated from our physical and ether body were not wholly imbued with the archangelic spirit.

Thirdly we are imbued with the spirit of the age, the spirit from the hierarchy of the archai. Anything arising from this remains really quite dark, shadowy in our mind. Present-day humanity does not have it at all except when people feel themselves to be part of history, the life of history. Oriental thinking has not at all advanced as far as this awareness of being an earthly human being. It has been the particular task of occidental civilization to feel ourselves to be part of history—in our case let us say as belonging to the nineteenth and twentieth centuries. In today's materialistic age this does not go far beyond the year and some external historical dates. We'll hear in a minute how little this really means where real life is concerned. It needs spiritual science to make us realize how the state of the human soul changes through the millennia, how human beings change, and how we now look back on earlier times and know that the people of the third post-Atlantean era, the Egypto-Chaldaean peoples, had a very different constitution of soul and of their humanity from the one we have today. We have this sense of being part of the whole evolution of humanity as an after-effect of our connection with the arche spirit during the time from going to sleep to waking up. From going to sleep to waking up we should know that we are connected with this third spiritual hierarchy.

How does our life from going to sleep to waking up, which happens every day, differ from our life between death and being born again? Every night as we go to sleep we are putting our physical and ether body aside provisionally, as it were, until revoked. The body is kept for us. We are then connected with the spirits of the third hierarchy. On waking we return to our physical and ether body. The situation is different when we can no longer return, having died. Then our physical and ether body is given over to the drives of earthly change and development—apparently so. We know that it is apparently so, having talked the other day about the fact that it seems to be so. As far as our experience goes, our physical and ether body is given over to the spheres of earth and sky. Yet in the time between death and rebirth we are not merely in contact with the spirits of the third hierarchy the way we are in sleep but we are in equally close contact with the spirits of the second hierarchy—the Exusiai or Spirits of Form, the Dynameis or Spirits of Movement, and the Kyriotetes or Spirits of Wisdom—and also the spirits of the first hierarchy—Seraphim, Cherubim and Thrones. As here on earth we direct our essential human nature towards the world and in the world periphery to everything to be found in the natural worlds, so will we then be aware—not outwardly but inwardly—of the higher hierarchies having an influence between death and rebirth. From a certain point of view this is the difference between human sleep and death. In sleep we are directly—and also indirectly—connected with the spirits of the third hierarchy, after death with the spirits of all three hierarchies, all the way up to the most sublime spirits.

With this in mind you'll also be able to see how human beings altogether have their place in the universe, as microcosm related to the whole universe, to the macrocosm. Let us get an overview of what I have been saying. After death our spiritual nature is inwardly connected with the spirits of the third hierarchy, those of the second hierarchy and those of the first hierarchy, just as here it is connected with the animal, plant and mineral worlds around us. When you get to know everything which the spirits of the third hierarchy do in the first place—they have other things to do as well but we are always only talking about some aspects of things, aren't we? The spirits of the third hierarchy are single individuals, each acting on its own but through its actions also together with others. If you bring to mind what these spirits of the third hierarchy bring about, it is first of all everything—first of all, as I said—that happens in the historical life of humanity [Fig. 3]. You may also put it like this: No one knows anything about the reality of humanity's historical life unless they have some idea of the true nature of history which in real terms is made not by human beings but by the spirits of the third hierarchy. It is they—angels, archangels and archai—who actually make history. Human beings take part in the work of this third hierarchy by gaining from it awareness of their individual nature, their humanity, of being historical entities on earth. Human beings have their place in the world because those spirits create historical life and human beings do in turn have their inner nature and their inner connection with historical life from these spirits. Historical life all around us, history as it is generally accepted, is largely a story that has been

[Handwritten annotations at top: Astral body - Angelic Hierarchy, Historical life of humanity / Etheric body - 2nd hierarchy - planetary evolution]

agreed upon, a mere reflection of the inwardly historical life, the course of which is created by the spirits of the third hierarchy.

We may now ask if the spirits of the second and first hierarchy also had tasks in a similar way—speaking of the Exusiai, Dynameis, Kyriotetes, Spirits of Form, Spirits of Movement and Spirits of Wisdom. Well, their task was much more comprehensive. Let us leave aside their connection with humanity to begin with. You will find it easiest to consider their task if you direct your attention to your ether body. You know, of course, that when you start from your I and move inwards you'll first of all come to your astral body. Through the astral body you are connected with the historical life of humanity. The spirits of the third hierarchy create and influence the historical life of humanity. But when you go further, down to the ether body, you find that this ether body is a most complex entity. In present-day life human beings do not know much of the whole complexity on which this human ether body is based. You will get some idea of everything which has to work on this ether body if you study *Occult Science*. There you find how the ether body evolved from the whole cosmos in the successive Saturn, Sun and Moon periods, consecutive embodiments of our earth, and how the spirits of the higher hierarchies played their part in this. To put it succinctly we may say from a particular point of view that everything in world evolution—a more comprehensive evolution—which our ether body is connected with, just as our astral body is connected with the historical life of humanity, is created and developed by the spirits of the second hierarchy, by Exusiai, Dynameis, Kyriotetes. To give you a clear picture I'll say that the spirits of the second hierarchy do all the things that influence the human ether body.

This really leads to something else again. When you wake up in the morning and enter into your ether body you are actually entering into a creature of the spirits of the second hierarchy. You also enter into your physical body which in the ancient mysteries was called the temple of man. Anything discovered about this in anatomy and physiology really and truly is merely the absolutely outermost

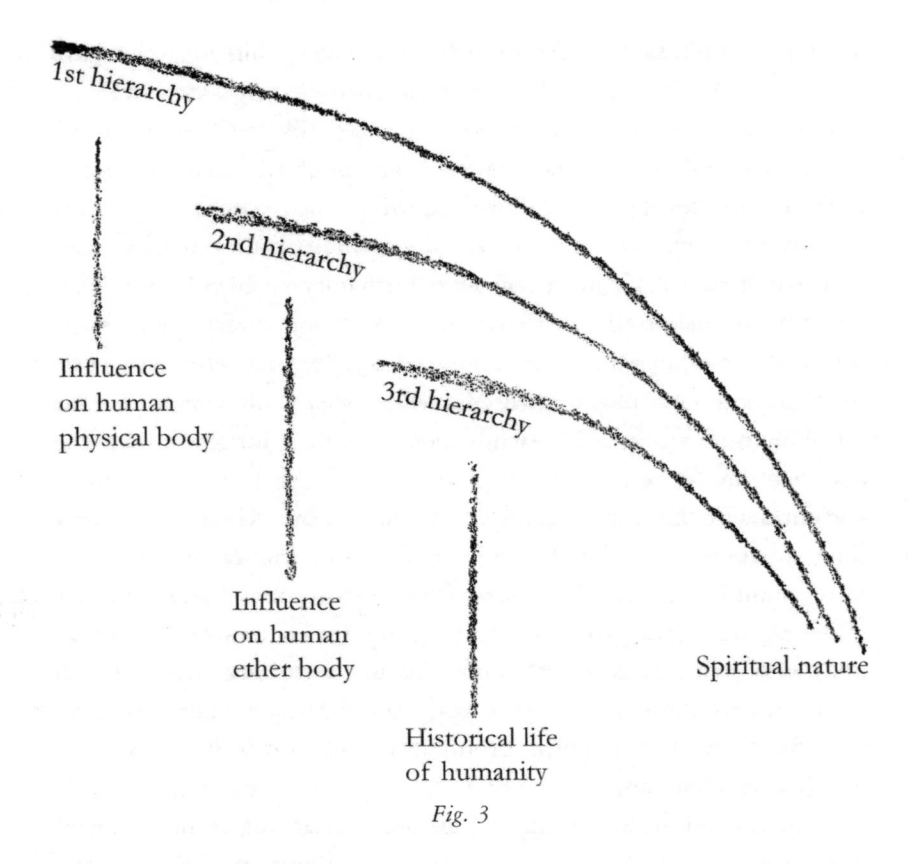

```
1st hierarchy
      |
      |
Influence
on human
physical body

        2nd hierarchy
              |
              |
        Influence
        on human
        ether body

                3rd hierarchy
                      |
                      |
                Historical life
                of humanity

                              Spiritual nature
```

Fig. 3

envelope or shell. We can only get an idea of this utterly marvellous creation which is the human physical body if we know that it has been created by the spirits of the first hierarchy working together. Entering into your physical body as you wake up in the morning you are actually entering into the work of the most sublime hierarchies. Consider, therefore, how things are arranged in life. Here, between birth and death, we enter on waking first of all into our astral body where the historical life of humanity takes effect. We also enter into our ether body, created by the second hierarchy. There much of the cosmos, the etheric life in the cosmos, is at work. And we enter into our physical body, created by the spirits of the first hierarchy. In our life between death and rebirth, however, we are not living with the creation but with the creators themselves.

Lecture 3 * 43

Here you have one of the marked differences in life between birth and death and life between death and rebirth. As you enter into your bodily nature here you are entering into all that is creature of the higher hierarchies. When you die you enter into the hierarchies themselves. You move from the creature to the creators. That is the situation.

Let us now ask, as we consider what has been said: What is the true nature of our earth? The things our ordinary geology or other sciences discover about the earth are again merely an outer shell. So what is the earth's true nature? You know that we have our physical body in common with the whole mineral world and in the waking state we are within a part of the earth. We have our ether body in common with the whole plant world, and in this respect are within a second part of our earth. We have our astral body in common with the animal world. The I we have for ourselves. We are thus within the three worlds on our earth, and they really make up the whole of our earth. It is the ground we stand on, as it were, not physically but in our essential human nature. It is something that cannot be seen; it stays supersensible. It is the ground we stand on, and the mineral world is its lowest part.

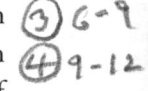

The mineral world is the lowest part of this ground we base ourselves on. You'll remember from *Occult Science* that the mineral world did not exist in earlier embodiments of our earth. The Moon did not yet have a mineral world, nor did the old Sun, nor indeed old Saturn. You can read it up in *Occult Science*. The mineral world only evolved on earth, the fourth stage of Earth evolution. I'd ask you to remember this. It is a difficult matter but it is extraordinarily important. There had to be three prior stages before the mineral earth evolved. We call those three stages the three elemental realms, with the mineral world the fourth. We might also say about the earlier embodiments: During the Saturn embodiment of the earth, first elemental realm; during the Sun embodiment of the earth, second elemental realm (the entities which were then mineral world had earlier been elemental realm); during the Moon period—not the present time, the old Moon period—third elemental realm. The mineral world arose as the fourth realm on progression to earth. Human beings bear this within them.

To be within the mineral world is to be in the fourth development. We bear this mineral world within us and it is this which makes us into visible entities. This mineral world is also the only one which is complete in us. When the earth will have come to an end, when it will have entered into another embodiment, human beings will be as complete in the plant world as they are in the mineral world today. They will then be in the fifth stage of development. I am saying that the earth will reach an end state and then arise anew—Jupiter period. Human beings will then relate to the plant world the way they do to the mineral world today. They will be in the fifth development. To be in the plant world is to be in the fifth development.

There will be a further embodiment of our earth. We call it the Venus stage or period. Human beings will then hold their own place in the animal world, not be animals but be in the animal world. As you know, this is different from being an animal. To be in the animal world is to be in the sixth development. There follows the conclusion, the seventh in musical terms, in the whole process of evolution. We call this the Vulcan embodiment of the earth. Man will then have reached the highest level of his evolution. He will finally be wholly human. To be in the human realm is to be in the seventh development. And the life of man goes through a total of seven stages of development.

Let us look at present-day human beings. As we have seen they are within the mineral world; they are not yet in the plant world. Life will be very different for them when they will be in the plant world. They will not feel themselves to be individuals but members of the whole of humanity. They will then, for instance, find it intolerable to have a certain degree of good fortune if someone next to them is suffering misfortune. Today people feel separate from others as if there were a screen between them. This will have to be so, otherwise they would never be able to develop their individual nature. But it will be different in the Jupiter world, where human beings will be in the fifth stage of development. There they will find it utterly intolerable if one person is happy and another unhappy, for they will not feel themselves to be an organism, to put it in abstract terms. Now they do not feel themselves to be an organism, but that is maya, illusion. A time will come, however, when human beings will be in the plant world and will be unable to bear individual good fortune if someone else is suffering misfortune.

This thought is behind the feelings of the spiritualists of whom I spoke yesterday. I told you that English spiritualists will have to fight a great battle in future times against the whole of popular English culture. The evil in this culture is utilitarianism. In Bentham's case this utilitarianism essentially led to the principle that has been called the maximation of happiness. This utilitarianism will fill people's minds more and more and that is why this way of thinking will only come to be spiritualized under opposition from those who are spiritually minded. That is the prospect for the future. The spiritually-minded will have to overcome popular culture, vanquish it to annihilation. And so I was able to tell you that Bentham arrived at his maxim out of his nation's culture, saying that the good on earth was the happiness of the greatest number of people. His worst opponents were the spiritually-minded in his own country who told him that this was a devilish definition, one which one could only produce if one thought of nothing but the present. Thinking a little of the future in evolution one would know that it was quite intolerable to think of the happiness of the greatest number, since the opposite to this would be the happiness of the least number, and that would have to be evil. Yet evil and happiness have nothing to do with one another; such contradistinction will be impossible in future when human beings will feel themselves to be within the plant world, part of the whole of humanity. Today we cannot cut away an important organ in the human body, for the whole human organism would then perish. In future, when the earth will be within the plant world, it will not be possible for a particular group of people to be suffering without the whole suffering. That will be a particular stage in evolution. Bentham gave a definition of happiness that has absolutely no future but only a present time, and this must be fought particularly by those who seek spirituality.

Yes, but why is it said to be the opposite when one says, 'Good defined by Bentham as the happiness of the greatest number, evil defined as the happiness of the lowest number'? These are not opposites in abstract terms the way people see it, but spiritualists do not think in abstract but in real terms. They do not ask, 'What is the opposite to this?' but think of the reality which evolves and that is not usually the general way of thinking.

Individuals will take part in the whole to an even greater degree when they are in the sixth stage of development, and particularly so if they are wholly human, wholly spiritualized human beings, in the seventh stage.

We have seen from this that the way we are now on the solid ground of our earth we do as human beings, in so far as we are creatures, really only get as far as the fourth stage of development. We have the mineral world and this is complete. The other worlds, the way they are today, will partly perish and human beings will develop them in a different way—the plant world as I have described it. We won't speak of the animal and human worlds today but on another occasion.

Today human beings find themselves in the fourth stage of development when they see themselves as creature among other creatures. They do, however, project into the other stages of development, for as we have seen, human beings are under the influence of the third hierarchy even when just asleep. This hierarchy is further advanced than they are; it is today in the fifth stage of development, and the other spirits have advanced even further. Human beings thus project into the higher stages of development. I would ask you to be patient and really think these subtle thoughts through, for you must now make distinction between thinking yourself a creature and thinking yourself the independent spirit which you are in sleep, for instance, or between death and rebirth. In so far as you do here think of yourself in your physical, in your ether body, astral body and I, you are thinking of yourself as a creature on earth and are in the fourth stage of development but are <u>projecting into the fifth, sixth and seventh developments</u>. As you live not just in your body but also out of your body, in sleep or in death, you project into the other hierarchies, and those other hierarchies are more advanced. So we are able to say that if we look on the earth and everything on it and in it as something created, then it has as creation developed as far as the fourth stage and we have developed with it, also as far as the fourth stage. But since we feel ourselves to be independent individuals, human beings, feel ourselves to be part of Earth evolution, knowing that our ether body has been created by the second hierarchy, and our physical body by the first hierarchy, we extend up into the other spheres, the other developmental elements.

The seventh stage of development is not the end, however. Evolution continues, and since we project into the higher forms of development we also project into an eighth form of development, the famous eighth sphere.[18] It is reasonable to say that in a way we do extend to the eighth development since we extend up to highly developed levels of sublime spirits and are thus in the divine realm or the realm of the spirits—call it what you will. We extend into this eighth development with the most subtle parts of our spiritual nature. This extension to the eighth development is a great secret but we can get an idea of a very slight, I'd say, not very intensive projection into the eighth development if we consider the following.

We know that the central point for earth is the Mystery on Golgotha. Looking back to this Mystery on Golgotha, how it happened in year 1 to 33 in our calendar, in the 747th year following the founding of Rome, we find it happened in the first third of the fourth post-Atlantean era. We refer to the time in the evolution of human civilization when it took place as the fourth post-Atlantean civilization. We know that the third period of civilization preceded the Graeco-Roman period. We are now in the fifth, for the fourth, in which the Mystery on Golgotha took place, ended in the fifteenth century. We are now in the first third of the fifth post-Atlantean period of civilization. Humanity evolves through the periods of civilization, but when we speak of them we are actually speaking of something in which human beings are not wholly involved. All of you are bound to have been incarnated in the ancient Egypto-Chaldaean period which was the third post-Atlantean age, then again in the Graeco-Roman period and now in the present one. But you only ever live through 80 years—if you reach the age of 80, all things being well—of the period, and there is a much longer period of time between your incarnations, the period from death to rebirth. Human beings thus share only part of the successive periods of Earth evolution.

You may say, of course, 'Ah well, human beings only go through part of it in their physical body; but it is not for nothing that they live in a physical body—they experience the world from the standpoint of the physical body because they would not be able to have the experiences which they have in the physical body when they are between death and rebirth.' Now anything experienced between death and rebirth when human beings are in the purely spiritual world may be rated more or less highly—we won't go into this today—but it is different from the things human beings experience here through their physical bodies, always in episodes of human evolution as a whole. They would not be able to experience them if it were not for development in the living body. People have quite the wrong idea when they are ascetic about the development of the body on earth, seeing it as an enemy of the higher human being. That is not so. It is something which gives human beings something which they cannot gain in any other way. Someone who despises life in the body, considering it to be something inferior, is utterly mistaken, for it signifies something most sublime, most important in human life as a whole. Spiritual science cannot go along with the mysticism or that wrong direction in Christianity—not the right but the wrong direction—where people despise what they call the mundane world. Human beings experience the world from a different angle between death and rebirth. They experience it in the way in which they are able—with now the creators themselves influencing them and not the creations which influenced them through physical body and ether body. It is a different experience.

It is because of this that we need to get to know not only the things perceived through the senses but also the supersensible during our time on earth. We cannot get to know the historical life of humanity, which results from the efforts of the third hierarchy, from the point of view we have in life on earth. And for our time—please note that I am saying 'for our time', for it was not so in pre-Christian times—for our time it is most important that human beings become aware that if they want to get to know themselves as part of history whilst here on earth between birth and death they must also come to know what the angels, archangels and archai bring about as historical life. Getting to know the world only in the way natural scientists seek to know it today, getting to know the world the way it is described in history, as if history were made solely by people and not by the spirits of the third hierarchy, is to get to know only the outermost layers of historical evolution. History can only be known by someone who is aware that whilst here in a physical body he must, as it were, see what the spirits are doing on earth which he gets to know in a very different way between death and rebirth—if I may use a term which has to be relative—personally, individually, in their heavenly deeds. We have to get to know their influence on historical life on earth.

But it has not always been the way it is now, in the age in which we live. Above all it was not like this in the third post-Atlantean era, before the year 747 in Egypto-Chaldaean times. We know that people's whole inner life, the whole state of their soul, was different then. Life from beyond the earth shone into ordinary human life, and people knew—though their interpretation was different from the one which we use in mythologies—that the spirits of the third hierarchy influenced their I and their astral body. They meant the spirits of the third hierarchies though they called them Osiris or Zeus or Apollo or Minerva or whatever. They knew that those spirits—they merely thought them out and interpreted them, but the figures thought out and interpreted actually were those spirits—had an influence. They might not have wanted to see them but they did see them inwardly for in those early times the mind was not deluded the way it is today.

Only the delusion about life existed, anthropomorphizing those figures, as it is said. People knew of those figures, however.

This is one of those points which changed the whole life of humanity. Today people do not know in their ordinary state of mind what plays into their lives. Man was born with a soul in that third post-Atlantean era, was born again in the fourth post-Atlantean era and again in our time. Human beings do not perceive what the spirits of the third hierarchy bring about as historical life, but they should get to know it, they really should! The people of earlier times came to know it in its mythological form.

Let us enter into such a human soul. There are more incarnations, as you know, but let us take three successive incarnations—one Egyptian, one Greek and one from the fifth post-Atlantean period of civilization. In the third, the Egypto-Chaldaean period of civilization that soul experienced the things which it could then experience because the spirits of the third hierarchy influenced life. This gradually dimmed down. Some would still experience it in the fourth, the Graeco-Roman period; many still experienced it in the proper way especially until the year 333 after the Mystery on Golgotha. Then it gradually disappeared. People then had to limit themselves more and more to the sense-perceptible world around them unless they went through such inner development that they came to know the spiritual world by another route and were thus able to ascend to the spirits of the third hierarchy.

If we look at such a soul as it now returns again, it comes with everything it had taken in during the third post-Atlantean era, in the Egypto-Chaldaean period of civilization. But let us assume that such a soul refuses in the present incarnation to consider the involvement of the third hierarchy in the historical life of humanity, saying to itself: 'What concern is it of mine what angels, archangels and archai have done? To me, history is something which human beings have done at all times here on earth.' Such a soul does not take into account that the deeds of the third hierarchy have played a part in everything human beings have done on earth. Let us now assume for clarity's sake—for some souls it also applies with regard to the fourth era, the Graeco-Roman period, up to the year 333—but for clarity's sake let us assume such a soul has come from the Egypto-Chaldaean period. Then it needed no effort to know something about the involvement of the third hierarchy, for this was a natural part of human life, and the soul would still bear this within it. Let us say, therefore, that the soul bears within it anything which it had been able to take in at that time. You would not have been able to tell an ancient Egyptian about this historical life—he would have no real concept of historical life—that human beings make history. He would have laughed at this, for he could see that the spirits of the third hierarchy were making the history, though he would think of them in his own inward way.

In this day and age people bear all this within them, but unconsciously so. It has gone down into the subconscious. They now believe that history is something which people on earth have made. This creates a strange state of soul, and I'd ask you to let this be very clear in your minds. Looking at such a soul in the present time we would say that it refuses to take its place in a real way in humanity's historical life. It says: 'I do not want to know of the involvement of the archai, the archangels and angels. I only want to know from physical evidence what people have been doing from those ancient times.' But a soul cannot develop further as a result but will in reality remain at the point where it was in ancient Egyptian times; it will have the maturity only of a soul in ancient Egyptian times. It is not prepared to take hold of reality. The angels, archangels and archai have continued to develop. They have done the things which humanity has since been able to experience. Such a soul will say: 'What the hierarchies have done up there in the spiritual world is something I'll not concern myself with. I'll concern myself solely with my own abilities.' Those abilities are, however, none other but those which it already had in ancient Egyptian times.

Numerous such souls live in the present time. Consider the strange position such a soul is in! Up to the year 333 a soul could not get into this position for the spiritual world was still coming in of its own accord. Now, however, souls may be in a strange position. They cannot refuse to accept reality. They are, of course, within the deeds of the angels, archangels and archai, but they deny this in their minds, accepting only the things which human beings have brought about here on earth.

This is a case where people as creatures are in the fourth stage of development. That stage involved everything which happens in creation. Since Egyptian times, therefore, everything human beings have done on earth is part of the growth stage of development. But man himself extends beyond this, and because he has not been able to extend consciously into the realms into which he does extend he is in his essential nature actually above the seventh stage of development. He is there within the eighth stage of development. It is possible today for souls to be actually in the eighth stage of development but fail to accept this because they do not acknowledge the work of the angels, archangels and archai in human history. They acknowledge only the fourth stage and so the eighth sphere remains unconscious within them. This is an extraordinarily important fact.

When a soul in this position develops a philosophy of life, what will it be? The individual ignores his own reality; he does not admit that he projects into a sublime realm of the spirit although he does in fact do so. He only admits that he is in the human realm. This stage of soul has only emerged clearly in the industrial age, as I have called it. It has only been since people were wholly in the industrial life that they came to ignore the fact in their philosophy of life that human beings extend up into the spiritual world, taking account only of the outward activities of human beings. This is something significant. We cannot understand the present if we do not know that there are numerous people today who extend into the eighth sphere with their philosophy of life but ignore this fact. They cause all the damage on earth which comes about when one extends into a sphere but denies its existence. By denying that they extend into the eighth sphere, into the eighth stage of development, man excludes himself from the good of this stage and gives himself over to the ahrimanic spirit of the developmental stage concerned. His thinking becomes ahrimanic rather than divine or spiritual.

Speaking of spiritual science, one must point to the facts, the truth of that world. The truth is that something like the materialistic view of history of Karl Marx,[19] for instance, who lived from 1818 to 1883, his philosophy of life, is wholly ahrimanic. The secret of that philosophy of life is that the projection of man's spiritual nature into the supersensible worlds is ignored and that because of this the human being falls prey to the ahrimanic powers. As soon as human beings exclude their conscious awareness from the worlds into which they project, they fall prey to the ahrimanic or luciferic powers, in this case the ahrimanic powers.

It is a fact that today very many people represent and fight for a purely ahrimanic philosophy of life. In doing so they evoke everything that will have to happen if the ahrimanic rather than the divine order spreads around the globe. Bentham's philosophy, which I spoke of yesterday, is initially an external theoretical version of this ahrimanic view. Marxism is another version and is also creative, configuring, and tremendously influential. People living a middle-class life, slow to change, know nothing of this and for decades have not concerned themselves with the elements of such philosophies which have developed in the social sphere. Marxism is an extreme version of this. It will continue to have an influence. Something which initially was meant to be just knowledge will be happening in life, to be absolute reality. Only one thing can be a help in this situation and that is insight, insight which generates a will to act.

Truths like these mean radical changes and are definitely not suitable for making your Sundays more exciting. Truths like these are deep down connected with the whole of present cultural life. Much will depend on people being prepared to consider the things that live in their thoughts in connection with the whole world order. For we have now entered into the cycle of time where we will not progress without getting into horrific disasters unless we realize how something which happens within the human being relates to developments in the whole cosmos.

Truths like these, when you find them in your search for truth— you can be assured of this—will be rather a shock at first. If you have a feeling for the way in which great truths bring great change in the world you will also know the shock they may be. Only superficial minds might think that it does not shock one to have to say: 'Ahriman is pulsating through people who many others thought'— and it was, of course, also true—'were honestly endeavouring to discover the truth.' It touches the heart, my dear friends! And when such truths are found one tries to cope with them. They are not made to go in one ear and out the other. Nor are they made to be found in solitary meditation and accepted as sensational. None of these truths are for such purposes. One has to cope with them; one must be able to discover how world evolution, as it is called, being there all around one, also in people's opinions, is in accord with the existence of such truths.

Someone like myself, who has seen how many people today—people can nowadays convince themselves of this through external facts—live with Marxism or Marxism-type views will certainly consider it necessary to go more into these things. There one will often say to oneself: 'Perhaps you are nevertheless under an illusion!' We need not put the whole of the spiritual world into immediate doubt, of course not, but when it comes to such concrete truths one does often say to oneself: 'Maybe you are under some kind of illusion here!' The profound sense of responsibility concerning truth must of course arise particularly when they are spiritual truths. One then tries to go deeper and deeper. In fact, however, there are not few but very many things that provide dreadful confirmation of what I have just been presenting as the ahrimanic nature of Marxism, for instance, and similar philosophies of life.

A while ago when I was speaking to you[20] I did rather challenge you. I said that time, as we experience it, is really a delusion and is in reality something quite different from people's experience. This, I said, was so because people did not see time in perspective. They experience space in perspective; trees that are further away look smaller than those nearby. We really must see time in perspective as well. Events further away in time must be seen differently from those closer to the present. The basis for this is that time truly is what investigators have always thought it to be—the most important medium for deceiving humanity. We imagine that the spirits of the higher hierarchies also move through time the way our own inner life does. This is untrue. In reality the essential nature of the higher hierarchies lies in times past, but they exert their influence from times past, just as in space it is possible to have a distant influence, using light signals or the like to influence others who are not too far away. Time is not what people think it is. Nor is it what philosophers like Kant consider it to be. In reality time is something quite different. Human beings think it is real but it is another maya, a great delusion. Above all, things which we think in our delusion about time to be in the past actually continue to exist. Time truly turns into something rather like a space. To see things as they really are one does not look on past events the way one does at objects in space. Time deceives us.

We know from spiritual science that the wellsprings of other great delusions in human philosophies of life arise because of the illusion about time. If there were any physicists among you I would be able to use the language of physics here. I would be able to show you, using physical formulas, that when physicists use time—'t' in short—in their formulas that time is just a number, something quite unknown therefore, not anything real but quite unreal. Only velocity is always real, but physicists see velocity as a consequence of time. You are not physicists, however, and unlikely to put your minds to this and so I will not go into this any further.

Time is delusion, which is a truth of great import, for the fact that time is delusion is the basis of many other delusions in life. We see everything the wrong way, for example, if we use time in the wrong way with regard to history. People tend to think that certain things that happened in the first three Christian centuries are now in the past. In reality they ought to think: 'The archangel or the spirit from the hierarchy of the archai which guided events at that time is still here; this continues to have an effect in another way.' Being past and gone is a delusion. Much depends on it that we get to know the perspective nature of time when it comes to spiritual reality, knowing that we have to be deceived about events in time just as—not believing this—we are deceived about events in space unless we allow for perspective. Just think how great the delusion would be if you were not to accept perspective, considering something distant in space to have the same power to affect you as something close by. You are looking at a distant mountain. Your health depends a great deal on the air around you and not on the air on the distant mountain. If you want that air to improve your health you'll have to go there. Essentially reality has to do with perspective when it comes to reality in life. And it is the same with regard to time. We are living in the right way in the present time if we do not think that events in the more distant past carry the same weight as more recent events.

If we consider the Egypto-Chaldaean period in the third post-Atlantean era, limiting ourselves to surviving documents and record them the way history written by fools does, the agreed-upon fable which they call history today, we are making the mistake in perspective. It really is of no significance in the present day what people did in Egyptian times. But the things which the angels, archangels and archai did—those are important. This will only emerge, however, if we use perspective. It is therefore a basic principle in spiritual investigation, not only today when we have to rediscover all these things, but it has always been a principle that time as such is maya. No one who knows the true nature of time has ever reckoned with time in such a way that it was taken to be true, that time itself was taken to be a genuine reality.

The strange thing which emerged was that Karl Marx—I have spoken of him, and millions swear by him today, though more or less in nuances, more or less in formulas, but that does not matter—Karl Marx tried to answer the question: 'What are the things of true value for humanity? What is it that is truly achieved in humanity?' He answered this question in an extraordinarily original way, for it had never been answered like this before. People had always looked at true value in some other way, not the way Karl Marx did. People would consider things to be of value to humanity, let us say, according to whether they had to be transported through long distances, if much intelligence had been needed to find them, etc. I once tried to explain this to you by saying that human labour must also be considered in qualitative terms and one must altogether look at it in a very concrete way. We consider the engineering marvel of the St Gotthard Tunnel. No one can build such a tunnel unless they know differential and integral calculus. Differential and integral calculus was invented by Leibniz, or, if this makes the English more happy, by Newton. The two of them were in dispute over the invention. We may say, therefore, that Newton or Leibniz also worked on the St Gotthard Tunnel. It certainly could not have been built without them. One has to put quite a different value on the work of Newton or Leibniz than one would on the work of someone who put one stone on another in the tunnel. This is a point to be considered in putting a value on human work, something of value for humanity. The theory of the value of human labour has taken different forms. Values have been put on labour, something of value in life, from all kinds of different points of view but never in the way in which Karl Marx did it. He included just one element in his theory of value. To him, everything that had value in human life had value only because it was condensed time, especially condensed working hours. The economic value, the value in the world economy, was measured in whether it could be produced in three, six or twelve hours. A major part of Marx's theory was based on this. The theory is so widely accepted today that you may find that when a member of a 'higher class' is speaking about labour from his point of view, a worker will get up, a real socialist, and say: 'Please read it up in Karl Marx'—he would not have the book with him, of course—'page 374, and there you'll find this or that.'

To judge life we must really know it or we will find there are constant surprises with one thing happening or another. The things that happen arise from impulses in the human soul. However, if one cares as little as people have in recent decades have been caring about what was really happening deep down in the human soul, one should not be surprised when the whole finally collapses and one faces disaster. I have been saying these things for a particular reason. It was the first time that very original something which is but the source of deception was made the measure of all economic values—time in form of working hours.

Take this from the standpoint of a higher perspective. People with insight into reality have always known that time is deceptive. Now someone comes along and says: 'But the things that are of value in the world have only as much value as the condensed working hours in it.' Surely this means in other words 'Your reality is therefore illusion, and only condensed time for labour has real value'? The people who want to be wholly materialistic, only basing themselves on reality, make the deception into reality even in the form which they give to time, and reality is overlooked.

This is just one example. I could give you many examples of things that are a comfort when one is taken aback by truths which strike like rolls of thunder if one has a heart for the life of humanity. But when one then studies these things in detail, when one focuses on someone like Karl Marx, knowing that his spirit was an ahrimanic influence, and asks him 'How does this go in detail?' one will indeed arrive at the ahrimanic element and feel that these are truths one may admit to oneself. Basically it is not easy to have to say to oneself that everything that is anachronism in the world today is coming into our world because people take a position which is outside the spiritual world and which then becomes the eighth sphere for them, and because they take the world only from the creature point of view. Here you will indeed realize, in all its gravity, what it means when I stress over and over again that it does not matter at all if someone speaks of something beautiful, something one is able to accept; what matters is what actually becomes of those good things said. Again and again I have to draw attention—you know I am not saying this from some kind of silly vanity—to the fact that it does not matter what the thoughts are which we have in mind but that we take care to see what effect those thoughts then have. You may have a truly marvellous thought. But if you have no idea of what effect that thought has in real terms then it may well have the opposite effect. I have been trying to make this clear for years, giving examples.

One example was in a lecture I gave at the beginning of the twentieth century.[21] I said—I am summing up in a few words what was a full exposition at the time, merely to illustrate my point—that more people than ever are today pacifists, talking most beautifully of guidance for humanity from their pacifist point of view. Pacifism has really never before had so many followers as today—that is what I said at the beginning of the century. I went on to say that this was a definite sign that we were about to enter into the greatest war humanity had ever known. To think as unrealistically about human situations the way people did there, considering the subject of those thoughts only, having little awareness of the true effect of the thoughts that live in the soul, an effect one can only truly grasp by considering the whole world—that was not the way in earlier times. People are only doing so in an age when all those things of which we have been speaking are spreading.

Why is it that something can actually set the tone for many people which is no more than thought content, but completely unrealistic, something which can never have anything to do with actual events? Thus Woodrow Wilson's[22] thoughts, no different from thought content in Egypto-Chaldaean times, the thoughts of someone who does not care that there is spiritual reality in history but merely develops a sequence of abstract thoughts. Why is this so? It is because of all the special characteristics of our time. Future historians will have to attach the name Woodrow Wilson to everything our time has produced by way of unrealistic thoughts which have had the opposite effect.

It is this which seriously affects our philosophy of life, which has to have that effect. And we must not look at it as relating to today and tomorrow but as something we have to look at in the light of the whole of cosmology, from the point of view of having been put in that situation. Answering such questions from the point of view which arises from a worldwide view will judge someone like Woodrow Wilson not from sympathies or antipathies but in a truly objective way. The anachronism is that many people today cannot go into this because it is uncomfortable to look things in the face. You cannot look things in the face without going into them more deeply. It has to be said that people who do not relate to historical life today are ignoring the actual history brought about by the third hierarchy. They therefore have nothing to do with the real impulses when they speak but essentially are dealing only in the empty husks of words.

A basic requirement in our time is that we get to know and understand that when we have the best and most beautiful ideas, perfectly adequate to explore the natural world all around us, we'll still never understand anything connected with history. History does not proceed the way natural life does; history proceeds through the activities of higher spirits. This has to be added to the other philosophies of life. Humanity lived with theocracy when people still remembered the way the theocratic order extended to their life in the past. Then came the metaphysical age, essentially developing official administrative systems in the whole world. Then came the purely materialistic age, the age of industrialists. This would take humanity into irreality where the spirit is concerned if it were not for the counterbalance of finding one's way again into all that is real, and genuine, though one can only contemplate this if one is able to rise to something which is hidden from people in ordinary life in the present time cycle. We have to learn to speak of supersensible things again if we want to speak of history. People talked a lot about historical ideas in the nineteenth century—well, we all know that you can't fell a tree with ideas. The followers of Ranke[23] and similar historians do, however, believe that humanity's historical life is brought about by ideas. It will have to be realized that this time, the merely metaphysical time, also has to be overcome. Otherwise a philosophy will prevail that is wholly limited to things perceived through the senses. Humanity must work to come to the spiritual. They will only be able to do this if to begin with they at least work their way from the unreal history of sequence in time to the real process which I'd say is particularly tangible behind the reality outwardly perceived by the senses in the case of history. People will then no longer produce social programmes or the like based on ideas that relate merely to outwardly apparent life. They will once again proclaim their social programmes that arise from the revelations of the spiritual world. The programmes people produce today differ a great deal from those revelations that come from the spiritual world.

We'll speak of this next time. I'll continue these contemplations next Friday; they cannot be taken to their conclusion that quickly.

Lecture 4

13 September 1918

I am going to continue with the theme which we have been considering for some weeks but in a more aphoristic way. I have always told you that the great problem when it comes to philosophies of life, is now—and I have always stressed the 'now'—that with the views that are generally held people find it difficult to build a bridge between the approach known as idealism and what we may call the view taken of the natural order of things. When modern people try and build such a bridge by seeking to understand how moral ideas, for instance—to take just one group from the sum of ideas—relate not outwardly but inwardly and in real terms to the views and concepts people develop on the progress of causal natural order, they end up in a kind of philosophical dualism, as we might call it from the spiritual-scientific point of view. This is something we've been stressing over and over again. People try to build such a bridge but they do not succeed.

We'll find it easier to look at things relating to this question if we compare this dualism of the present day with something similar which existed in pre-Christian times. It was something which we might call fatalism. Until the second and third centuries before Christ—and later even more so, though it came to be more and more anachronistic—people were literally compelled to take a fatalistic view. Essentially fatalism was also the basis of Greek philosophy. In more recent times all fatalism has really been anachronistic. It is out of place in the present age. We might say that the ancients were seduced into fatalism. People of more recent times and particularly the present were and are seduced into dualism.

Let us be clear in our minds why the ancients could so easily submit to fatalism. We know that the state of mind of human beings has changed radically in the course of evolution, and it is superstition to assume the kind of successive evolution which is assumed in common or garden Darwinism, for instance. The state of mind has radically changed and history is here more than anywhere else a fable that has been agreed upon. The ancients' state of mind was such that they never really saw nature the way we do today, and on the other hand things of mind and spirit were not as conceptual, based on ideas, as they are today. The idea which the ancients had of nature was that they amalgamated nature and spirit in their mind; for the spiritual they took images from developments in nature to form their ideas. The ancient teachings of the gods were myths fully imbued with ideas taken from the natural world perceived through the senses. Speaking of nature, the ancients would not use the dry, abstract terms we use today but speak of elemental spirits that sustain and bring about the phenomena of nature.

This was not because they expressed themselves in a very childlike way. It was because they saw things in a real way, because of a very real state of mind. People of old did not see nature the way we do now, which is under the influence of modern science even for those of us who are not scientists. They did not see it in the abstract way, wholly in accord with ideas, in which we have to see it today. In this mingling of nature and spirit they induced their own fatalism; for with natural phenomena imbued with the activities of spirits, as recently described, all life was of course intentional in the outward way in which human actions are intentional. It was an image, but the people of old had no other image, and that inevitably led to their deceptive fatalism.

A different state of mind evolved in time. We have characterized the change in the state of mind from all kinds of different angles; today we'll look at it from a quite particular point of view. Let us consider the question which we shall, however, only be able to answer on the basis of everything which we have been considering in the last lectures: What, objectively, do people see when they follow the natural order, and what, objectively, do people think up in their minds when they speak of spirit today? I am now not saying that we speak of spirit in spiritual science; I am speaking of the way in which people in general are today speaking of spirit, with more or less of one or another nuance.

We know that even those who are not theoreticians—we'll leave the theoreticians aside—will in wanting to understand the natural order arrive instinctively at the way in which substances and forces work. I am now not speaking of natural-scientific theories of substances and forces but of how simple the average person today quite instinctively imagines nature to be, basing his view of natural phenomena on processes which are material and rich in forces. This is where people are taken into an illusion—we know this if we look at these things, investigating them in a truly objective way. For everything that can be said about the nature of matter and forces in that case is illusion. This is not entirely due to faulty thinking; it is simply due to the present state and constitution of the mind. We are no longer speaking of maya or illusion as people did in Indian philosophy, for instance, for in ordinary life we have no insight into the real facts. We have no insight into the real facts and are therefore really always under an illusion when visualizing nature. This is the one thing.

The other is this: How do people see the spirit today? This is something which is very much adrift in abstractions. You will find this easier to see if you take one particular philosophy or another. It does not really matter at all which one you take. You can take one that offers a confusing play of words like Eucken's,[24] or one resting on more sound foundations like Liebmann's,[25] you can consider one which is more to the popular taste, like Schopenhauer's,[26] and so on. People speak of the spirit in today's philosophies. If those philosophies are not purely positivist, like Comte's, which we got to know the other day, if they are not materialistic, the philosophers will at least speak of spirit. But what do the philosophers speak of, calling it spirit, in the present state of mind? Assuming a certain substantial and force-related order, and running it like a net through the phenomena of nature, people make their view of nature into an illusion. In the same way everything said about the spirit from the generally accepted point of view today is essentially a hallucination, and the accepted philosophies are really only a sum of unrecognized hallucinations. Basically people are constituted in such a way today that in their minds they are adrift between illusion when they look at nature and hallucination when they consider the spirit. What philosophers dream about the spirit, seeking to construe a certain view of it from nothing but concepts, is really just a sum of subtle hallucinations, subtle, yes, but nevertheless hallucinations. These are forms that arise from the inner human being for reasons which we won't go into today and as such do not really have anything to do with reality.

I have on quite a few occasions drawn your attention to phenomena from the world of facts which clearly show that all the things people may have in their minds need not have much to do with reality. To make my point I pointed out that a whole number of philosophers are naive enough today to say that human beings must be considered to be made up of body and soul. Even the world-famous philosophy of Wundt[27] is about body and soul, the opinion being that it is free from prejudice. But what is the whole of Wundt's philosophy—I have spoken of this before—or what are other philosophies in reality? It merely implements what was agreed on at the Eighth General Council, held in Constantinople in 869, that one must not—this is approximately how the definition of the resolution goes—in speaking of the human being refer to body, soul and spirit but that the spiritual was merely a quality of the soul principle, and it was only permissible to speak of body and soul. The trichotomy of body, soul and spirit was considered heresy throughout the Middle Ages. Theological philosophers would quake in their boots when reality forced them even just to hint at body, soul and spirit, for that would be heresy. Philosophers are subject to this view to this day.

They merely follow the dogma established at that Council in Constantinople and they believe themselves to be free from prejudice when in truth they are implementing a resolution by the Council. We have to consider things without illusion; we must look at reality. Our young students are everywhere in philosophy learning something that was decided on at the Council of Constantinople.

Now I certainly am not saying that the things taught today are a direct consequence or effect of that resolution. The dogma established at the Eighth Council in Constantinople was in turn only thoughts expressing more profound changes that lay hidden below the surface and are still in progress today. All who want to establish dogma—be they the good philosophers at the Council of Constantinople or the good professors at today's universities—all those tissues of concepts are essentially mere conceptual hallucinations that rise up in human beings and have so little reality to them that the underlying reality cannot be truly grasped. The soul constitution of modern man is such that he is swinging to and fro, as it were, between the hallucinatory nature of his concepts and the illusory way in which he sees the natural world. He is therefore in danger of falling into dualism. He'll always be in danger of being able to take any ideas he is able to think up only into the hallucinatory sphere of concepts that do not come close to reality, or take anything he thinks up concerning nature only into the illusionary sphere of views on nature which also has nothing to do with true reality but is illusion. Human beings simply are not made to discover 'truth', as they call it—a word—directly, to find it easily, I'd say. They have to start with something which in life can bring dichotomy, doubt, scepticism and then penetrate to the truth. In the present cycle of evolution human beings are compelled to rise from that to and fro between the hallucination of philosophy and the illusion of their view of nature to the true reality, to genuine reality.

Now we might ask—I am, of course, speaking more or less in aphorisms and it will need the whole to see the connection: 'What may we say is the most immediate reason why the people of old fell more into fatalism and humanity of more recent times are more liable to fall into dualism when it comes to their philosophy of life?' We are in danger of this when we give ourselves up to mere play with concepts, or we might today also say mere dialectics.

You will, of course, object: 'Modern humanity with its sense of reality is not at all made to fall into mere play with concepts.' Ah, but you are quite wrong! Future ages, when our own age will be seen more objectively, will realize that such inclinations to play with mere concepts, to theorize, never existed more for humanity than they do at the present time. Today people like to escape reality, turning to mere play with concepts. But when you leave reality and start to twist and turn your concepts, to link them, separate them—the moment you have moved away from reality you are indeed in danger of either fatalism or dualism. What matters, and what we must develop for ourselves today is a sense of reality. I have often emphasized this from various points of view and must do so again.

It is not exactly easy to develop a sense of reality, especially also when it comes to spiritual things. It is particularly when it comes to spiritual things that we are caught up more than we think in mere play of concepts, in playful dialectics. Something which seems to be external illusion is very apt to encourage illusory notions as soon as it plays into the moral and spiritual life. People will always seek to theorize on certain things. They seek to theorize on good and evil, on freedom or necessity. When it comes to the most important questions in life, we may say, people are really dreadfully inclined to give themselves up to mere play of concepts, of words. When you come across discussions on philosophies of life somewhere or other it all tends to be just within conceptual dialectics. What is more, people deceive themselves by thinking that they have concepts when in reality they cannot have concepts at all. Side by side with the concepts they also have their sympathies and antipathies for certain concepts and against others. It is according to their sympathies and antipathies that people create one or another conceptual complex for themselves. I won't go into this, however. In the great majority of discussions, which are a play on concepts in form of questions, people do not concern themselves with reality.

To be clear about what is meant here let us take a fact often met with in life—hatred, the existence of hatred. One wants to explain such a thing as the existence of hatred in human nature. People very often try to explain this and similar things by merely playing around with concepts. Hatred exists as a mental phenomenon, a psychological reality. Yet going into these things one soon finds that certain concepts one develops with regard to this do not really capture every nuance of the hatred phenomenon. We can only understand such things if we try to get from the world of illusion to the world of true reality. Hatred is something which enters into the human soul from a deeper world of reality. So one has to ask oneself: 'This hatred, is it the same in the world of reality as it is when it presents itself in the human soul?' If it is something different in the world of reality than it is in the human soul we shall soon realize that we evidently will not arrive at a spiritual view of it if we merely come to know the hatred in the human soul. If one looks for hatred in the cosmos, using the methods of spiritual science—now not in the individual human being, for hatred enters into the individual human soul—if one looks for it in the cosmos it will be something completely different. The element which comes to realization as hatred in the human soul is also to be found out there in the cosmos. One merely must not be deceived into looking for the kind of forces of nature which the illusion in modern science is looking for. One must look into the reality that lies behind nature; there one does find the equivalent of the hatred. But in the cosmos this hatred is something which differs greatly from what it is in the human soul. In the cosmos hatred is a power without which individualization could never happen. There could be no separate identities, human or otherwise, if the power of hatred did not exist in the cosmos. I am not speaking of the illusion of atoms repelling one another but of something real. Hatred does arise in the cosmos but there it must not be judged morally the way it is when it enters into the human soul. In the cosmos hatred is a power behind all individualization. The whole world would otherwise blur into a single whole, which is what nebulous pantheists desire. No entity would stand apart, differentiating itself, if the principle did not prevail throughout the cosmos which human beings initially do not see in the cosmos though it plays into the human soul, assuming the particular form which we come to know there as hatred.

Now the question arises: How does humanity relate to this cosmic principle? I did already hint at this in one particular respect. Today we'll add to this in an aphoristic way. When discerning philologists—philology has also been made abstract today and has grown mediocre—but when discerning philologists studied the languages found among the native Americans, when 'civilized' people (I am putting this in quotes) had reached America and discovered the native Americans, the more discerning philologists found that the languages of those peoples showed a remarkably transparent logic. There were many languages, as the philologists assure us and as is indeed true, where the finer points of Spanish and Italian are to be found in the development and differentiation of those languages. Such things were found among the natives of Greenland. Undoubtedly those natives did not have the intellect of which modern man is so proud. This modern intellect also would not get very far if it took up the development and creation of languages. There is plenty of evidence of what the modern intellect comes to if used to be creative in language. Objective common sense did indeed rule in human souls that were still native and had not yet developed the modern intellect. I did the other day show you how objective common sense prevailed in language creativity. The common sense which prevailed there did not yet come to human beings who were as highly individualized as today's worldly rationality is. It came to human beings who were less individualized at the time, less separate in their identity, influencing them more as cosmic rationality. In those early times people were not the savages of whom modern anthropology creates illusory ideas. They were part of a whole organism—metaphorically speaking, of course—and came to be individualized bit by bit. They were members of a whole organism and did still give expression to cosmic rationality or common sense, or we might also say that cosmic rationality came to expression in them.

There you have a definite indication of how the cosmic principle influences the human soul. You can also transfer it to a special phenomenon such as cosmic hatred which finds its way into the human soul. We know that in the spiritual sphere it will be necessary to speak of certain polarities, much as we do in the sphere of nature. How did that cosmic rationality which we have in language come about? Humanity is no longer creative where language is concerned; only remnants of this are to be found today. How did that cosmic rationality enter into the human soul? How did it become individual? Seeking to answer this question we come to everything we call ahrimanic. How does something like the phenomenon of hatred enter into the human soul from the cosmos? There we arrive at the luciferic principle which is the polar opposite of the ahrimanic. People feel embarrassed to speak of Ahriman and Lucifer today but do not feel embarrassed to talk of positive or negative electricity or positive or negative magnetism. The fact that they feel embarrassed is due to a modern superstition.

Even if it is clearly understood that this fact exists, that spiritual entities, things of a spiritual nature, did indeed enter on the one hand as the luciferic principle in such elements as hatred, or as the ahrimanic in things such as language or also thinking, we must on the other hand also clearly understand the significance of things in the world at large. When my view of hatred is that I call it the basis for the great beginnings, that there can be individualization, separation, that we do not have everything in one great original stew, I am referring to the phenomenon, the fact of hatred in the far distant past, in a past when man did not yet exist in his present form; I am referring to a very, very far distant past. I am giving you a view of hatred as it was in a far, far distant past when the human being had not yet differentiated out from the rest of the world order. We might speak of the different realms of nature, know how they developed into mineral, vegetable, animal and human worlds—you only need to read my *Occult Science, an Outline*. We can speak of these natural worlds. If we do so wholly in terms of their reality and not the illusion, then the power of hatred lives in all of it, but in the way I have shown you, as cosmic hatred.

There came a time in evolution when something which otherwise is general cosmic fact played into the human soul. It entered into the human soul through luciferic, ahrimanic powers. It was then in the human soul, taken out of the cosmic, the cosmic as it had developed from earlier times to this day.

Making a diagram of the cosmic principle from the past to the present moment [violet], we know—having talked so much about the law of the conservation of energy or of matter, a law which in fact does not exist—that anything which is real in a purely natural way in the present, including matter, will come to an end. We know that anything which today has a here and now that can only be seen in the spirit is the seed also for future matter or substance [red]. Taking the spiritual view we have to say that everything which is now order of the past has flowed from the spiritual. Everything which has thus flowed out will come to an end. The order of the future will only flow from the spiritual henceforth. It could never become fixed natural order if there were such a thing as conservation of energy and of matter. The most powerful of all superstitions ever to have existed is that there is conservation of matter and of energy. The spiritual, which today makes itself known only in thoughts, is the seed for the natural order of the future just as the small seed of a plant which only makes itself known in a small way in the present year's plant will be the plant of the following year.

This means that man himself fits into the world order in a conflicting way. Our attention is drawn to man in this conflict when we seek to understand the whole situation, when above all we want to find the transition from cosmic hatred to the hatred in the individual soul, the hatred which shows itself in human nature. As you know, when we look at a human being before us we are able to say: forming

violet   red

Fig. 4

ideas, feeling and acting out of the will—that is his nature. He shows himself to us to have idea-forming, feeling and will-based nature and these make up a whole. But all the beautiful things said about this in philosophy will not get us anywhere unless we are also able to make clear and accurate distinctions. Even the sharp-witted psychologists of our time are beginning to realize that we don't really know anything much about acting out of the will. I have explained to you how we act out of the will. For today is is enough to indicate that present-day psychologists also have to say to themselves that we don't know much, really, about acting out of the will. Even when awake, human beings really sleep through the way they act out of the will, such being its essential nature. We might also say that human beings do not reach down as far with their souls as acting out of the will. They believe—I spoke of this as a concrete fact when discussing Augustine—that they are right within their essential nature when they form ideas. It is not something they can say, however, when it comes to acting out of the will. In waking life people know as little about the way in which some intention connects with even just the complicated mechanism of a hand movement or of the legs walking as they know about their living body or their environment when they sleep. Acting out of the will is something we sleep through at the present time. When we use the methods of spiritual science and penetrate from mere idea to action, we learn from the facts, though these are spiritual facts, how it happens that human beings sleep through the way they act out of the will today.

We'd really be in a very bad way with our thinking, our intellect, if it were not for the other circumstance which I have mentioned and which I'll shortly consider in more detail. We'd really be in a very bad way with our thinking for basically it is always childlike where our essential human nature is concerned. In the course of life between birth and death our thinking gains some knowledge about the immediate present in the world; nothing about past and future or at most some hypotheses, though these do immediately fall apart if one gets really serious about them. This thinking is indeed the seed for the future. Just as a plant seed is something which does not really have much significance today but will at best have next year, so does our thinking today have no value in real terms. It relates to what it could be in real value the way a child does to an adult. Thinking is really wholly made for the future, but only what is going to become of it will have real significance in future. The actual content, the substance of thinking, only has seed value today. However, if we use spiritual science to enter into will-based action, seeking to perceive the subject of it—it is just an activity—but seeking to perceive the subject of our own will-based action, it will be something which bears within it awareness of the most far-distant past, of the cosmic past. You will never understand world evolution using only the intellect, unless you enter into will-based action with vision in images, inspiration and intuition. It is only in the human will to act, which at the same time builds up the whole human organism, that we find a subject which holds the memory of the cosmic past just as you have memory of your ordinary life.

The difference between the human intellect and the human will to act is that the human intellect will at best only develop a memory for one's individual, personal life. The will to act, out of the reach of the human intellect, holds the memory of the cosmic past. Human beings bear the memory of the cosmic past in them but without spiritual-scientific investigation they cannot reach it with their intellect. We may say, therefore, that on the one hand human beings have the will to act as a faculty, bearing within them—figuratively speaking—the memory of the cosmic past. As intelligent beings they bear within them only the present, for the intellect is but seed for the future and not yet something for the present. With reference to the will to act the human intellect is just like the tiny seed in relation to the whole plant. Having the will-to-act faculty we are as cosmic spirits based on the whole of the past because we are individuals. As intelligent human beings we are in the present and we prepare to grow into the future.

Our will-to-act faculty may thus truly be said to relate to the intellect the way a very old person does to a child. The human being with the will to act relates to the thinking human being the way a very old person does to a child—with the necessary extension of time, of course.

What can balance this out? Cosmic common sense, which I have earlier and on many occasions called the ahrimanic principle, influences the thinking human being. If we had to depend on ourselves as human beings, without Ahriman's influence, the situation for our intellect would be very different at the present time. The Roman Catholic Church might be highly satisfied with a humanity that had only the measure of the intellect which today arises from human nature itself. Relative to the potential which man has in the whole cosmos, this intellect is childlike, just as our will to act is very old indeed.

The ahrimanic principle influences our thinking—and our thinking cannot be thought of in evolution without the involvement of the element of speech, for instance. The luciferic principle influences our will to act. The ahrimanic principle penetrates us by winding our intellect, which in evolution as a whole is still relatively weak and childlike, up higher and higher, to a certain sun height. But there is also the other side of the coin—we have an intellect which is not really arising from us, we have an intellect which we might roughly compare not to a plant which rises from the ground and then has the seed but to a plant which has another plant set upon it, which does not bear seed but is another plant, another, more perfect plant.

Our intellect is arranged, organized ahrimanically. Because of this it tends to blind us. As spiritual scientists we do not, of course, say that we should not use this intellect, seeing that it is ahrimanic. It is merely that one must look at things without illusion, be clear that the human intellect is a powerful light, and may shine even more strongly than the intellect which is coming forth from human nature today is able to do. The intellectual principle can deceive human nature, placing things into a certain sphere for them where they are dazzled. When human beings use their intellect to cast light on this, it is like a blinding light. And it is really because of this that human beings make things into illusion.

Just as the ahrimanic principle influences the intellect, so does the luciferic principle influence our will to act, so that it goes to sleep, really goes to sleep. The ahrimanic principle enlightens our seedlike intellect. The luciferic principle lulls, puts to sleep our will-to-act subject which really bears the memory of the whole past in it, with the result that people know nothing of that past.

This, taken at a somewhat deeper level, is the basis for dualism in man. The dualism must be bridged but cannot be bridged if we turn merely to theories. We have to turn to the facts themselves, the facts of spiritual life, knowing that our intellect has a different prime origin in the world than our will to act. The situation with them is like having a child and a very old person standing side by side. We would be artificially deceiving ourselves in setting up the abstract notion 'man' which really is nothing but an abstraction, and in saying, 'The child is a human being and the very old person is a human being.' Such concepts suit people today because they mix everything up. Thus the soul is said to be uniform today, thinking that as such it has the same prime origin as intellectual thinking and a loving will to act. But, as I have just been indicating, we must make distinctions if we really want to understand the human being. The philosophy of life we think up using only the intellect will therefore never get anywhere near reality. It remains hallucination for it arises from an intellect filled with a spirit that is not of this world—with the ahrimanic spirit which does not belong in the world order which we behold with our eyes. The same holds true in its own way for the will to act, for this is filled with luciferic spirit.

People have always had a feeling for this or given expression to it. Hardly anyone realizes, for instance, that in the Old Testament there is already some idea at least of this polar opposition of ahrimanic and luciferic. I am saying it is not much realized because people will nicely read chapter after chapter in the Bible and there, too, make no distinction. No distinction is made between the Book of Job and the Pentateuch [5 Books of Moses]. Yet the distinction between those books does give a first idea of the polar opposition between ahrimanic and luciferic which we need to grasp. Moses poses the question as to the evil in human nature, that is, if I may put it like this, how cosmic hatred, human hatred influences human beings. Moses enquires into evil. He then presents the Fall in a magnificent picture. We know that hidden behind the Fall is the entry of the luciferic principle into human nature. Then a certain consequence is connected with Moses' view that really all misfortune and even death is due to this human sin—or pre-human sin if you prefer. We may say therefore that misfortune and death are the consequence of sin.

The Book of Job presents the radically opposite view. In the first place you do not have a serpent but a purely spiritual entity, an ahrimanic spirit approaching the divine spirit. And in Job we do not have someone like Adam, who is capable of falling into sin, but indeed someone who is said to be 'perfect and upright'. How does that spirit who approaches God want to achieve his aim of having Job fall into sin? By bringing misfortune upon him! It is exactly the opposite. This spirit wants to bring misfortune on Job so that he will fall into sin. The misfortune has come, and misfortune is said to lead to sin. According to Moses, misfortune comes from sin, in the Book of Job sin comes from misfortune. Views are in radical opposition in the more pagan Book of Job and the Jewish Book of Moses. But, as I said, people read one thing after the other and do not pay attention.

Today it is absolutely necessary that people are not misguided into the idiotic 'self-knowledge' which is so often said to be desirable but that they truly come to know themselves and objectively know how to distinguish between intellect and will just as they learn to distinguish between hydrogen and oxygen. Otherwise they will only apparently overcome a certain dualism.

Things that happen in one period of time have always been long in preparation. And we can really only study the things that stand out as being particularly significant in an era. Wanting to be thorough in building a bridge in the present-day dualism, let us above all consider on the one hand the hallucinatory nature of the intellect, which is connected with everything of which I have been speaking, and on the other hand the illusory nature of natural phenomena, which I have also been discussing. These take human beings into a kind of inner conflict in life. Two streams are active in them and they must aim to let there be only one. One stream is particularly seductive. It is the stream which arises from the relationship which people have in their souls with the natural order. A person of our time who sees reality for all things to be of the same kind—an anatomist, to take an obvious example, or a physiologist—will take the human body today and distinguish only outwardly, not inwardly, between the individual members of this body. I'd say he puts the heart beside the liver and investigates both organs only externally, not taking account of the time perspective of which I spoke the other day. In fact we will only learn properly about the nature of the heart and of the liver if we proceed in a genuinely spiritual-scientific way in embryology, learning to distinguish in time the beginnings of the heart in early embryology. We also cannot simply put them side by side and say they consist of cells. On the one hand this is correct and on the other it is nonsense. We know very well that something can be correct and a nonsense at one and the same time.

However, in the scientific stream efforts are made today to explain the natural order, taking no account of things being at different times but putting them side by side, and this leads to abstraction. Then the temptation is particularly great to put things side by side—cause, effect; cause, effect—abstract illusory causal order! We know from things I told you last year and also this year that this is not the way to look at nature, that nature only becomes explicable if one looks at it in the first place as reflecting something which is spiritual. Then you arrive at the true theory of metamorphosis, at genuine Goetheanism. Then the human head is seen as something which reflects an infinitely distant past, and the organism of extremities as something which points to a distant future. There something which exists on its own is seen not merely in a causal chain but as imagination, the image of something which is behind it. We will not understand the human head if we merely look at it as growing out of the rest of the human organism. In reality it has been created out of the whole cosmos and in a different way from the way in which the organism of extremities is created, for instance. In physics, everyone would think it ridiculous if one were to explain that the compass needle always points north because there is a force inside it that makes it point north. No, one realizes that there is one pole and the other pole because the cosmos, earth's magnetism, gives the compass needle its direction. Yet when it comes to man or to any organism, they say everything grows from it in a straight line! Just as the compass needle points north on one side and south on the other for cosmic reasons, so does the human head point back to an infinitely far distant past and indeed into past times when the earth had metamorphosed itself, and the organism of extremities points to far distant futures, but now for temporal cosmic reasons. The orientation is cosmic and it is in time. This will be the ultimate development of genuine Goetheanism—rising from mere illusory causal order to seeing nature through vision in images. Recognizing that what we have before us is the image of something else we rise above mere illusion.

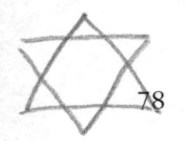

But we must not stop at nature. We need a correlate, something to complement it. Someone who talks about nature in that way would again be a fantasist if he were to take nature in that way and not on the other hand declare: 'Such spirit as is said to be the opposite of nature in more recent philosophies is also hallucination and again we must not stop at this.' All that lives today has developed slowly and humanity has gone through all kinds of different stages, gradually advancing, I'd say, to the point where the human soul is in the process of gaining insight into the spirit. We can distinguish three stages in this. Just as we can say that our understanding of nature is still very confused today, and strive towards the stages of insight which in my *Knowledge of the Higher Worlds* are called Imagination, Inspiration and Intuition, so we can say that the human soul principle has gradually developed intellectually through three stages of being truly within the spirit, so as to truly grasp things in mind and spirit.

These are the three stages. Living with an idea of the spirit, which is, of course, something hallucinatory because one takes the spirit as it is at the present time, and does not realize that it is seed for the future—living with the idea, dreamlike, having some idea of the spirit. The second stage is prophetic vision where something of the future is truly experienced in visions—like those of the ancient Hebrew prophets—and something does already live in there of knowing that the mind and spirit has the quality of being seed for the future. The third stage—little understood as yet, but there is a depth to it—involves taking an apocalyptic view of the world. All of these stages are preliminary to gaining the spiritual-scientific view, though this must, on the other hand combine with the vision of nature in images—otherwise it would, metaphorically speaking, float in the air. Seeing nature in images raises us beyond the illusory aspect of natural science. A realistic attitude to the process which goes through having an idea, an inkling of the future, vision of the future—prophetic vision, apocalyptic vision—raises us above the hallucinatory element in the life of mind and spirit.

We absolutely must not take the spirit the way it is taken in more recent philosophies. That is the human mission in the present time. We must not take nature the way it is taken in the naive view of nature nor in the theoretical natural science of today. No, we must lay aside the illusions we have about nature, as it were, and perceive the way in which it is but an image of something else. And we have to realize that the mind and spirit is mere shadow image in the way in which it presents itself in modern philosophy. Then a bridge is built between the ordinary way of seeing mind and spirit and the ordinary way of seeing nature.

And there will be a third thing. Mere discussion has never served to overcome such things as dualism, only looking at the facts, but it must be all the facts, and then finding a third element to go with the two. The symbol used must therefore represent a trinity. We do, of course, understand today that these concepts again refer to something which floats on top. But we have to have concepts. They do no harm so long as we do not overestimate them. We are speaking of normal humanity, of the luciferic and the ahrimanic principles, and also making a representation of this. It is to be the central focus of our building. Auguste Comte also had an inkling that there had to be a view that was threefold by nature. He spoke of the trinity to which I referred the other day. This genuine trinity which will encompass the view of mind and spirit and the view of nature and thus truly overcome dualism must also have the spiritual science with anthroposophic orientation within it. One cannot therefore arrive at a genuine anthroposophic spiritual science unless one also gives serious consideration to the light and shadow sides of present-day natural science, and science of mind and spirit. These things have to be taken seriously. Merely throwing things together and establishing theories will not achieve anything considering the seriousness of the present-day situation.

Life does not proceed in a general mix but is differentiated and individualized. Anything striven for in future must be striven for in a differentiated way from the beginning. It is still widely the bad habit today to treat everything the same way. When someone has a political theory today he will also shape everything else according to that political theory—philosophies of life and so on, treating everything the same, all based on his favourite theory. That is how it is in our day. Life proceeds in a differentiated way. Only someone who knows this will be free from illusion. The future lies not in striving for a general mix of life but for marked differentiation, for a life in mind and spirit as true knowledge, a certain inner life of which people have little idea as yet, a life which in the thinking of earlier times may be called a religious life, and for political life. Throwing everything together, regulating one thing the way one does another, one falls into the kind of error of which I spoke last year, or indeed two years ago.[28]

Things run in separate streams. On one side social life according to socialism, on the other religious life according to freedom of thought, and scientific life according to pneumatology, the study of spiritual entities and phenomena and the nature of the human spirit. The three must work together in a living way if the future is to offer a certain healing power in human evolution, not a paradise on earth, there being no such thing, but a certain healing power. It would be anything but good, however, if people were to think of external life in pneumatological terms, for instance, establish religious sects and fill them with pneumatological life, that is, run political life from the pneumatological point of view. That would bring nothing. Nor would it bring anything if religious communities were to do politics in the old sense. Just as the hands cannot do the things the head is able to do, nor the legs, so pneumatology cannot do what socialism should be doing, nor religion what socialism should be doing or indeed pneumatology. What matters is differentiation of certain things, but not just in theory but in actual life.

I want to conclude with this today, taking it further tomorrow. As I said, it is meant to be merely aphoristic, adding some new aspects to the basic issues with which we are concerned.

[For the words Rudolf Steiner spoke after this, see Note 29.]

LECTURE 5

14 SEPTEMBER 1918

I have heard of and met present-day mystics who have sought to gain insight into human nature in the following way. I want to tell you the result which they believe they have obtained. They say something like this: 'Looking at human beings as they walk about on earth, their whole existence is something of a riddle. In their soul existence they go far beyond anything they are able to represent in their whole existence as human beings, revealing themselves, as it were, in the relationship to other people. One therefore has to assume that human beings are something quite different by nature from what they appear to be as they walk about on earth. They have to be a comprehensive cosmic spirit which in its inner nature is much, much more mighty than is apparent here on earth. There must be reasons why they have forfeited life in the great cosmos and been banished into this existence on earth,' as a follower of mysticism going in this direction told me, 'to learn to be modest, to make no demands and even to feel small here, but in reality they are great, mighty cosmic spirits though in some way they have come to be unworthy of living as such cosmic spirits.'

I know that many people will simply laugh at such ideas. But those who take a deeper view of life know that such a mystic idea ultimately also arises because it is so very difficult to solve the riddle of life. This difficulty is increasingly coming to awareness, especially so as more human souls seek to enter deeply into true reality. I do not, of course, intend to say anything about this idea which people who are following a particular form of mysticism have. I merely wanted to show it to you as something which has also found a place in human souls as a concept. One could just as well present a dozen other abstract, more or less philosophical or mystic solutions to the human riddle.

If one then tries to fathom why different people seek to clarify, often in highly unusual ways, what man's existence on earth really is about, one will arrive at various things. Above all one discovers that when it comes to the great questions about human existence people are not prepared to fulfil one thing for themselves, though on lesser occasions they will definitely admit this on every possible daily occasion. People will admit on every possible occasion that one should not obscure the truth for oneself by wishful thinking, and that anything one wished were true cannot be the standard for the objectivity of truth. In ordinary life, on the small scale, anyone will immediately admit this; on the large scale we see, as it were, human inability to arrive at a philosophy of life that is in accord with reality exactly because people cannot help themselves to bring in their wishes when it comes to grasping the truth. And it is usually wishes which we might call unconscious wishes that play the greatest role, with people not even admitting that there are wishes in their souls. Yet those wishes are present in the soul; they remain subconscious or unconscious. Exactly this would be the task for spiritual-scientific training—to bring those wishes to conscious awareness and so to become free of illusory life and enter into the sphere of truth.

Such unconscious wishes come into play particularly when the most sublime truths of life should take effect, life truths concerning the nature of human life itself, let us say this ordinary human life in the physical world between birth and death. An approach that is genuine, objective and in accord with reality must always look at the whole course of life if that life is to be understood. Imagine that such a study of life which is in accord with reality would give a result which the individual would not wish to have at all, not even in subconscious wishes. The individual would then do everything he could to overcome that unwelcome result by using sham logic.

Essentially nothing in life on earth as we consider it suggests that the truth must be in accord with human wishes, not even unconscious wishes. It might rather be the case that the truth, also about human life, is something which is not in the least pleasant.

Spiritual-scientific investigations show that this is indeed the case. It is, of course, possible to find a higher point of view from which things may appear different again. But for the life which people would like to have here on earth, truthful observation shows that it certainly is so, that the truth about the human being is exactly such that most seekers of comfort in life must feel a slight frisson of horror—even if subconscious, but you'll know what I mean—a slight, unconscious, sometimes very powerful subconscious frisson of horror. One must then look at the whole of human life.

We know that when we look at it carefully and objectively the whole of human life falls into different periods. You can read about these periods in my small publication *The Education of the Child*. We know that one will only understand the human being if one looks at life initially from birth to second dentition, then from second dentition to sexual maturity, from sexual maturity to the early twenties, up to the twenty-first year on average, let us say, then again until the twenty-eighth year. One can understand human life just as one seeks to understand anything in natural science if one considers the periodicity of human life in seven-year periods.

Significant things happen in every one of these periods. Yesterday we referred again to the position which man takes in life and how he relates to the cosmos. I reminded you of the image of the compass needle. The form of the human head does, for instance, go far, far back to an infinitely distant past; the form of the extremities points to a distant future, just as the compass needle points north at one end and south at the other.

The relationship to the cosmos is, however, a different one in every one of the main periods in human life. The principle which is active in us during the first seven years is essentially very different from the principle which prevails in the second seven-year period. Everything which comes more or less to expression in the seventh year in that the whole of growth builds up as if on a shore, everything piling up as the permanent teeth emerge, comes from the powers of the cosmos in the first seven years. And then there is something which human beings hold back as they develop, on reaching sexual maturity, something which gives them a tinge, in a way, as they develop and gain sexual maturity. This develops because certain powers of development, which are wholly established in the cosmos, develop in the human being during the second period, and so on.

The situation is such, however, that we have to say: The different elements in the whole human being are always interacting. Children also develop some soul activity up to second dentition, and this is particularly important in those early years of life. Let me just remind you of Jean Paul's words[30] that undoubtedly we learn more that is of value for life from our nurse at the beginning of life than we do from all our professors when at university. There is something very true, very right in those words. We merely have to put the right value on things. We learn a great deal in those first seven years but intellectually as it were and also otherwise the things we learn stay down in the dullness of inner life, a life which is still largely a life in the body. Read it up in my *The Spiritual Guidance of the Individual and Humanity*.[31] You'll see that one can also put a different value on a child's life in the first seven years. A wisdom that is far from minimal prevails in the human organism in those years. When a child has come into the world the brain is still fairly undifferentiated. It only differentiates out in the course of time. The structures which develop in the brain do really and truly, if you study them, reflect the influence of a wisdom that is more profound than anything we manage to come up with later in life when we design a machine, for instance, or do some kind of scientific work. We will, of course, not be able to achieve in conscious awareness later on what we did achieve when we first came into the world. Cosmic sense, rationality, is then active in us, that cosmic rationality we also spoke of when speaking of the development of language. A great cosmic wisdom is truly active in human beings in the first seven years of life.

In the second seven-year period this cosmic wisdom goes in the direction of tinging the human being with the quality which then leads to sexual maturity. There cosmic intellectuality is at work though as yet only to a small degree. One would like to say that whatever is left over and not used in the inner human being—well, it rises up into the head. The head also gets something, though usually this is what you would expect. The head gets what can be spared in the inner human being, in the unconscious sphere of the inner life. And development then continues in seven-year periods.

People do not normally study the whole of human life, 'normal' life as they call it. It needs some dedication to study normal human life, devoting oneself to the true human being himself and then also to the great cosmic laws. It may sound odd, but one cannot understand the principle which is at work in human beings in the early years, the first seven years, definitely not when one is a child, but also not as a young man or woman, not even if one imagines oneself to be understanding the whole of life in one's twenties. One cannot understand it. It is possible to gain some understanding of what goes on in childhood when one looks for this insight inwardly in the human being, in inner experience, roughly between one's fifty-sixth and sixty-third year. Only advanced age, when one is very old, provides opportunity to gain a bit of insight into what is active in us in the first seven years of childhood. This is hard to accept, for today people want to be full human beings when hardly out of their teens. It is not acceptable today to have to admit that there is something in this world, something which actually concerns us personally, where one has to be well up in one's fifties to understand it. As to developments in the years when people move towards sexual maturity, from the seventh to the fourteenth year, one will only be able to understand some of it more of less between the forty-ninth and fifty-sixth years, in the early fifties.

It would be good if such truths came to be accepted, for they would help us to understand life. The truths one usually posits about the human being are what people wish. They merely do not realize this, the wishes being unconscious. As to the things that happen from sexual maturity to the twenty-first year, one gets some inwardly experienced insight and will be able to form some opinion about it between the forty-second and the forty-ninth year. Between the thirty-fifth and the forty-second year it is possible to gain some insight into developments in the twenties, up to the twenty-eighth year. What I am saying about these things is based on genuine observation of life. This has to be made by training oneself in the spiritual-scientific method of observation and not in the kind of frippery way of gaining self-knowledge which is often given that name today. One must develop genuine insight into human nature. It is only in about the time from one's twenty-eighth to one's thirty-fifth year that one can have experiences which can be understood at the time when one is experiencing them. A certain balance then exists between understanding and thinking. In the first half of life one may think or envisage all kinds of things. For true understanding of the things one can envisage in the first half of life one has to wait until the second half of life.

This is an uncomfortable truth, but that is how life goes. I can even imagine that there are people who say, 'Well, if human beings are so precisely defined in their inner laws, where do they have free will? Where's their freedom? Where's the awareness of their humanity?' Yes, I can imagine that someone feels unfree because he's not able to be in Europe and in America at the same time, that someone feels unfree because he can't fetch the moon down. But the facts do not go according to human wishes, and the facts must be faced even when someone gains insight into himself. It is not for nothing that we live a life that modifies itself, metamorphoses itself. We live this life in such a way that every period in life has meaning and significance in its relationship to others. We live a normal life, as we call it, beyond the sixties—we'll talk about early death also from these points of view tomorrow—and in a way only come to understand in the second half of life what was active within us in the first half of life.

People would be much more certain and sure in getting their orientation in the world if this truth about life could be more widely accepted. For they would then build on a secure foundation in life. Today people basing themselves not on objectivity but on wishes do often simply say, 'Ah well, one has to learn things until one is in one's twenties, but then you are ready and ripe for anything in life.' They completely overlook the inner connections in life. To get to know life is indeed an inner task. And when it comes to this intimate task we must not forget that wishes must be silent and objectivity must be taken into account.

A degree of balance came to exist in the course of human evolution. Things had been very different in earlier times, and I have spoken of this before. You'll remember how I spoke of human evolution from the Atlantean era to this day, how humanity grew progressively younger.[32] A degree of balance arose because it came to be in the course of evolution that one element became related to the other. If that had not happened one would simply have to take life like this: someone who was only in his twenties would simply have to believe someone who was in his forties about certain truths which one can only grasp in a living way in one's forties, as I have described it for you. It is not entirely like this, for in the course of human evolution the concepts themselves, the ideas, have become such that one can gain some degree of sentience to convince one in one period of life about another. If one has sufficient devotion to let people in their forties and fifties tell one of their life experience, providing, of course, that they have had some—people tend not to have any today—if one lets oneself be told the experiences in life when one is younger, then one does after all not have to depend on belief in authority today; this has already come about in evolution. By giving it thought—young people are able to think—there is more to the nature and character which the thoughts have assumed than something that merely appeals to belief. There is indeed a certain possibility that one will also understand. Otherwise we'd have to say that human beings think when they are young and understand when they are old. But there is something there which can give one more than conviction of faith, purely authoritative conviction. This balances things out to some extent.

Take what I have said as a truth for life. If you take it as a truth for life it will cast light for you on practical life. Just think—if what I have been saying exists in life, is thought and felt and people are sentient of it, how this will be reflected in the way people relate to one another! How it will create elements that link one soul to another. Someone who is still young looks at the old person in a particular way if he knows that that person is able to experience things, and compared to someone who is merely able to think this means that something that was thought is also understood. One will then take a very different interest in the things someone of a different age is able to tell one if one looks at life in such a way. And one will still be interested, even at a greater age, in all the youngsters and even children around one. You'll remember how often I've said that even the wisest can learn from a young child. No doubt the wisest person will happily and lovingly learn from a young child. He may not be able to learn about morality or other philosophies of life, but he would be able to gain infinitely much wisdom exactly from the young child especially with regard to cosmic secrets. These still come into their own in a young child in a way that is very different from later on in life. The interest that links one soul to another will grow tremendously if such things are not just abstract theories but the wisdom of life.

It simply is a characteristic of spiritual science that it elevates, strengthens and increases the bonds of love which essentially must rest on the bonds of mutual interest between individuals. Ordinary rational wisdom can leave people dry, as dry as some academics are. Spiritual science, if its substance is truly grasped, cannot leave people dry but will always, whatever the circumstances, let human beings love others, strengthening and increasing mutual human interest.

Today I intended to tell you about some things that are not nice to live with but are the truth, facts. One will not progress in spiritual science unless one gets used to looking facts boldly in the face even if they are uncomfortable.

Another fact—already evident from what was said yesterday—is that the kind of intellect we are able to achieve in the present human cycle is altogether only suitable for providing insight into a limited time span. I really do not envy the people who light-heartedly set about translating Aeschylus, even Homer, the Psalms and so on. Honestly, I do not envy them. That people can in our time believe that all those middle-class pretensions in Mr Wilamowitz's[33] translations of Greek plays truly represent Aeschylus—anything of that kind simply is a sad sign of the times. People are not able to observe as soon as it somehow gets to be on the large scale. They often also do not have the patience to observe things on the small scale. It would be a good thing to try, simply as an exercise, and observe things on the small scale. Let me give you an example of a rather childlike small matter.

The other day I read an essay in the international journal published here in Switzerland[34] in which the socialist writer Kautsky[35] particularly complained of a Russian socialist having quoted him so badly that the opposite of what is said in Kautsky's books was given as Kautsky's view. It was highly unlikely, considering the nature of the subject matter and the nature of the people involved, that Kautsky's text had been deliberately falsified. I then read the Russian's essay and also had to say that it was odd how he represented Kautsky's views. I formed my own opinion even as I read, for I found it interesting that such a thing was altogether possible. As I read on I soon realized what must have happened, and this was confirmed later on when that author apologized, though I only saw this later. He had not read Kautsky's work in the original German but in a translation into Russian. Writing his essay in German he had back-translated it. So this is what had happened—translation from German into Russian and back-translation. Because of this the opposite of what it had said in the book came out and was quoted.

It needs no more than this when something is translated from one language into another, quite honestly so, to change things into their opposite. There need not be any funny business involved but essentially only the principles according to which translations are done today. It is a small, childish observation I have been mentioning. Someone who has the patience to observe such and similar things in life should not really be surprised to be told: 'It is impossible to understand Homer simply with the powers available to us today. We only think we understand.'

Well, that is looking at the matter from outside. There is, however, an important inner aspect to it. The state of the human soul was so very different in the days of Homer that modern people are also far removed from the possibility of understanding Homer. The present-day state of the human soul is such that it is very much tinged by intellectuality. The state of soul in Homer's day was not. People today cannot rid themselves of that tinge if they stay in that ordinary everyday state of soul. It is more compelling than people think and more powerful than they are aware of. They live with abstract concepts, Homer not at all. But people find it difficult to reconcile this with their subconscious or unconscious wishes. They thus say to themselves: 'Well, having the understanding which is normal for the present time one has to forgo understanding anything which originated in the days of Homer or even just Aeschylus.' This renunciation is not at all in accord with people's subconscious wishes. This is where spiritual science must come in. It does not stay at the ordinary state of soul but evokes a comprehensive state of soul which allows one to enter into states of soul which are of a different kind from the normal states of the present time. With the means of spiritual science it is once again possible to enter into something which is not accessible to the present state of soul. This renunciation, resignation would be of tremendous importance for people today so that they say to themselves, 'The understanding we are able to have extends only through a limited distance in human evolution.' It is also important to think of this when it comes to looking to the future.

You can be as explicit as you like today, write or say things clearly, note down what has been said, but this will not continue for much longer. In the near future times will move faster—if I may use this paradoxical phrasing—than was the case in the past, and it will then be quite impossible to understand anything we say or write today the way we understand it. Once again it will only be for a certain period towards the future that our understanding will be such that people can understand what we now say and write. Historians refer to documents, only wanting to rely on physical documents. But it does not depend on the existence of documents if we do or do not understand but on whether our powers of understanding go that far. Our powers of understanding do not at all extend to times that are further away. And if we then do not have that resignation, we'll arrive at Kant-Laplace theories or the like. I have spoken of this on quite a few occasions. What really is a Kant-Laplace theory but the helpless attempt to use the intellect of the present time to think about the origin of the world in spite of the fact that our normal state of mind and soul is now so far removed from this origin of the world that anything thought up in our present understanding of the world about the time that should be covered by the Kant-Laplace theory cannot be anything like the actual origin of the world. The knowledge that it is necessary to resort to different ways of gaining insight if one goes beyond a certain distance in time is something which spiritual science must also provide. People are unable to gain insight into past times beyond a certain limit unless they resort to spiritual-scientific research, unless they try to use different senses from those to which the intellect is bound.

Taking note of what I have just been saying I think you will realize how narrowly confined the horizons must be for present-day people unless they are prepared to resort to other stages of investigation, to other stages of gaining insight, when it comes to the things which the ordinary intellectuality, which really sets the tone today, cannot reach to gain comprehension. We know that it is possible to rise to imaginative, inspired and intuitive insight. These methods take us into different stretches. They alone can extend the island of existence which we are able to survey in the present-day state of mind and soul.

Everything which encompasses the present-day state of soul is really bound to the human I. You can read up on this in my *Theosophy*, *Occult Science* and so on. Human beings also bear other elements of their essential nature in them—astral body, etheric body, physical body. But the ordinary present-day state of soul does not extend down into the astral body, nor the ether body or the physical body. For anatomists are only able to see the outer aspect. Inner insight does not go beyond the I, let alone perhaps the physical body. One has to be able to follow the human being full of understanding from within. The insight into life of which I spoke at the beginning of today's talk is a first step in that direction, the things one is able to understand in the second half of life are a beginning, though a feeble one. For a better start one will have to rise to spiritual science. When one grasps the human being inwardly one goes down from mere intellect to acting out of the will. Yesterday I said that the subject of acting out of the will, the principle in us which is actually doing it, preserves the cosmic memory. Whatever man could develop if he had the will to do so as he develops normal wisdom of life in the second half of life would be a start of this going down process. It would not cast light on much but it would enlighten him about what human beings need to live. But if he then goes down with the higher insight he has developed, this entering into his own essential nature would open up the cosmic memory for him. Then something different from the Kant-Laplace theory would emerge, for instance the reality of our physical nature. As you know, the physical body is the oldest part of us, going back through four incarnations of the Earth, to the Saturn period. It is possible to learn from the ordinary wisdom of life which opens up in the second half of life what needs to be done to enter more deeply into essential human nature. Man is an image of the world, and in gaining insight into this image he is able also to get to know the world.

People are usually governed by subconscious or unconscious wishes when light-heartedly or taking the easiest possible line they think up something like the Kant-Laplace theory when they should really say to themselves that the subject is not accessible to their thinking. Here we are once again—approaching the tasks that lie ahead by moving in circles, I'd say—touching on what prevents people today from building a bridge between ideality and reality, which is our present theme.

People have sought through the ages to overcome these problems. But it is difficult to be really clear about these things because it is awkward, because people do not like to face the real facts. People are in the habit of accepting half the story and not the other half. A typical example is this. Karl Marx once said that philosophers had so far only endeavoured to interpret the world with their concepts; but we needed to change the world, and one really had to find thoughts that would change the world.[36] The first part is absolutely right. Philosophers have endeavoured, in so far as they are philosophers, to interpret the world, and if they were a little bit intelligent they would not think that it was possible to do anything but interpret the world. Yet the very archetype of all philosophical philistinism, Wilhelm Traugott Krug,[37] who taught in Leipzig from 1809 to 1834 and wrote many books ranging from fundamental philosophy to the highest levels of philosophy, demanded that Hegelian philosophers should deduce not only concepts but also the development of the pen—which greatly infuriated Hegel. Resignation is needed also in this field, saying, 'Of course, we are as whole human beings called upon to change the world in so far as the world consists of human lives.' But the kind of thinking we do in the present time, gloriously adequate and truly perfectly suitable for understanding the natural world, this thinking is utterly unsuitable for getting us anywhere when it is a question of letting action based on the will come into effect.

This is an uncomfortable truth. For if one understands this one will soon no longer say that whereas philosophers have so far endeavoured to interpret the world what matters is to change the world—secretly hoping that one can contribute to this in some way with some form of dialectics. Instead people say to themselves that the philosophers have only been able to interpret because they are able to refer to things. With nature it is enough if we just interpret it, for—thank God, one would like to say—the natural world exists without us and we can consider it enough just to interpret it. Social and political life does not exist without us and there we cannot say it is enough merely to grasp it in concepts which are suitable only for interpreting life and not for shaping it. There it is indeed necessary to advance from mere theorizing—which is largely hallucination, as I have shown yesterday, and is very much a hobby today—to real life. Real life with its facts demands that we do not take it in the linear way which people are used to taking today. Yes, ideas which one person conveys to another do lead to something; but they do not always lead to the same thing. Absolute truths do not exist, nor do absolute facts. Everything is relative. And the effect of something I put in words depends not only on whether I consider it to be true or not but also on what people are like in a particular era, how they react to it, if I may put it like that. Let me give you a significant example, one which it is most important to consider.

Going back to about the fourteenth century of the Christian era we find that before that century it was possible to speak to people of mysticism. Mystic concepts still had the impetus then which served to educate people and give them impulses. The oriental population of Asia, the Indian, Japanese and Chinese peoples have still preserved much of these faculties, for certain sections of humanity will retain earlier qualities or faculties at later times. We can at present still study things, and this had also been the case with European peoples in earlier times; but the whole state of the human mind and soul has changed. Someone who passes on, presents mysticism today, for example, must understand that an era is coming closer and closer where the way in which people react to the presenting of mysticism—proper mysticism, that of Meister Eckhart,[38] Tauler[39] and the like—teaches them the things which Lucifer calls forth in them, things that lead to trouble and strife. It would seem that there is no better way of preparing a sect for trouble and strife, disagreement, for abusing one another but by pious mystic speeches. Well, if you think of the straight line this will seems downright impossible; but it is a factual truth. It is so because it is not just the content of anything said but the way in which people react to things. And one must know the world. And above all one must not base one's views just on one's wishes.

Let me once again remind you of the conversation I once had with two Roman Catholic priests in a town in southern Germany.[40] They had attended a lecture I had given on the Bible and wisdom. There was nothing the two priests could really object to. But even if there is nothing to object to, priests cannot simply accept that. They have to raise some objection. So they said, 'Yes, in substance we would be able to say the same, but we say the things we say in such a way that everyone can understand them. You are only saying them for a number of people who have a certain level of education. Anything we say has to be understandable to all.' My answer was, 'Well, you see, it does not matter what you think is comprehensible to everyone and what I think about it. Our theoretical views as to what people understand are irrelevant. What matters is that we study reality. And there you can easily make a test for reality. Let me ask you, when you use these methods and present in your church today what you think everyone can understand—does everyone go to your church or are there not some today who stay outside? The fact that some stay outside counts more than your belief that you speak for everyone. The reality is that some stay outside. Your belief that you speak to all is your belief. I speak to those who do not go to your church, for it is my opinion that one must accept reality, and that one can also speak to those who do not go to church but nevertheless are justifiably looking for the way to the spiritual world.'

A commonplace example to show the difference between thinking in a way that accords with reality, letting reality dictate what one's views should be, and the way most people think they know things they have just dreamt up and wish for and swear by. Someone who investigates reality is also prepared at any moment to abandon something he considered to be right and give his thoughts a different direction when the facts teach him the truth. Reality does not go as much in a straight line as people would wish.

So it can certainly be the case and will be more and more the case—that is the trend in the evolution of human nature—that members of a sect will grow more and more quarrelsome and cantankerous as one seeks to teach the most pious mysticism, the most heartfelt mysticism. But it is equally wrong to teach people one-sided natural-scientific views. It needs great mental acuity to gain insight in natural science, and as you know I am not at all inclined to give less recognition to the natural-scientific truths than anyone else. But there is also the fact that if only natural-scientific truths or truths of the natural-scientific kind were taught to the world, the mental acuity used to find natural-scientific truths would greatly contribute to condemning people to be unfree. Where one-sided mysticism would lead to more and more trouble and strife, one-sided natural science in the present-day sense would cause inner lack of freedom, to being inwardly bound. So you see that it is properly thought through when we say that in spiritual science one must endeavour not to be one-sidedly mystical nor one-sidedly natural-scientific. Justice must be done to both, neither overestimating nor underestimating the one or the other. We must advance from duality to trinity. Spiritual science will of its own accord avoid the either-or and accept the both-and, one casting light on the other. You know it is always a bad thing when someone of a natural-scientific bent inveighs against mysticism; as a rule the things he says will be downright silly. In the same way it is downright silly for someone purely given to mysticism, knowing nothing about natural-scientific insights, to inveigh against natural science. To inveigh against mysticism—to ring the changes—is something which really only a mystic should allow himself to do, and only someone who knows natural science should permit himself to inveigh against natural science at one point or another. Then the things said will be what they are said to be, as they can be properly assessed. But it will always be a bad thing for natural science to be bad-mouthed by someone who knows nothing about it, perhaps believing himself to be a great mystic, or when a natural scientist knows nothing about mysticism and denigrates it. In the field of spiritual science it has been said many, many times that certain truths must seem paradoxical to people because they go so much against the standpoint of being at ease in ordinary life.

Today I have been speaking about a whole number of things which have surged up against your souls unresolved, in a way. I have spoken of some facts of life that will have to be admitted if one also wants things to be different. Some who are today considering themselves to be great people, capable of much, have no idea of these truths of life. And that is exactly what lies behind the great catastrophes in our time, that there is this great need to get to know this life and people do not want to know it.

Tomorrow we'll consider some things that will resolve some of the contradictions which quite rightly surged up against your souls today.

LECTURE 6

15 SEPTEMBER 1918

Looking at human life in spirit and soul one cannot use some ideas that are widely accepted particularly in present-day life and present-day views. One such idea which is not a good one concerning human life in spirit and soul is for instance the idea of evolution, the idea that one thing evolves from the other, or rather one state from the other. To avoid misunderstanding let me stress that I do not say something now about the idea of evolution being of no use. We did make extensive use of it yesterday, for example. But when one is speaking about human life in soul and spirit—and not in soul and body—the idea of evolution serves no purpose. Yesterday we were speaking of life in soul and body, how it progresses from birth to death; there we do need the idea of evolution. The situation is different when we speak of human life in spirit and soul. If one is speaking in accord with reality, concepts or ideas other than evolution will serve.

Human life in spirit and soul, the way we know it within the outer reality perceived through the senses, involves thinking, feeling and doing, or acting out of the will. To understand the course of life in spirit and soul according to thinking, feeling and doing as we go through life, we must take note of the following. Living in thinking, feeling and doing—that is in feeling something and what has been felt coming to expression in thought, or perceiving something in the outside world which then comes to expression in thought, or doing something, letting will become deed—thus going through life in spirit and soul, the relations must always be considered which exist between spiritual entities. Wanting to describe the element of spirit and soul within which human beings exist with their soul, we must not shy away from speaking of connections that exist between entities of spirit and soul.

Let us assume, for instance, that someone is more of a thinker. Well, the activities of thinking, feeling and doing are never completely separate in real life. So if someone is a thinker and forms ideas, the will is involved in the thinking; the will is involved in the process of thinking. And also when we will, when we do something, thought is involved in what has been willed and done. The situation is that people are sometimes more thinking and less doing when they think, when they reflect; or they are more doing and less thinking in taking action, or also when they give themselves up to some feeling they experience. But talking about it the way I have just been doing is merely a very superficial characterization. One has to use a very different approach if one wants to come to the reality of these things. One must then, for instance, consider this: I am perceiving something or other in the outside world; this encourages me to form ideas about it. I am not taking action; my will intent is limited to directing my bodily nature towards the outside world and perceiving that world, letting thoughts follow one another. My activity is more reflective, perceptive, and in reality this means that I enter into a spiritual region where certain spirits have the upper hand which incline more towards the ahrimanic nature. Figuratively speaking I am sticking my head into a region where spirits who are more of an ahrimanic nature have the upper hand. Instead of saying, and this is merely in accord with seeming reality, 'I am reflecting on something,' I would have to say, in speaking the truth, 'I am active in a spiritual region where spirits have the upper hand over other spirits, damping them down, as it were, and in thus having the upper hand keeping those in balance which are more inclined towards ahrimanic nature.'

When one says something like this it does at first sound vague, indefinite. But one cannot put it in any other way but the way they are in the spiritual region. Our language has been created for the sense-perceptible world. It is, however, possible to present such things in images by taking the process out of the human being, as it were, and moving it more into the cosmic sphere. For initiates the fact which one characterizes in outward terms by saying, 'I am reflecting on something which has stimulated me,' is figuratively expressed more or less as follows.

Human beings live cosmically within the cosmos. I have spoken these days of the compass needle which cosmically points north and south and does not determine its direction from within. Human beings are orientated within the cosmos. They live in such a way that we are in one way considering their orientation by saying: 'Cosmically they are orientated in such a way that their orientation may change and swing to and fro among different signs of the zodiac [Fig. 5]. The orientation changes, going towards Ram, Bull, Twins, Crab, Lion, Virgin, Scales, Scorpion, Archer, Goat, Water-carrier, Fishes. Their orientation is also such that initially there is a main direction, so that if we base this on the zodiac, the head is orientated upwards,

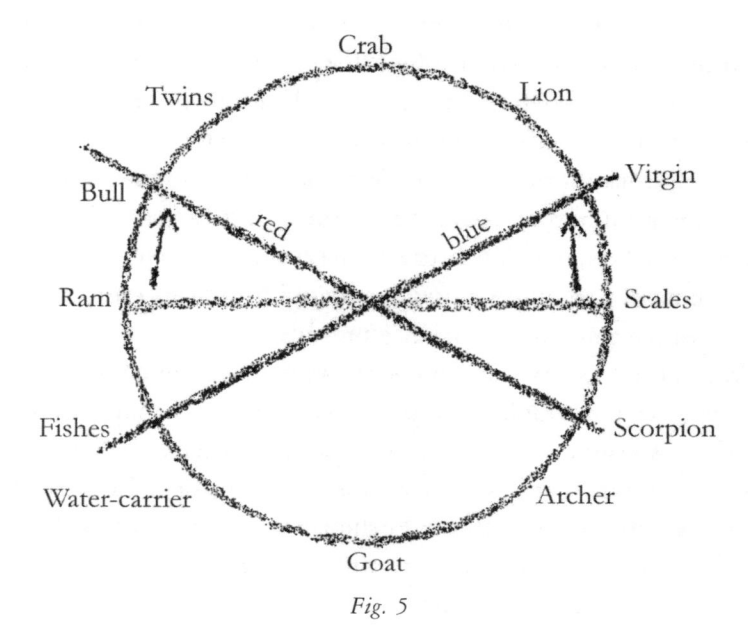

Fig. 5

the extremities downward.' We may say, therefore, there is something like a balance beam in this orientation, separating the upper from the lower [Fig. 5].

What would the cosmic orientation of the human being be—if we were to look at him in a way in which I would not wish you to be now—so that he neither thinks nor acts, but simply gives himself up to his general feeling of life, half asleep and half awake, not being passive nor active but passively active, slouching along in life. A lot will then also be going on inside him but he won't be aware of this. If we wanted to characterize this condition—as I said, I would not want you to be in it now—we would say that the beam is horizontal. But if he were in the kind of state of soul in which I'd hope you to be—reflective, stimulated and taking in the things that are said—the beam would have to be in a different position and we'd have to say, 'All the souls sitting in this room, or at least a number of them, enter into a region where certain spirits raise the beam on one side.' In physical life, if there were excess weight moving the beam we'd say the beam is going down. But we are now speaking of the spiritual; there we have to say that the beam is rising. When someone is 'reflective', certain spirits in the region which he then enters raise the beam from Scales to Virgin [blue]. I then have to draw the beam so that certain spirits which incline towards ahrimanic nature raise it like this. So that would be the human being musing, reflective [beam extending from Virgin to Fishes]. We may ask, therefore, 'What does it mean when a human being is reflecting?' It means that he uses his position as a human being in the whole cosmos in such a way that he uses the powers in which he swings to and fro to enter into a cosmic region where this state of balance prevails.

So you think yourself in a reflective state; thinking yourself in that state you have to think to yourself that your—if I may now put it like this—spiritual space into which you then enter is within a region where a struggle that has come to rest is taking place; the spirits here on the left would fight those on the right, and vice versa. But the struggle is not actually going on when your are in a reflective state; it has come to rest. This means, however, that certain spirits with ahrimanic tendencies have the upper hand. When a beam is at rest though at an angle, and is no longer swinging to and fro, something is dragging it down. That would be the real situation which corresponds to reflection, to thinking activity.

Thinking as we call it in ordinary existence based on the senses is merely maya, an illusion. You have to describe real thinking cosmically by asking about the whole position of the human being within the cosmos. This position of the human being in the cosmos that gives you answers as to what certain spirits in the spiritual world are doing will also answer and tell you what thinking activity, reflection, truly is. Essentially therefore the way we speak of thinking in ordinary life is an illusion. To describe it in a way that is in accord with reality we'd have to say, 'We are in a region where thoughts arise in our thinking space because certain spirits inclined towards the ahrimanic have raised the scale on one side.' That is the actual thing which happens.

Let us consider another thing that happens in the human soul and spirit. It is that we act, but not wildly so, that our actions are full of intent, of thoughts. The way one thinks of this in ordinary life, describes it in ordinary life, is again mere illusion. For when we do things, act, we also enter into a certain cosmic region. But now the situation is that certain spirits which incline towards luciferic nature make the scale rise in the opposite sense, so that we must now draw the beam like this [Fig. 5, red]. The arrow would indicate the direction in which those spirits lift the beam from its resting position. Acting out of the will, with real intent, we are orientated in a region of the cosmos where the beam is held like that by luciferic spirits. This had been preceded by rest, and as soon as we enter into the region of doing, of acting, the luciferic spirits begin to make the beam tremble; we then enter into a kind of struggle which is taking place in the cosmos. The luciferic spirits begin to fight ahrimanic spirits, and the unstable position, with the beam shifting, reflects the struggle which is truly taking place between ahrimanic and luciferic spirits in our will to act. So the 'will to act' we speak of in our ordinary speech and define with our ordinary ideas is mere maya, illusion. We talk of the will to act in the right way when we say, 'When we act out of the will we are in a region where the world balance beam has been raised [Fig. 5, going from Bull to Scorpion]. This did, however, happen without us. We enter into a region where the beam has been raised without us. So we go into exactly the kind of region where rest begins to change into movement, begins to change into rhythmic play.

In the first of our Mystery Plays[41] I indicated something of this nature. It did of course have to be indicated in dramatic form—that we must not imagine that something happens merely in the human being who thinks or feels something in soul and spirit. No, cosmic powers are set in motion. The way it is presented on the stage is that great cosmic events take place whilst Capesius and Strader behave in a particular way. They really do, not in the sense-perceptible but in the supersensible world; in the sense-perceptible world one can only present these things to the senses the way they have been presented in the play. It is, however, stated quite clearly in the play that the way people behave here, as we describe it, is really only a reflection of something real. Significant events take place in the cosmos when a human being wills or thinks even the least thing in his soul. We can never will or think something inwardly without entering into regions where spiritual struggles take place or spiritual struggles come to rest, or spiritual battles have already been fought as we enter into the outcome of the struggle, and so on.

What I have just been describing is part of human soul and spirit nature. It is, however, hidden from the life which people live between birth and death. But in the spiritual sphere it is the truth. In a different context I did say that these days in relating to the world in an intellectualistic way, as is the custom in the world, human beings are actually living in hallucinations. Basically the ideas we have of our thinking, feeling and doing are hallucinations, and the reality behind it is the way we are able to show it on the stage in this way. It is the things I have just been describing which really are behind anything that goes on in our mind and soul. Reflections are revealed to human beings which to them seem to be thinking, feeling and acting out of the will.

As soon as we look at human beings as they truly are in spirit and soul the concept of evolution no longer applies. It would be complete nonsense to say that human beings only grow reflective at a particular age and are given up to a raging will nature before that, and that the one evolves from the other. Nothing evolves like this in the region of the spirit. All we can say when we see that a child has different ideas, feeling and will than does an old person is that the child enters into a different spiritual region where the struggles between the different spirits take a different form. You do not get the kind of development or evolution in the spiritual region of which we spoke yesterday. In this spiritual region we only understand things past if we say that the picture of the struggle, of the relationship, of the changing relations between the spirits whom we seek behind the higher hierarchies is different from the picture which we have in the interactions of the hierarchies when speaking of the present. Yet another picture results when we speak of the future. We see different pictures of the relationship between the different spirits in the hierarchies depending on whether we are considering past, present or future. And it would be very wrong to say that the picture of the struggle of the future evolves from that of the struggle in the past. In the spiritual region these things are, in a certain respect, side by side, not one after the other. Because of this one cannot speak of evolution but only of a spiritual perspective, something I did already refer to in another context. We may say, therefore, that when we consider the human being in spirit and soul it is pointless to say that he is first a child, goes through second dentition, that he then reaches sexual maturity and so on. The development seen in body and soul is bound up with a spirit and soul principle where one cannot speak of evolution but only of transitions in the interrelations between the spirits of the higher hierarchies, moving from one picture to another.

You cannot gain a real insight into the relationship between the temporal and the eternal unless you consider what I said in my lectures yesterday and today. Yesterday I showed how human beings as entities in body and soul are within the evolution of time in such a way that they will indeed have to be old before understanding what has been happening within them as children. There we are fully concerned with development or evolution. We have to acknowledge, however, that in spirit and soul human beings are not at all in a process of evolution, that the concept of time in the form in which we know it in the life perceived through the senses does not apply at all when we speak of human nature in spirit and soul, that we are wrong in applying the concept of time to the sphere of the higher hierarchies. There everything is eternal. Things do not proceed in time there but we are dealing with perspectives in which we have to see the struggles and changing relationships. The concept of time does not apply to the changing relationships in the higher hierarchies. We are merely presenting the nature of the higher hierarchies figuratively in using the time concept. Because of this you can see in my *Occult Science* how careful I have been in indicating that things do, of course, have to be presented in time in the images given, especially where I was referring to the Saturn and Sun periods where it has been described like that, but I did distinctly say that the time concept is only applied figuratively to anything preceding the Sun period and half the actual Sun period as well. You can read it up in my *Occult Science*. Those comments of seemingly secondary significance in the book based on the science of the spirit, are of the greatest importance, for they provide the basis for understanding the difference between things temporal and transient and things eternal that go on for ever.

If you consider what I have just been saying you will be able to say that yesterday I attempted to describe essential human nature for you purely in time. The concept of time played a quite considerable role in what I said yesterday, the role being that it does depend on time if one has a certain ability to understand, speaking of the time one has lived through before reaching old age, or time not yet lived through, in which case one is still a child. Everything we discussed yesterday was strictly based on the concept of time. We described what in the light of spiritual science is the basis of essential human nature in body and soul. Today I have been speaking of the things that are the basis for the human being in soul and spirit. This can only be spoken of by going into the region of eternity, describing it in such a way—and this is difficult to do—that the concept of time does not apply in this region in which we are as human beings in spirit and soul.

So in this respect we truly are discordant creatures. As we develop through life we know that we must calmly and patiently wait until our bodily and soul nature is mature enough to understand things. On the other hand we are all the time in the region of eternity where we do not develop and, as it were, look just once, in childhood, at one location in the region of eternity and in advanced old age at another location. Here on earth human beings live in such a way that the things that happen in the region of eternity are radiating down into the things that happen in time and the two mingle.

In the knowledge gained by the initiates, things that mingle must be kept apart for they can only be understood if held apart. In that science, the things that are in the region of eternity have always been called the upper ones, those in the region of transience the lower ones. Living here on earth human beings are from this point of view a mixture of upper and lower and will never gain any kind of insight into essential human nature by looking at the mixture. They will only gain insight if they know how to keep the things that mingle apart. So you will find it understandable that when it comes to the aspect which life on earth offers you cannot in your normal state of conscious awareness establish that things are the way I did say today. Someone who wants to base himself only on the ordinary conscious mind may say: 'Yesterday you told us something about the human being which we cannot see, which is not anything real at all, for human beings do not develop in the way you described yesterday. Some are very mature when young,' and so on. This objection is, however, raised from the illusory point of view. Reality is as I have described it yesterday and today. People fall into dualism today because they do not see the lower principle being as fluid as I have presented it yesterday. The initiate must free the lower principle from its rigidity and make it flow. In ordinary life people look at someone who is before them; the initiate must consider the process which takes place between birth and death. He must see the human being in a state of flux.

Then again, as the initiate considers thinking, feeling and doing, which is in a state of flux, he has to stop the flow and look at the aspect which is bound to the body and therefore appears to proceed in time in the region of eternity, the region where things are side by side, but spiritually side by side. People strive for the knowledge of the initiates and are happy to admit also in outward terms that the environment we observe, the environment evident to the senses, is maya, a great illusion. But when things get serious they prefer not to consider this but seek to stay with maya in describing both the upper and the lower region. Nice diagrams are called for that follow the pattern of maya concepts, and go up into the spiritual world with them or move down, above or below the conscious mind. People say, 'Well, you don't describe things so that I can understand them.' But all there is behind this is this: 'You are asking me to arrive at different ideas than the ones that exist in maya. You ask me to arrive at ideas that are in the region of reality.'

Another objection may be: 'What does it matter to me, what goes on in the lower part? One will also manage quite well by just applying the concept of time in earnest to human evolution, or by looking at the region of eternity in life.' People might say this if they stay in maya, if they develop ideas that come from the mixture and do not go beyond maya. Well, you can just about live, be able to live in a sleep state, if you stay in the region of eternity. In the first place, however, any concepts or ideas you produce here, however great the acuity, however much they could hold their own among today's scholars, will only allow you to just about live, but you cannot die with them. No one can die with the concepts produced here. And this is the point, as soon as one touches on this secret, where spiritual insight gets really serious. Concepts produced without the knowledge which initiates have, these ideas, will after death take one into a wrong ahrimanic region. You will not enter into the region of human principles, a region which you are in fact destined to reach, if you are not prepared to develop concepts like those which the knowledge gained by the initiates provides.

In earlier times higher spirits would in supersensible ways teach human beings who had atavistic clairvoyance the concepts of initiation. A kind of supersensible teaching existed—essentially until 333 after the Mystery on Golgotha—which prepared people not only for life but also for death. Since then need has arisen for human beings to make their own efforts to gain insight and so prepare their soul that it can go through the gate of death in the right way. There is nothing more frivolous than to say about the knowledge of initiates that one might simply wait until one comes to the region after death and see what the situation is. In the science of the initiates one is told that anyone who waits like that is sinning against life. For you would get a terrible shock if an initiate—this is an impossibility—were to tell you the kind of monstrosity you would be born as if you had that attitude in your life between death and that birth, saying that you'd wait and see till you're born on earth and then you'd see the creature which lives in the blood covered in flesh. Yes, there'd be a beneficent influence, but they would not relieve you of the need to prepare for yourself the powers that would save you from being born a monster. Higher spirits will protect you there. This spiritual life between death and rebirth—say the spirits who teach there—exists not only for our region; it exists so that the region of the lower principle be prepared in the right way so that no monsters arise there but truly well-formed human beings.

But life on earth, too, exists not only for the earth; it exists in order that human beings may be able to die in the right, the human way. Human beings must here on earth prepare their lower nature so that they will not enter into an ahrimanic region which is unlawful. There are of course also lawful ahrimanic regions, but this would be an unlawful one that would not be in accord with their human nature. So that is the first thing.

The second thing is this. You can, if need be, live as an isolated individual—but in reality one does not live as a single individual—

by ignoring the region of eternity, but you cannot live within the human social order. The human social order is guided and led by the spirits in the higher hierarchies. And if you enter into even the most minimal human relationship—our whole life consists in relationships between ourselves and others—and anything you put into this relationship does not come from an awareness of being within the spiritual region, the region of eternity, you will ruin the social contact. You are then having a part in bringing about the catastrophic phenomena of destruction and annihilation around the globe. Social or political views not coming from the spiritual are destructive, annihilating. Only a view where one is taking account of the region of eternity will enliven anything evolving in the political, the social and altogether human community life. That is the great, solemn truth and the knowledge gained by the initiates must make more and more people aware of it.

The signs of the times are such today that the time has passed when sublime spirits taught supersensibly, which was the case until 333, lessons people did not have to attend to consciously, for they were largely given in sleep or in a twilight state. Today human beings have to learn the things they need from other human beings. They must simply put aside the arrogance which makes them say that they can always develop their own opinions. In the region of transience they need to grasp such things as this: old people have something to say to the young which only they can tell them. And if one grasps this, why should one not also grasp that there is knowledge gained by initiates which one human being learns from another. This is also a leaven in the social life that must develop in future, that people take in things which they are not able to perceive for themselves at some time or other—now speaking of the region of time—from other people. Yesterday I told you that through evolution in time the arrangement is that one need not accept things on mere authority but that in the ideas which arise within one you can indeed have a kind of conviction welling forth from your own inner life.

I emphasized in a number of my books that belief in authority should not flourish in the soil of spiritual science. But one thing must be certain for all who truly base themselves on the science of the spirit: you are not a initiate by simply being cock on the dung heap and begin to crow about your own convictions at any time in life. You can set up all kinds of programmes which you think will rule the world, but never produce a body of knowledge which will truly flow into the life and activities in the world. The knowledge of the initiates will be needed more and more for all life and activity in the world.

In earlier times initiation was like a thinking given to people; as we move towards the future people must with all their will turn towards the knowledge which comes into the world through initiation. All kinds of wishes, subconscious wishes, will go against this. It is not easy for people to develop the great seriousness needed to enter in the right way into everything that is demanded by everything that has been said.

It is really quite difficult to tell people today how much they need to be of good will because they often see this good will as a heartless will. Someone who truly enters into the meaning of spiritual science will know that moving towards the future there is no other way but through the science of the spirit, through initiation, to create soul substance that can go through the gate of death in the right way and can find its right place in human social life. You can come to live in it and then the counter thought will come. So a person has entered into this kind of life and there are others whom he loves for one reason or another who do not want to know about this great challenge in our time, about turning to spiritual life. He will then wish that these other people shall also be blessed, and it seems heartless when the full truth relating to this is stated. But someone who is of good will in this sphere will know that there is no good will in closing one's eyes and saying 'Well, they do not want to know about spiritual life but they can also be blessed without it.' What one has to say is, 'Every effort must be made so that spiritual life may come to the earth.' We must endeavour to be positive and not so much follow thoughts that are so closely bound up with wishes, thinking of the situation of people who do not want to know, but with good will give our selves up to spiritual life in the endeavour to bring this spiritual life into the world and so take humanity into the state of blessedness, if I may use the term, of being in harmony with the spiritual world.

Behind the attitude often called 'loving' lies not only superficiality but also a failure to see things as they truly are. Someone speaking from initiate knowledge today does not do this merely to bring theoretical insight to the human soul but is speaking from a warm heart, with love for humanity. He knows how much the signs of the times indicate that the next great task will be to speak to people of this spiritual life, and to work in such a way in the life of people that this spiritual life will reach the human soul. It will, of course, call for some degree of courage to face up to human evolution in time. The views of the upper and the lower have to be clearly understood as they have to be today and as far as possible must also be presented to the human soul.

If you look at the whole of life the way it is looked at in a prejudiced, illusory way today, yes, then you won't talk of the whole of life; you'll really only talk of a very small part of life. I have tested this. I know the existing Goethe biographies, for instance. They do tell us all kinds of things which Goethe has done, thought and envisaged between his birth and his death. But when this Goethe soul went through the gate of death, everything written from the point of view of today's illusory philosophy of life did not have the least significance for the region into which the human soul enters after death, which represents a different blend between the region of eternity and the region of transience. For this, too, is transient. The human being will be born into a new existence. For in the region into which human beings enter through the gate of death we can do nothing with everything known through the illusory philosophy of life, through the illusory biography recording the life between birth and death. There the only question that matters is: 'How did the soul speak to the cosmos?' Things a person has told others, even if they have been the most beautiful things here on earth, will not have been spoken to the cosmos unless they have themselves arisen from spiritual insight.

The things Goethe had lived through had been spoken to the cosmos if we look at his life in such a way that we describe the seven-year periods especially with regard to his life. How much he changed from one seven-year period to another! How remarkable that the great change in his life came within a seven-year period when he went to Italy, or at least made the decision to go to Italy! The things that happen from one seven-year period to another under the region which creates the biographies in the ordinary sense speak into the cosmos; something can be done with them when the human being has gone through the gate of death.

What Goethe said as the spirits from the region of eternity influenced him, which can be described the way in which I have described it today, does in turn relate to the region into which one enters after death. Describe Goethe's life from the point of view which results from the spiritual way of looking at one seven-year period after another: what Goethe felt when he wrote words like 'Things you wish for in youth are yours in abundance in old age'. If you look at Goethe's life from the point of view of transience and come upon words like these which Goethe wrote as a motto at the beginning of a chapter in his works, 'Things you wish for in youth are yours in abundance in old age', if you come up to such words with spiritual-scientific insight you are, as it were, coming up against the eternal Goethe. And if, again in a spiritual-scientific mood, you come on something of Goethe's where something coming from the region of eternity enters into his words, from the region where the hierarchies let their interplay proceed, you come on something which is the eternal Goethe. To get to know not only the temporal in the world but the eternal, which one can only get to know by the roundabout route of spiritual science, is the task set for us when we take up the science of initiation. Things from earlier times must now be seen in the light which can come from the present-day science of initiation.

There is something in the Roman Catholic Church which we may compare with the effect which a red rag has on a certain creature. If a Catholic who today is often considering himself to be dyed-in-the-wool could speak up against some kind of philosophy of life—it would be a philosophy of 'emanation', presenting the world from the emanation point of view—then this philosophy would be condemned (perhaps less for the man himself but certainly for the faithful sheep for whom he writes or speaks). All one has to do is to attach the predicate 'emanating' to a philosophy of life! Our staunch Catholic opposes this emanationistic philosophy with the creationistic philosophy, the philosophy of creation from nothing. Now again dualism would be used, putting the emanationist philosophy that acts like a red rag on one side, the creationistic philosophy, creation from nothing, on the other side. One adopts the creationistic philosophy and rejects the emanationistic philosophy. Emanationism has specifically come to be known in the Occident by way of gnosis. The way it has become known in the Occident—the literature on which it is based has largely been destroyed—this emanationism is already a kind of caricature and the great misunderstanding arises because essentially only the caricature is known in the Roman Catholic world. For their theory of emanation, with one aeon arising from another, with the less perfect or the less sublime aeon arising from the more perfect aeon, exoterically usually known as gnosis, has already been corrupted. It goes back to a philosophy of life that was of a completely different nature, one that was still possible in the times when spiritual teachers from the supersensible world taught humanity; emanationism which, as I said, has already been corrupted, points back to knowledge which in the old way related to the region of eternity, the upper element. When it comes to this upper element one can, in a way, defend emanationism, not in its corrupted form but in the form where only a perspective in time is spoken of and not an actual process of evolution. And as there was no reference to evolution one also could not speak of something arising out of nothing for that would be an evolution, even if evolution at a radically extreme point. There one cannot speak of one thing arising from another but in the way we also did not speak—as we talked about the region of eternity today—of an emanation, an arising, but of changing relationships among the spirits which have the quality of eternity.

When we talk about the region of transience we can certainly speak of evolution, but then also of the extreme case of evolution of which we have essentially, implicitly, been speaking a great deal these days. Surely it means continuous creation from something which to the world is nothing when we say that the present ideals are the seeds for the future, and the present realities are the fruits of the past. Rightly considered this gives us the true, uncorrupted creationism. The challenge for people today is this: to see what was meant by emanationism in the right light and apply it to the world of spirit and soul; to see what true, uncorrupted creationism is in the right light and apply it not to the creators but to the creation, to the element of body and soul. The salvation, the redemption of the philosophy of life is to acknowledge the duality, see through it and not jumble things with dualistic orientation together in a nebulous way, to see the region of eternity in the right way and also the region of transience and be able to tell them apart. Then we'll be able to say: 'When I look at the reality that lies before me it is a reflection and at the same time also a consequence. It is a reflection in that it belongs to the region of transience and is governed by evolution, a consequence in that it belongs to the region of eternity and is governed by that which results when we see the things we have today been characterizing for the life in spirit and soul in the right way.' Someone who puts things in the right way will not say that creationism is right and emanation is wrong, nor that emanation is right and creationism is wrong. He will know that both are necessary factors if we are to grasp life in the full. The overcoming of dualism cannot be done in theory but only in life itself. Someone who is looking for a way out between the region of the upper and the region of the lower, the region of transience and the region of eternity and does so in theory, using concepts, ideas, notions, will not succeed, he'll always end up in a confused philosophy because he is using the intellect to look for something that must be looked for in life. In life, however, one is only looking for the truth if one knows: 'You have to turn your attention on the one hand to the region of eternity, there to perceive what admittedly does not present itself in external reality, and then also to the region of transience, there to consider all human beings and all creatures in a way which actually contradicts outward reality.' Equipped with both, the reality you approach, experiencing it in a living way, will come together from the elements which originally gave rise to it—the consequence of the region of eternity and the reflection of the region of transience. This is how we grasp it in life if we do not want to have a theoretical philosophy of life that is all concept and idea, but are ready to have two philosophies—one for the region of spirit and soul, the other for the region of body and soul, and do not want to have a theory for the source that feeds life and makes it fertile but have the two live together. Then and only then do we escape the dualism.

This is the challenge facing humanity today. It is not a matter of having founders of religions appear to teach spiritualism. It is not a question of some founders of scientific sects making their appearance who teach materialism. What matters is that we see matter materially in evolution, the spiritual immaterially, spiritually, in the region of eternity, and see reality in the two coming together. Letting the spirit illumine the material, letting the material harden the spiritual—this is what must become part of the future philosophy of life. There is no need for philosophers who give people definitions of the truth, nor definitions of what science teaches so that a 'monistic' harmony is established. What matters is that the dualism between truth and science is recognized, looking in a life that is alive to the relationship between truth and knowledge and so arrive at a living rather than a theoretical epistemology. Not truth or knowledge but both truth and knowledge—the knowledge sustained by the weight of truth, the weight of truth illumined with the light of knowledge, acknowledging that man is dualistic in the world and can only overcome such dualism as needs to be overcome in his life, in growth and development. It is not Kantianism, the belief that whatever lives in the outside world is not the thing in itself, but truth and knowledge which future humanity must make its task also in philosophy, recognizing that everything around us is maya, but maya because as human beings we take this position in the world which is dualistic. We create maya by doing so and we overcome maya in life in that we ourselves come alive, and not with theory or notion.

That is what I have also written in my *Truth and Science*[42] and my *Philosophy of Spiritual Activity*.[43] A new edition of the latter will be available shortly. I have made some additions; the text has not been changed but considerably expanded on certain points.

It is a question, therefore, of understanding the signs of the times and on the basis of this cultivating spiritual life in all kinds of fields of human activity.

Lecture 7

20 SEPTEMBER 1918

There is no need, really, to celebrate the fifth anniversary of laying the foundation stone for our building. And there is particularly no need for this among the people who have been more or less close in space to the building through those five years. These are disastrous days and for that reason, too, one certainly has no time for special celebrations, nor should the celebrating of anniversaries become a habit in our movement. Only a few words shall be said on the subject.

The building could not be finished in the time which some people may perhaps have expected when they attended the foundation stone ceremony or were involved in some way or other, perhaps in their thoughts. But that is not the essential thing. The essential thing with this building, even if it is still incomplete today, is that it actually does exist. Even if it were less complete than it is, the essential point would be that it does exist and looking at its forms one can see the spirit in which it is meant to exist. We have talked about its design, its nature, on a number of occasions. The fact that the building exists is something we really want to register as a fact, a fact which in a way is also an obligation for us. It simply is not one and the same thing if our spiritual-scientific movement would have existed without this building over the last five years or if it exists with this building. It is not the same thing, absolutely not the same thing. The building is above all a landmark for our movement. In a sense it shows to people far and wide that there has to be such a movement in the world. It is also an obligation, as is evident to us from the way the outside world sees this building. The outside world would have been much less aware of the whole of our movement if the building did not exist. It simply is a fact that at the present time visible signs mean a great deal to people. Considering that a good deal of our work for the spiritual-scientific movement will no doubt consist in fighting hostile movements, it has to be acknowledged that the existence of the building contributes quite a bit to the existence of powerful hostile movements. People would pay less attention to us if the building did not exist.

It is therefore not enough to feel a degree of satisfaction that the building has come into existence. Considering this building to be our own affair we must also have a feeling to go with this—like the south pole belongs to the north pole or the north pole to the south pole—that it is our responsibility to stand up for the anthroposophical cause in the right way. I'd like to say that we should not really feel pleasure or satisfaction with regard to the building unless we are at the same time doing everything in our power to stand up for the anthroposophical cause. For the building would cause the destruction of our cause if sufficient strength could not be found to defend it. I would say that if we did not have a building we could have the luxury of merely belonging to the anthroposophical cause, for there would be no visible sign which attracts the attention also of people who need visible signs. But if we take pleasure in the building, if we feel satisfaction about it, we must also accept a certain obligation to stand up for the cause of anthroposophy.

The most serious misunderstandings are, of course, connected with the anthroposophical cause itself, but we shall also hear of countless misunderstandings of the worst kind where the building is concerned. You only have to meet someone now and then who has visited the building or talks about it and you'll see what misunderstandings there are. Many other things also show us how something positive affects people, and our building is something positive. We won't get very far by seeking to correct ill-intentioned attacks in a negative way; but we'll go a long way if we endeavour to present the positive to the world in the right light. People who have been to the building—the evidence for this exists—and who have let it speak to them, have seen something positive, and they, or at least many of them, have not formed a bad opinion of the cause that is connected with the building. We just have to be careful not to attach all kinds of mysticisms to the building when people come to visit it. The building will have its own effect if we objectively interpret it as the artistic reflection of basic spiritual-scientific facts and basic observations. It will definitely compromise the building and the whole of our cause if you seek to impose all kinds of mystical things on people.

My intention has been to speak of some such practical things. The most important thing is that we remember the laying of the foundation stone five years ago, the significance of this building which is intended to stand before us in liveliest sentience of the inmost nature of the anthroposophical cause. We have frequently uttered thoughts on the building and will also do so on all kinds of occasions in future. Today we take the thoughts that come to us when we look back on the occasion five years ago when we laid the foundation stone and make them part of the feeling that connects us with the building.

I have often spoken to you of how the human soul has changed in the course of human evolution, how short-sighted it is to think that today's state of soul can be understood if we do not look back on the transformations which this human soul has gone through. We look back—I need not recapitulate—on the different periods of Earth evolution, and have on a number of occasions characterized the post-Atlantean era to show how the state of the human soul has always been changing in this post-Atlantean era. It is particularly in speaking of these things that we must move from abstract to concrete thinking. We must try, ever more intensively, to answer the question 'What did things really look like in the human soul in those earlier times?' We are looking back on a primal period when—we may say so in more than a figurative sense—divine teachers were imparting the sacred secrets of existence to human beings. And we know that from then onwards human beings have found many different ways of learning about those secrets of existence. The ideas formed in the human soul did indeed change again and again through the ages. Ideas we have living in us today and put in words at any moment also lived in earlier states of soul; but they lived there in a very, very different way. Many of our most common concepts were utterly different then. Today I'll refer to two common concepts living in the human soul today. People are at any moment referring to them in words that are part of their vocabulary; they also lived in the human soul in the past, but in a completely different way. I want to speak of the concepts 'space' and 'time'.

Space is the most abstract thing people can think of today. They do not have much idea of space today! Three dimensions at right angles to one another or, if one reads textbooks of philosophy, how far physical objects extend, and there are also other definitions of space. But all this—consider how dry, cold and abstract it all is! Three dimensions at right angles to one another, or indeed everything that is said about space in geometry—dreadfully abstract, dry and conceptual! So conceptual that in art the whole of space—with time, by the way—has become subjective shadow, merely looking at the sensory phenomena. This abstract concept of space, which modern people know very little about except that it has length, width and height, this abstract notion was a very different thing in the distant past, with some idea still existing today for a few particularly sensitive people; but only a trace of it remains today. Yet we do not have to go all that far back—to the sixth, seventh, eighth pre-Christian centuries—and it will be fair to say: At that time space, the way people experienced space, was something very different for the human soul and not the dry abstraction which space is for the human soul today. In early Greek times the human soul still knew something when experiencing space which it could connect with, which it could feel in a living way. It felt itself to be in something that was alive when it felt itself to be in a space.

At most only a trace of this remains for humanity today. A few people have traces of sentience—I'll come to this shortly—of being present in space as a person, as a human being. But the people of those earlier times were saying something by which they meant a significant relationship between them and the universe as they distinguished between above and below, left and right, in front and behind. The living relationship people had with the three dimensions in those times do indeed have terribly little to do with our abstract three dimensions which really do nothing but be at right angles to one another—truly boring if you can do nothing for all eternity but be at right angles to one another like the three dimensions in geometry. The living experience which people meant in that past when speaking of above and below, left and right, in front and behind, really has terribly little to do with those three dimensions.

Above and below—it was something full of life when people in ancient times were still sentient of how they were first a young child and came upright from below up, when they felt how life consists in unfolding in the direction from above and below. Life consists in living the direction of the above and below. It is just a short distance which we move away from the ground in normal life as we grow, unless one lives in the ahrimanic times of airships or the Atlantean times—though in those times it was not very far above the ground, as you know from my description of Atlantis—feeling oneself to be living in the above and in the below, and not just above and below. The contrast between above and below was felt in those early times to be the contrast between the world of conscious awareness and the world of objects, the conscious and the unconscious world. People were deeply sentient of how subject relates to object when they experienced above and below. Above—and ever higher and higher above are the worlds of the gods; below are the worlds that are opposite to the gods, and the human being has his place in the above and below.

Even with someone like Goethe—you only need to study his *Faust*—you still find remnants of that awareness of above and below. Humanity was then also sentient of left and right. We have to speak in abstract terms about left and right today. The people of early times genuinely learned something when experiencing left and right, a genuine world of observation. The above and below is the line from infinity to infinity or from conscious to unconscious. Left and right—in experiencing left and right people felt the connection in the world between meaning and form, wisdom and form. Just draw an axis of symmetry; anything to the right of it and to the left of it will together give you the form, and you cannot connect the one with the other unless you do it meaningfully, relating one to the other.

If above and below were pointing to the mysterious relationship which human beings have to the spiritual and material worlds, the experience of left and right is the relationship of human beings to the world as it spreads in the form. They would feel themselves to be in this second element of space as they related left and right to one another, letting wisdom prevail in forms symmetrically arranged in left and right. This experience of meaning in form, of wisdom in form, in all possible variations, this feeling oneself within this harmony of meaning and form, wisdom and form was to the human beings of those early times what for us today is the abstract second dimension. And the above and below and the left and right come together in something which is the plane, which cannot yet exist in sense-perceptible form, needing thickness, needing in front and behind if is it to exist in the sense-perceptible world.

And in this third element, in the in front and behind, the people of old sensed the material making the leap into the spiritual. Above and below, left and right they would still sense as something spiritual. There can be no physical existence if something is just above and below, left and right; it is just an image, and has to be an image in space. It needs thickness to be material. In those early times people had a lively awareness that when you grow you take a few steps up from the ground in the above and below direction. Walking, you can move freely and are in your will element—in front and behind. Between them is the moving-in-complete-freedom to left and right as you stand still.

The people of those earlier times were sentient of these three opposite pairs which in their nature are part of the whole universe—

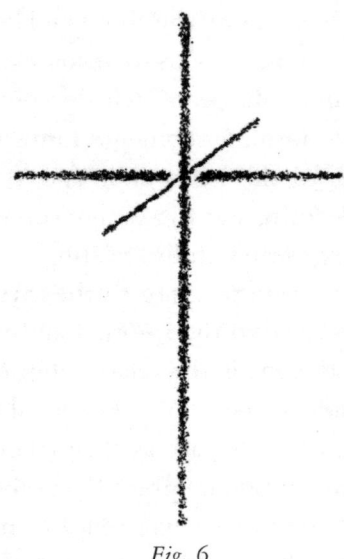

Fig. 6

this 'stay where you are' with regard to left and right, this stepping out into the world with regard to in front and behind, this slow upward movement along the above-below axis. Living in the above and below they were sentient of everything we call the intelligence, the rationality, of the universe being active in the whole cosmos. For them, all intelligence alive in the universe was interwoven with the above and below. Being able to be involved in this intelligence of the universe as they grew from below upwards they also felt themselves to be intelligent. Participation in the above and below was to them also participation in cosmic intelligence. Participation in left and right, with meaning and form, wisdom and form interwoven, was to them the feeling which is alive and active throughout the world. Standing quietly, surveying the world, was to them the connection between their own and the world's feeling. And walking through space in the in-front and behind axis was to them the unfolding of the will, taking one's place in the universe, in the world will, with one's own will. They felt their life to be interwoven with above and below, with left and right, with in front and behind. Conscious and unconscious elements: above and below, wisdom and form; left and right, spirit and matter; in front and behind. That was the sentience in those earlier times.

At the same time, however, those earlier people vaguely felt—I'm putting it in extreme terms—'If one stands on one's head, the below will be up above and the above will be below.' But that is also how it is with the antipodeans, and if one sees oneself as part of the earth—the below is above, the above is below. And so it is also possible to imagine that one day, thanks to something or other, anything which is on the right will be in front, anything on the left will be behind. These directions are just as alive and active in space as they are in a sense indistinguishable, interweaving. In those earlier times, when people were aware of living in that threefold space, they felt that the divine in its threefold form reigned in space. The divine spirit reigning in space made human beings aware of the divine in eternity.

The people of those times experienced—and what I am saying now is something they truly did experience—the divine in space in its revelation, tripartite by nature. It was the image for them of the threefold god—Father, Son and Spirit—or whatever name the threefold god was given. The trinity truly is something that was not thought up, it is not an invention. The trinity with all its particular characteristics was experienced in image when people had living experience of tripartite space.

Lack of clarity may prevail, in a sense, when it comes to above and below, and the way right and left may also turn into in front and behind. Under certain circumstances lack of clarity may also affect the interrelationship between God, Son and Spirit. However, when in the sphere of transience, in the sphere of space, people were living with the three dimensions not in an abstract, geometrical way, which is what we do, but in concrete living experience of how the divine comes into its own in space, when they were at the same time also aware of transience, they would relate this transience to the element of eternity, and tripartite space became for them the image of the tripartite spirit.

Living down here on earth I am living in the trinity of space; but this trinity of space is in image proof of the trinity of the divine origin of the world. That was more or less how people thought in the past. Today space has become abstract, and only a few people are sentient of the depth dimension, the thickness dimension and the way they arise: above and below, in front, behind; left and right the dimension of the plane. Even philosophers do not offer much living experience of this. Yet a few individuals who think about things and are not wholly asleep will realize that the depth dimension arises only on unconscious observation which is not that far below conscious awareness. People do still experience seeing the depth, but that is the last, shadowy remnant of that living experience of space.

In the religions which have developed, true understanding of trinity was preceded by understanding for the oneness of the god. Understanding for the oneness of the god has much the same origin as understanding for the trinity of the god through space.

Spiritual science finds its things from the divine facts themselves. Foolish people will come and say that some external proof or other does not exist. Well, we have told a few things about this and I could tell much more, but we won't spend time on it today. Let me just point out that perhaps it is simply that today's 'science' is so unscientific that proof cannot be found. Let me tell you just one thing, in a way also as an outward proof that people in past times had the sentience I spoke of today. Why did the rabbis of old also call God 'space'? Because in earlier times people had the sentience of which I have been speaking also in Judaism. If science meant genuine thought in the different fields, countless riddles would be found but these are at the same time genuine proof, external proof of what has to be found in spiritual science, though in this case from the spiritual facts. One of the names the rabbis have for God is 'space'; space and God are one and the same.

The oneness of the divine is similar in origin to the trinity of the divine. This is because of living experience of time. For people in earlier times also did not experience time in the abstract way we do today. Concrete, living experience of time was lost even earlier than concrete living experience of space. If you read Plato[44] or Aristotle[45] not the way many a schoolmaster does today—I have on several occasions referred to the note Hebbel had made in his diary[46] about a schoolmaster faced with the fact that the reincarnated Plato was at his school and lo and behold, the schoolmaster was at that time just reading out one of Plato's Dialogues in class, and the reincarnated Plato was given really bad marks by the schoolmaster. This is what Hebbel wrote in his diary. So if you read Plato and Aristotle with real, deeper understanding you will everywhere in their works read how people really still had a good feeling for this in pre-Christian times, in the sixth, seventh and eighth centuries before Christ. It had faded to some extent by the time of Plato and Aristotle but one can still clearly sense this getting a feel for space of which I spoke. The living experience of time was lost even earlier, however. It was very much alive in the second post-Atlantean era, the ancient Persian age. Zarathustra's disciples would have felt a shudder, of course, if one had said to them that time goes in a line which runs evenly from past to future.

In the time of Gnosis people still had a shadow of the feeling—scarcely recognizable, however—that time was a living thing. People would not say that there was such a line going from past to future. They would speak of aeons, of the creators who had been there in the past, with the later ones coming forth from them, with one aeon always handing on the creation impulses to the other. The image they would have of time was more or less that in the succession of hierarchies the spirit who went before would always hand on the impulses to those who came next, with the next always brought forth, as it were, by the preceding one. The preceding one would encompass the one that followed. People would look up to the one which had gone before as being more divine than the one which followed. 'Later' was felt to be ungodly, 'earlier' more divine. Living experience of and learning about time included looking at the change, with the development going from divine to godless. Everything would fall apart if the godly and ungodly were not to interweave and be a whole, and that is identical with our present-day abstract notions of past and future.

But in the image of time, looking back and embracing more and more comprehensive elements until one comes to the Ancient of Days,[47] people were sentient of the image of the god who was one. The old experience of time provided the basis for monotheism; the old experience of space provided the basis for the trinity. That is how the state of the human soul has changed; something that was full of life has grown abstract and dry. Paradoxical though it may sound, modern man is undoubtedly thinking of something abstract when speaking of space, and, I think, he thinks of a living relationship when speaking of a friend. But that concreteness, that elementary living experience which speaks from friend to friend today, to give an example, is still abstract compared to the intense experience of the world which people had in earlier times, living with space and time which were images to them of the one god and the trinity.

So we have grown dry and abstract when it comes to space and time, and something else must take their place, something of which we must have living experience, making it part of our inner life. We must learn to be sentient of the dualism, the contrast in the world of which I spoke last week. Just think of someone seeing only the ruffled surface of water. Essentially it is an abstract line. What is concrete here? Water down there, air above it. And in the interaction of the two, of their forces, we get the maya, the ruffled surface. That is how we are as human beings as we look at ourselves within maya. If we look at ourselves in a real way we must also see ourselves right here—water below, air up above. Water below—we see it as we observe transient development as I presented it here last week. The human being develops so that ideas he may have as a child would only be understood in old age. The ideas he has at sexual maturity he

Fig. 7

will understand a bit earlier, but still only when old age is approaching, and so on, as I presented a human life where it is only in old age that one is able to grasp what one has been in childhood and youth. Life proceeds like this, not seemingly but in reality on the surface. I told you that perhaps one does not need such an overview even today in order to live, but one does need it in order to die.

That is the idea of the lower; the idea of the true upper principle, the region of eternity of which I spoke last week,[48] goes with it. There the human being does not develop but also has the principle that belongs to the region of eternity all his life, from birth to death. But today we are unable to consider how the lower and the upper interweave unless we grasp the lower at the point where it threatens to grow rigid, where it threatens to harden; if we then grasp the upper where it threatens to evaporate, to grow spiritual; unless we grow sentient of the opposite nature: divine—luciferic—ahrimanic. In earlier times people had something that was alive in their souls as they spoke of their experience of space, their experience of time. In future human beings will have to develop inner concepts, inner idea impulses: divine—ahrimanic—luciferic.

Lecture 8

21 September 1918

In last week's lectures I said that efforts must be made, with the help of initiation science, to progress from the seeming reality which is really all around us all the time to genuine reality. I also said that the endeavours which most people find they like, the endeavour to find a uniform, rational theory for the world, actually lead away from reality, taking people straight into delusion about reality. Instead one must endeavour to distinguish between two streams in reality, especially when it comes to understanding human nature, and then connect anything that can be known about either of the streams with the other.

Let us briefly review what has been said so far about these two streams in seeking insight into human nature and then try to gain the necessary requirements for a view of reality on this basis. Human life really proceeds in such a way that people will only in the second half of life be able to understand what they went through in their thinking and in their inner life altogether in the first half of life. I told you that good sense is active in us in the first seven years, from birth to second dentition; sense reigns in us but our own human powers are not enough to let us grasp what reigns in us then nor anything we may have learned in those early years; we do not grasp it if limiting ourselves to the one stream which we need to consider. If human beings had to depend completely on themselves as earthly human beings they would only be able to grasp what they thought, felt and did up to second dentition when they reach a considerable age, the late fifties and early sixties. We thus are only ready to gain self-knowledge relating to our inner life in childhood when we reach a good age. The powers which enable us to grasp what we lived through so sensibly in early childhood are only born at that late time in human life.

We then have a second period in life which extends from second dentition to sexual maturity. Just consider—we have written about this in *The Education of the Child in the Light of Anthroposophy*—what human beings go through in their thinking, feeling and doing until they reach sexual maturity. Their own human powers, the powers which man has on earth, would only enable them to understand what they have been going through there when they are in their late forties and early fifties.

And anything we live through from sexual maturity into our twenties could only be grasped with our own human powers in the late thirties and early forties. Anything we think up, if you like also by way of ideals—the importance of it, the value for life—could only be grasped, using our human powers in life, when we are in our thirties. Anything we live through from roughly our twenty-eighth to thirty-fifth year stands on its own, can be more or less grasped. This middle part of human life has a certain balance; there we can think up and understand at the same time—not so in the other stages of life.

You get an idea of human development in one life if you think this through; you will get an idea of how human beings develop in their time on earth. Gaining self-knowledge, seeing that we are bound to time, would really only be possible if we always waited until the requisite age is reached to understand what we were thinking at an earlier stage of life. Human life forms a whole. As individuals we would not know anything of real significance about ourselves as earth creatures unless we were to look back in old age, unless in old age we were to look back on what was developing in us in our youth.

This is the one side of human beings, one mood in human life. With regard to this stream people are wholly subject to time; they simply cannot do anything but wait until the time is ripe. However, I did tell you that human life is not really the way we live through it in maya existence. It is human life if seen only in relation to time. Yet what is said about the progress of human life in time is absolutely real. For at a pinch, if one wants to stay superficial, one can live with the things we live through between birth and death, but one cannot die with them. For everything else we learn in other ways, are taught by others, things we learn because humanity has acquired them in the course of history, in short the things you as a temporal human being learn in other ways than by looking back on youth in age will initially be lost when we die. We do not take things from that one stream with us through the gate of death. We take with us only the insights gained by doing so at the relevant age. And don't think that you are not doing what I am referring to! Those of you who are older are already looking back on earlier stages in life in their subconscious. It does indeed happen, even if it is at the subconscious level. You would not be taking anything of your external temporal life through the gate of death if that were not the case. People pay no attention to this in the age of materialism, but everything which the age of materialism can teach people cannot be taken through the gate of death. Only things you have gone through by understanding in old age what was going on in the whole of your being when you were young has significance for the world. That is the one stream.

The other stream is brought about in that human beings exist in more than body and soul. In body and soul their existence proceeds in time in the way we have just been considering again. But human beings also live in spirit and soul. And with this they exist not only in the realm of time—as we have just been characterizing it—but are also entities of spirit and soul in the realm of eternity. There, however, they are again something completely different from what they appear to be. There they do not develop or evolve, there they are the same from birth to death. But their thinking, feeling and doing is something completely different from what it appears to them to be. Their thinking and part of their feeling consists in entering into cosmic regions where battles of the gods are fought, as I described it to you a week ago, and their doing, acting out of the will, and part of their feeling consists in entering into a different region in the cosmos where battles of the gods are fought. To reflect, I told you, is to enter into a particular region of spirituality and take part in certain battles of one kind of spirit against another; in the same way acting out of the will is to take part in certain struggles, although in some instances the struggles have come to rest. A profound truth shown in *The Portal of Initiation* is that great things happen in the cosmos as things happen in our spirit and soul.

Human beings want to have no inkling in the age of materialism of the body and soul aspect which proceeds in time. Nor do they want to know of this aspect of spirit and soul which lives in the realm of eternity though it looks very different from their thinking, feeling and doing in ordinary life and, seen in the light of reality, takes the form of battles in the spirit. It may sound paradoxical to someone who thinks as a materialist, but when you take a thought it is something completely different from what you see if looking at it yourself in maya. Let us assume you have a thought—let us say one of the kind which we mentioned yesterday—you have a thought about space. The moment you think of space—even if merely abstract, the way people do at the present time—the moment your mind fills with thoughts of space your soul is in a spiritual region where Ahriman is fighting a tremendous battle against hierarchies of a different kind. You would not be able to have the thought of space without living in a region where Ahriman is fighting other hierarchies. And when you develop the will to do something—perhaps 'I want to go for a walk'—however insignificant the action may be, as soon as you let the will become deed you are spiritually in a region where the luciferic spirits are fighting the spirits of other hierarchies. What happens in the world at large is, seen from the point of view of initiation science, something very different from the shadowy reflection we perceive when as human beings we live in maya between birth and death. For the maya we perceive is nothing but something which may be compared with the ruffles on the surface of the sea. I gave you this image yesterday—the waves ruffling the

Fig. 8

surface of the sea essentially is something which would not exist if there were not the sea underneath and the air above. The forces which evoke the ruffling of the waves are within the sea and in the air. The ruffling is but a reflection of the way in which forces from above and below come together. Our life in maya between birth and death thus is nothing but the coming together of those spiritual battles that truly take place in the realm of eternity when we think, feel or act out of the will, and the evolutional progress in time which takes place in such a way that we only understand what we did think up in our youth once we have reached old age. Essentially our life is a nothing unless we consider it as these two true realities coming together. These two true realities are there behind our life.

Now behind our life there is not only the progress in time where we would need to wait and wait before we could understand something we thought of earlier in life, nor the things that go on in eternity, taking the same course for the whole of our life between birth and death. No, we ourselves are within this reality, and our being in it also appears only as a reflection. The whole relationship we have to the world appears to us only as a reflection, an image. To perceive the truth always means that one must gain the strength to perceive it; it will not come to us if we prefer to remain passive. To perceive the truth means to see ourselves as we are within the two streams—in the realm of time and in the realm of eternity. And being in the two realms and living a life which compared to the true powers has no more significance than the ruffled waves on the oceans have with regard to the air and the flowing waves below, we live our life between death and birth, and then also again between birth and death. The forces and powers make us their concern as we live in this way. For there always are tremendous powers which on the one hand endeavour to tear us away from the ordinary life on earth which proceeds in maya, and other powers that make every effort to tear us away from the realm of eternity.

On the one hand—let us hold firmly on to this—we have the progress of life in time where in our understanding we only grow mature late for what will be our future. There are forces and powers that sought to limit us to what we are as human beings, wanting to shape us in such a way as human beings that this will happen for us. This means, therefore, that there are forces and powers which want our life truly to run that way, also in maya, also in earthly life in such a way that as children we live through one thing or another but understand nothing of it, living in sleep, as it were, until our twenty-eighth year, then begin to have some understanding of what is going on at that time, and then, once we have passed our thirty-fifth year, begin to understand earlier things. There are powers that want to make us into purely temporal human beings, individuals who live more or less like a plant, in sleep, in the first half of life and only grasp what happened during that sleep when we look back in the second half of life. There are powers that want to make human beings into dreamers in the first half of life, and in the second half of life into someone who remembers those dreams and so gains self awareness only in the second half of life. In practical terms, if those were the only powers that had an influence on us, it would mean that in our souls we are only born in our early thirties or at most in our eighteenth year. Before then we'd walk about as if drowsy in sleep.

If this were just as those spirits wish it to be we would be torn away from the whole of our cosmic past. As I have shown in *Occult Science*, our present existence has its basis in our having gone through a cosmic past—through Saturn, Sun and Moon periods. As we went through those periods, spirits from the higher hierarchies—who had a particular interest in having human beings arise in the cosmos—

spirits who are the creators of humankind, evolved us and placed us in the earth world. In earthly existence we are according to the one stream human beings of the kind we have described for that world. The forces and powers are there which wanted us to be such earthly human beings only. If they were to win they would tear us away from our Saturn, Sun and Moon past. They would preserve us in life on earth, they would make us into nothing but earthly human beings. That is the aim of certain powers, the ahrimanic powers. Ahriman seeks to make us into pure time-people, seeks to tear our life on earth away from our cosmic past. He seeks to make the earth into a completely separate entity and to make us wholly telluric, utterly earthly.

Other powers seek to achieve the exact opposite. Their aim is to tear us away completely from our life in time, to give us a thinking, feeling and doing which drips down solely from the region of eternity without our doing anything to bring it about, and then maintain it throughout life. If they were to win, the whole of our life in time would dry out. We would finally—actually very soon, it would have happened long since if these spirits had won—shed, lay aside, our physical body nature, our nature in body and spirit, and we would be nothing but spectres. Our task, in so far as it comes from existence on earth, would not be done. We would be drawn away from existence on earth. These spirits consider the earth to be too bad. They hate the earth, they don't like the earth, they want to lift human beings away from the earth; they want to make them exist in the realm of eternity. They want them to eliminate everything which proceeds in time, the way I have shown it. These are the luciferic spirits. Their aims are in the first place the opposite of those of the ahrimanic spirits. The ahrimanic spirits seek to tear human beings and the whole of their earthly existence away from the cosmic past, and preserve the earthly principle. The luciferic spirits seek to cast away the earth, everything that is earthly in human beings and make them wholly spiritual so that nothing earthly influences them, so that they will not be filled with the nature and powers of the earth. They would wish to have man as a cosmic spirit; they would wish that the earth dropped away from evolution, that it be cast aside in the universe.

Ahriman wants the earth to grow independent and be man's whole world. The luciferic spirits want the earth to be cast aside, thrown away by humanity, and that humanity be taken up into the realm where the luciferic spirits themselves are, where they have their existence in the world of sheer eternity. To achieve this the luciferic spirits are all the time trying to make the intelligence which we have as human beings automatic, and they also seek to suppress our free will. If intelligence became purely automatic, if free will were to be suppressed, we would be able to use automatic intelligence and do what we are meant to do not according to our own will but according to the will of the gods. We would be able to be purely cosmic spirits. Such is the aim of the luciferic spirits. They want to make us into pure spirit, as it were, into spirits that do not have their own intelligence but only cosmic intelligence, and no free will of their own, in whom all thinking and doing proceeds automatically, as in the hierarchy of the angels and in many respects in the hierarchy of the luciferic spirits themselves, though there in another respect. The luciferic spirits want to make us pure spirit; they want to cast away the earthly aspect. Instead they want to create an intelligence for us that is utterly and completely uninfluenced by any kind of brain and in which there is absolutely no free will.

The spirits gathered around Ahriman want exactly the opposite. They want to cultivate the human intellect, cultivating it more and more in such a way that it will be more and more dependent on all earth existence, and they want to develop particularly also the human will, everything therefore which the luciferic spirits want to suppress. The ahrimanic spirits, or rather the spirits that serve Ahriman, want to develop just this to the full. It is particularly important to remember this. Human beings would arrive at some kind of self-sufficiency. They would be dreamers in their young days, but they would be someone quite bright in old age, understanding many things from personal experience. They would, however, receive no revelations from spiritual worlds. Let us accept the fact that anything which makes us bright in youth has come from revelations; personal experience only comes with age. And the ahrimanic spirits want to limit us to this personal experience. We would have free will but would at best be born in spirit and soul only in our twenty-eighth year. Just consider—as human beings we are really between the two directions of will in the spiritual world. And as human beings we have, in a sense, the task to live through the world in such a way that we follow neither Ahriman nor Lucifer but find a balance between the two streams.

It is possible to imagine that people feel shudders down their spine even in this materialistic age when they hear what is actually going on deep down in human nature. People do shudder at this and it was therefore arranged in the world order that divine teachers provided superconscious knowledge in earlier times so that people did not have to take a position relating to the battle in the spirit. Initiates were thus able to keep silent in the outside world about those struggles. There have always been people who know, knew, about the battles which in a way take place behind the scenes in every human life. There have always been individuals who have become convinced that life is a matter of worming one's way through a struggle, that life holds a danger. Yet it also came to be more and more the principle that one would not guide people to the threshold, to the Guardian of the Threshold so that they would not have to feel that shudder down the spine, if I may put it in such commonplace terms.

Those days are over, however. Times will come in future Earth evolution when the children of Lucifer will have to be separated from the children of Ahriman—either the one or the other. To know that we are in this situation and will have to conduct life in this knowledge is something which today one has to say is a vital necessity for the future of humanity and which has to be understood.

Anyone wishing to live life in such knowledge will in a way, I'd say, have to develop cosmic sentience. What does it mean to develop cosmic sentience? It means one has to learn to see the world in a somewhat different way from the one we are used to seeing in the light of maya. When one goes about in the world with initiation science, feelings arise which do not exist for as long as one lives merely in the knowledge of maya. Feelings arise which ordinary people will consider not just paradoxical but foolish, sheer fantasy, but they are as justifiable as possible, especially with regard to the truth. If one is armed with initiation science as one faces another person, one swings to and fro between sentience of two things. 'Human being,' one will think, 'you are swinging to and fro between two possibilities—either you give yourself up entirely to the temporal and grow mineral, rigid, being nothing but an earthly human being and losing your cosmic past. Or you volatilize in spirit and become a spiritual automaton. You do not achieve your goal as a human being although you are spirit.'

We might say that when you have a person before you in this way you are really always having two human beings before you, one who is in danger of growing petrified in his form, growing dense and rigid in form and growing together with the earth, and the other in danger of casting out everything that tends towards mineralization, hardening, and growing quite soft, like jellyfish, and ultimately dissolving as a spiritual automaton in the universe. These two human beings present themselves to those who are armed with initiation science when they study a human being. You're always afraid, I'd say—forgive me but one has to take such words as the language offers, and some things do sound paradoxical when you point to the sphere of reality—that all the people you meet might suddenly turn into those strange figures you sometimes see on rock faces, knights on horseback, as if brought forth from the rock, or other figures in the mountains, sleeping virgins and so on, that people might turn into such things, merge into the earth's mineral world and only live on as mineralized forms. Or they might cast out anything that points them towards mineralization and be like jellyfish—the organs which have condensed might swell up, ears might be giant size, also encompassing the larynx, winglike organs might grow from the shoulders and grow together with it all; the whole would be as soft as a jellyfish but as if dissolving out of its own billowing wave form.

One would have such sentience, cosmic sentience, I'd say, not only with regard to people if one approaches them with initiation insight but one will ultimately apply this cosmic sentience to everything. As you will have noticed, the tendency to grow rigid, turn to stone, comes from Ahriman; the tendency to volatilize, to be first like jellyfish and then dissolve comes from Lucifer. It is not limited to anything we encounter in human beings but extends to everything abstract we encounter. You grow sentient of all things that go in straight lines as ahrimanic, all curved lines as luciferic. The circle is the symbol for Lucifer, the straight line for Ahriman. Look at the human head; this has the tendency—you can see it if you look at a skeleton—to petrify, grow bony in the form given to it by the earth, to stick with that form. It is ahrimanic. If the powers active in the human head were to be active in the whole human being, people would assume the form of Ahriman as you see him in the sculpture over there, and would be all head nature, all personal intelligence, egotistical intelligence, and wholly self-willed, with the will reflected in the form itself.

Looking at the other human being, not the head one but the human being of extremities in the wider sense, we get the impression that if the powers active in the rest of the human being were to be active in the whole human being the human being's form would be like the figure of Lucifer in the sculpture. Wherever we look, everywhere, whether in the life of nature or in social life, equipped with initiation science we would be able to look into the ahrimanic and the luciferic principles. We just have to be sentient of the ahrimanic and the luciferic. To develop such sentience is indeed necessary in developing towards the future of humanity. People must learn to feel: 'Luciferic spirit prevails throughout the world. This luciferic spirit prevails also in all human social life. And this luciferic spirit wants above all to remove from the world everything that is law in the world, any law human beings have ever established. In human social life nothing is more hateful to Lucifer but everything that has a whiff of being law about it.'

Ahriman wants to have laws everywhere; Ahriman just wants to write down laws all over the place. On the other hand human social life is woven from Lucifer's hatred of anything by way of law and Ahriman's sympathy for laws, and we won't understand life unless we grasp its dual nature. Ahriman loves everything that is outward form and can grow rigid. Lucifer—'the Lucifers'—love everything unformed, anything which dissolves form, growing fluid and mobile. We have to learn from life to establish balance between the principle that wants to grow rigid and the principle of getting fluid.

Look at the forms in our building.[49] Everywhere straight line is taken into curve, balance is sought; everywhere the attempt is to let something which is growing rigid dissolve into fluidity; everywhere rest is created in movement but the rest is set in motion again. This is what is so very spiritual in the building. As human beings of the future we must endeavour to configure something in art and in life, knowing that down below is Ahriman who wants everything to freeze, and up above is Lucifer who wants everything to volatilize. Both principles must, however, remain invisible, for in the world of maya there can only be the ruffling of the waves. Woe betide if Ahriman or Lucifer were on their part seeking to push their way into something that wants to be life! Our building has therefore developed into a state of balance in the universe that has been wrested, lifted out of the realm of Ahriman and the realm of Lucifer. Everything culminates in the central figure of the group, the Representative of Man, where everything luciferic and ahrimanic is to be extinguished. That this is so, that it has been taken away from the only thing that should remain spiritually, is shown in the group, where the luciferic and ahrimanic spirits are shown as opposites in balance, so that people may come to understand it.

That is the prospect we must put before people today so that they come to understand that they must find the balance between ahrimanic and luciferic. The ahrimanic always makes us move in a straight line in spirit and soul; the luciferic always guides us into wavelike or circular motion and makes us manifold. Ahriman is tweaking our ear when we tend one-sidedly towards monism, wanting to declare the whole world to be a single whole; Lucifer is tweaking the lobe of the other ear when we become monadists, one-sidedly so, declaring the world to consist of many, many atoms or monads, all different. Basically, for anyone with insight, one finds that when monists fight pluralists, monadologists, the human being involved in the dispute is mostly not responsible for the situation; behind him is Ahriman to tweak his ear if he is a monist, providing him with all the excellent reasons, all the logic he thinks is his own to support his monism; and when someone is a follower of Leibniz or another monadologist it will be Lucifer who provides all the excellent reasons for the manifold nature of spiritual entities. What we have to look for is a state of balance, oneness in manifoldness, manifoldness in oneness. It is more difficult than to look for oneness or else for manifoldness, just as it is altogether more difficult to look for a state of balance than for something or other on which one may rest at ease. People turn into sceptics or mystics. The sceptics feel themselves to be free spirits able to doubt everything; the mystics feel themselves to be imbued with godliness, lovingly and perceptively embracing everything within them. Essentially sceptics are merely disciples of Ahriman, mystics merely disciples of Lucifer. Humanity must endeavour to find the balance—mystic experience in scepticism, scepticism in mystic experiences. It matters not if you're Montaigne[50] or Augustine; what matters is that Augustine casts light on anything that is Montaigne, and vice versa. Bias makes human beings deviate towards the one stream or the other.

What actually is 'the luciferic'? It really exists to make us headless, taking away our own intelligence and free will, and the luciferic spirits, the luciferic element, really wants us to die in our twenty-eighth year and not grow old. It is better, by the way, to say 'the luciferic spirits' but 'Ahriman', for although Ahriman has hosts of followers, he presents as a single whole, since he strives to be such; the luciferic element presents as manifold because that is what it aims for. This is why one puts it the way I have been doing in today's lecture.

If things were to be just as Lucifer, the luciferic spirits, want, we would turn into children, young women and young men, would have good knowledge of eternity fed to us drop by drop, but we would develop sclerosis in about our twenty-eighth year and soon begin to dote, so that anything we can develop by way of human insight would be cast up as sclerosis, and anything we take in in our youth could be spiritualized. The luciferic spirits want to take us straight to the spiritual world and not let us go through Jupiter, Venus and Vulcan development before we become cosmic spirits. They consider this unnecessary. Their aim is to take human beings away from the earth and to the divine and spiritual goal with everything they have developed on Saturn, Sun and Moon. This is a stream in which man is to be taken forward as fast as possible; it is a precipitate stream. The luciferic spirits want to rush ahead with us and take us into cosmic spirit nature as soon as possible. The ahrimanic spirits would wish to wipe out our past and take us and the earth back to the starting point, extinguishing our past, preserve us as we are on earth and then take us back to where we were as human entities on Saturn. It is a retrograde movement. Life ultimately is made up of a precipitate and a retrograde movement, and we must find the state of balance between the two.

Do not say that these things are difficult, for that simply is not the point. Yesterday I showed you how in earlier times people had experiences of space and time, experiencing them in a concrete way. To us they are abstract; to them they were concrete. We must learn to look at our surroundings in such a way that we see everywhere this interplay in processes of growing rigid, evaporating, running away and throwing back, linear and curved held in balance. One can be asleep with things simply seen in the world. If we are wide awake in looking at the world it will threaten, in everything it is, to grow rigid or evaporate as soon as the balance is lost.

You can be sentient of various things when looking at the group sculpture. You can feel the Representative of Man at the centre, the lines and surfaces and forms where everything luciferic and ahrimanic has been extinguished. The forms are there, but as far as possible the luciferic and ahrimanic quality has been eliminated. You can see Lucifer and Ahriman given form. You can sense this contrast in the central human being, in Lucifer and Ahriman, and you can go through the world feeling that you will find the like of this everywhere in the world. Someone who really makes the quality his own that lives in the feelings which one can develop in looking at this trinity will gain a great deal that will enable him to perform a kind of autopsy or dissection of life. Much will be revealed in the world if we look at it in the way in which these feelings arise when considering the trinity of the central human being or Representative of Man, Ahriman and Lucifer. The trinity revealed itself to the ancients in their feeling for space, the oneness of the divine in their feeling for time. The most sublime of cosmic secrets will have to reveal themselves to future humanity if they are able to be aware in a concrete way of the processes of growing rigid, evaporating, running away, pushing back, of linear and curved, of love and hatred where they are according to their laws, and so on. To see the pendulum swing everywhere in life, that is what matters. For life is not possible unless there is that pendulum swing within it. If you have a clock with a pendulum you can, of course, avoid the swings by stopping the pendulum; but the clock will be of no use to you then; the pendulum must swing if the clock is to tell the time. This is how there must be the pendulum swing in life. Note must be taken of it everywhere. We'll continue with this tomorrow.

Lecture 9

22 September 1918

If we bring to mind the overall meaning rather than all the detail of the last lectures, including the one given yesterday, we can say that in the civilization which must energetically take over from our own in future it will be demanded that people look more deeply into true reality, and that above all slogans or catchwords—or, better, catch-theories—like monism, idealism, realism and so on come to an end. People will have to realize that the maya reality, the reality of outer phenomena all around us, is a combination of two real worlds, and, it is fair to say, two worlds that fight one another. To look at reality is something very different from following the world of phenomena around us theoretically, the way it is done in natural science.

Let us get down to practicalities and take a concrete example. I think you'll agree that everyone will think that the materialistic philosophy of life which has spread among civilized nations mainly from the 1860s or 1870s and the materialistic way of life which results from the ideas in that materialistic philosophy of life also make human beings more materialistic under their influence. Looking at the phenomena in the world superficially people think that the ideas human beings get into their heads lead to something which looks like an external realization of those ideas. But that is not how it is. As soon as one considers the successive configurations in real terms it is not at all true that the world somehow arranges itself according to the ideas which people get in their heads. And one will only realize that this is not the case when one understands that human beings have the two sides to them of which we have spoken and that the ahrimanic and luciferic principles are indeed interfering with one another all the time in the way I have described. It is only because of this that the following is possible.

Let us assume that people were giving themselves up to materialistic ideas for a sufficiently long time during an era, as has happened in our era. Led astray by those ideas people would also develop some kind of materialistic way of life in their conscious will to act. The consequences would not arise in the part of the human nature which is the vehicle for conscious life. Initially this vehicle for conscious life would not have the deep-reaching influence on human life which one would be inclined to think if taking a superficial view; no, the effect comes at the unconscious level. Schematically you can visualize it as follows. Materialism lives in the conscious head nature of the human being, and at the unconscious level the part of our nature which only goes through its metamorphosis when we have gone through the gate of death and live on for our next incarnation on earth, though we do already bear it within us, is something which is as yet incomplete—this lower nature as we may call it is the vehicle for the unconscious inner life. Strangely enough, it is growing more and more spiritual under the influence of materialism. Thus the real consequence of materialistic ideas, the real consequence also of a materialistic way of life is that man's lower nature is growing more and more spiritual. You therefore have to imagine the following. If you go really deeply into ideas of energy and matter and believe only in them, and if you arrange your life in such a way that you say, 'Food and drink and then, after death, nothingness,' and do everything you do in this style, materialism will truly become your way of life and the lower nature will then grow more and more spiritual.

But then this lower nature which is growing more and more spiritual demands that something else influence it, for it cannot make the progress which it must make through world evolution on its own. The consequence of having only materialistic ideas and materialistic sympathies in the upper nature of the human being is that this upper nature cannot influence the lower nature of the individual and that the lower nature is therefore exposed to other influences. Upper nature being powerless, lower nature is exposed to the influence of the luciferic principle. The luciferic principle does not come into its own in the reality perceived through the senses, as I told you yesterday. The luciferic entities are spirits. They enter into the lower nature of human beings when this grows more and more spiritual under the influence of materialism, and it is exactly because of materialism that nothing from the human beings themselves can enter into their lower nature. The paradoxical truth is that a materialist era is in reality always the preparation for a spiritual though luciferic culture.

Let us also look at the opposite situation; let us assume an ecclesiastical truth not filled with spiritualism but resting purely on tradition takes hold of people or was intended to take hold of them. Abstract idealism is related to such an ecclesiastical truth. Belief is limited to abstract ideals, especially in the moral sphere, and there is no feeling for the way in which the abstract ideals arise. For however excellent such ideals may be they will serve no purpose unless one has a feeling for the way in which they may turn into powers. Purely religious and purely idealistic ideas mean that the lower nature of human beings grows more and more materialistic, whilst materialistic ideas encourage spiritualism in man's lower nature. Purely ecclesiastical views based on tradition with no spiritual aspect or abstract human idealism encourage lower human nature to grow more and more material. I'd say that the typical figure showing this material progression due to traditional, abstract ecclesiastical views—please forgive the drastic choice of words—is the fat prelate given up to traditional ecclesiastical views, his paunch growing larger and larger in the process. It is merely a comparison, it is not a fact and not a law of which I speak; I merely want to illustrate, but it is in line with a reality which is behind these things. This process of lower human nature growing more and more material does, however, lack sustenance if there are only traditional or abstract idealistic notions in the head. A humanity which establishes such a civilization is predominantly exposed not to its own head nature but to the ahrimanic influences. We therefore have to say that abstract religious elements, abstract idealism, essentially encourage materialism, a materialism with ahrimanic orientation, whilst materialistic ideas encourage a spiritualism with luciferic orientation.

Essentially all these things arise because genuine reality is something completely different from the apparent outward reality. Now, however, it behoves us to get to know the genuine reality, its laws and nature. Social science, the science of human beings living together, and of the historical life of humanity will have to be imbued more and more with a spiritual science which truly builds a bridge in the way I have indicated in these lectures between the natural order and the order of the spirit—building the real bridge and not the abstract one of monism. For this it will, however, be necessary that certain laws of the true reality, laws of which people are also not made aware by initiates who are not thinking in the right way for the present time, do get more and more widely known.

One such law you may think of as follows. You know, if you follow the true meaning of my *Occult Science, an Outline*, when humanity, as we call it at present, did actually first appear on earth, this humanity also has a cosmic history in the sense reiterated yesterday—Saturn, Sun, Moon history—but to begin with its earthly history was recapitulation, and earthly humanity first appeared at a quite specific time. Reading it up in my *Occult Science* you'll find that this humanity appeared at the very time when the mineral world arose clearly and distinctly on earth. We know that the mineral world, as we now call it, did not exist in the same way during Saturn, Sun and Moon time. The three realms which preceded the mineral world were there. The mineral world came into Earth evolution and at the same time as this macrocosmic fact of the mineral world appearing in Earth evolution man appeared in his present form, in the form which his body has at the present time, in his present bodily configuration. This bodily configuration only developed fully in the course of time, but the potential for it appeared at the same time as the mineral world in Earth evolution. In a sense, therefore, human beings established a connection as earthly human being or, in becoming earthly human being, between the fourth level of existence, which then developed into the I, and the mineral world. We might also say that in the human microcosm the I corresponds to the macrocosmic mineral world.

We know, from simple superficial observation of the natural world, that the cosmic mineral world is crystalline in configuration. Our children have to learn the different crystalline forms at school, getting to know them first according to the laws of geometry as these can be shown, and then in the way in which they actually occur in the mineral world—octahedron, cube and so on. Looking at these geometrical configurations of the mineral world we essentially have the configuration which is utterly the mineral world's own. This crystallization, or better these crystalline forms, are in a sense inherent in the mineral world, utterly its own. And in integrating the mineral world into its cosmic evolution the earth did at the same time take in the tendency to crystallize its mineral matter in the forms that belong to the mineral world.

There is a counter-pole, a polar opposite, to this form principle in the mineral world. I would ask you to consider the following. Let us approach an important fact of life in an image. You are no doubt all familiar with the common phenomenon of some substances dissolving. You know that if you put a certain amount of salt into a certain volume of water the water is capable of completely dissolving the salt. This is then no longer in its solid form but has dissolved in the water. You also know that solid salt would be of no use for certain purposes in practical life and it is necessary to dissolve the salt in liquid. Now the tendency of minerals to crystallize in Earth evolution must not stay connected with this earth just as salt must not stay in its solid form for certain practical purposes. The cook must be able to change the solid form of salt into its dissolved form; she must use solvents, otherwise the salt would serve no purpose. In the same way the tendency of minerals to crystallize must be dissolved in the cosmos. So there has to be a counter-tendency, a polar opposite, which will ensure that this crystalline tendency has dissolved, is no longer there when the earth has reached the goal of its evolution and will be about to change into its next form, the Jupiter form. Jupiter must no longer have the tendency to crystallize minerals. This tendency must be reserved for the earth's body, and must cease when the earth will have come to the end of Earth evolution.

The polar opposite to the tendency to crystallize is the tendency which is imprinted in the human—and not the animal—form. Every dead body which we give to planet earth in some form or other, burying or cremating it or whatever, every dead body in which the human form is still active as purely mineral form, every dead body from which soul and spirit have departed counteracts the mineral crystallization tendency just as negative electricity counteracts positive electricity or darkness counteracts light. At the end of Earth evolution all human forms imparted to the earth during this evolution—the forms I say and not the substance, for it is the power that lies in the form with which we are concerned—will have cosmically dissolved the tendency to mineralize, to crystallize in the process of mineralization.

You see how again a point is added where the bridge is built between two streams in the world, a bridge which cannot be built with natural science. In natural science one investigates the changes to the human form after death in purely mineralogical terms, applying only the laws of mineralogy; one looks only for the things that are connected with the earth's tendency to crystallize, treating the dead body in the same way. It means one will never discover the significant role which the dead human bodies, their form, plays in the earth's economy. The earth has changed enormously from the middle of the Lemurian age, since mineralization has begun and hence the tendency to crystallize. Anything on earth that is less mineral, tending less towards crystallization than in the middle of the Lemurian age, is so thanks to the dissolving forms of human bodies. The tendency to crystallize will have gone completely when the earth has reached its final goal. All the human forms given to the earth will have acted as the polar opposite and dissolved the crystallization. There the event of human death is also seen as a purely physical phenomenon in the whole of world economy. There the bridge is built between phenomena such as the phenomenon of death which otherwise make no sense in world economy and the phenomena which are referred to in natural science today.

It is important that we develop such views more and more, views that give the natural-scientific view its true and proper character. What I have been telling you is a natural-scientific fact like any other natural-scientific facts discovered today. It is, however, a fact which cannot be discovered with just natural-scientific methods. The present-day methods of natural science must of necessity remain inadequate and therefore cannot encompass all phenomena of life. Natural science must therefore be complemented with spiritual science.

When laws as comprehensive as this one will be known—laws saying that human forms given to the planet earth will dissolve the earth's tendency to crystallize—the laws will also make the human mind ready to enter more deeply into the reality of spiritual evolution. Someone who thinks and investigates only in terms of present-day natural science cannot bridge the gulf between natural science and social and political science. Only those who know the great laws established on the basis of spiritual science that relate to the great things in nature (as I have just been showing) will find it possible to cross the bridge that goes from natural science to the humanities, above all to the historical and political life of humanity. Natural scientists will not hesitate to say that polarity exists in nature. They will distinguish between two forms of magnetism, one of the north, the other of the south; they will distinguish between two forms of electricity, positive and negative. When it will be possible one day to take natural science more along the proper lines of Goetheanism, natural science will also be more Goethean than it can be today when it is so hardly at all. The law of polarity will be known then as the basic law in the whole of nature, the way it did already figure in the ancient mysteries, then on the basis of atavistic methods of investigation. In the ancient mysteries everything was based on insight into polarity in the world. In natural science itself, that is in investigating the natural order, modern scientists are perfectly happy to acknowledge the existence of polarity; but they won't touch this polarity when it comes to the human order and the cultural order. Yet in the spirit and its orders, which also include man, the principles we call luciferic and ahrimanic fully correspond to the north and south magnetism or the positive and negative electricity which are accepted in natural science. People will never know how to establish real harmony between spirit and nature until the true things, a concrete polarity of the ahrimanic and the luciferic, are found in the order of the spirit. True reality cannot be found in abstract concepts which are simply transferred from nature to spirit, but only by entering deeply into the spirit itself, and to find the corresponding polarities in the sphere of the spirit.

It has to be the same with the other facts of nature. You cannot simply study facts of nature and then say you are basing a spiritual order or philosophy of life on these natural-scientific facts. This will not get you anywhere. To study spiritual life in its reality, even just the phenomena of life where the spirit has an influence, you have to resolve to study the spiritual orders themselves. Things that happen at some period of time, arising from human souls and human activities, cannot be explained using natural-scientific methods. In reality you can only understand them if you use the methods of spiritual science to elucidate them.

If you want to consider certain phenomena of our present civilization, for instance, you must clearly establish to what extent the luciferic element plays a role in our present civilization and to what extent the ahrimanic principle does. I made the attempt in 1914, before the present catastrophe came upon us, in the lectures entitled *The Inner Nature of Man and Our Life between Death and New Birth*,[51] a course I gave in Vienna before this war began. Let me quote the important passage where I spoke of the key issue of today.

'This spiritual science has now made its appearance in the world because human evolution makes it necessary that penetration of the spiritual worlds and their conditions lives more and more in human souls, instinctively at first and then deliberately so. Let me tell you something which is completely perceptible to the senses so that you may see how people will more and more reach a point where they can judge the true content of life on the physical plane only if they also know the laws of spiritual existence. It is entirely in the world of maya but of tremendous importance. Looking at the world of nature we see the strange spectacle that everywhere only a small number of seeds are used to continue the life of a species, and a vast number of seeds perish. We look at the vast numbers of fish embryos in the ocean. Some grow into fish, others perish. We look out over a field and see countless wheat grains. Only a few of them will be wheat plants, the others perish in serving human beings as food and being used in other ways. Much, much more has to be produced in the natural world than the amount which truly becomes fruit in the steady stream of existence and then germinates again. It is good that it is like this in nature, for out there we have the order and necessity where anything which comes away from the stream it belongs to— the stream of existence and of fruiting which is based in itself—serves the other continuous stream of existence. Human beings and animals would not be able to live if all seeds truly bore fruit and achieved the development which is inherent in them. There have to be seeds which are used to establish the basis, as it were, from which life forms can grow. If we take the maya point of view it merely seems that something is lost, but the truth is that nothing is lost. The spirit is at work in this nature and it is due to the wisdom in the spirit that nothing is really lost within the creative world of nature. It is spiritual law, and we must look at the matter from the spiritual point of view. We will then discover that anything which seems to be taken out of the stream of existence in the world does also have the right to exist. This is rooted in the spirit; it will therefore also have the right to exist on the physical plane in so far as we live a life in the spirit.

My dear friends, take a very obvious situation. Public lectures must be given on the subject of our spiritual science. The audiences come together simply because of the announcements. The situation is rather similar to that of the grains of wheat, only some of which are used in the continuous stream of existence. One must not shy away from facing the fact that one has to speak of the streams of spiritual life before many, many people who have apparently come at random and that only a few of them will enter into this spiritual life, become anthroposophists and go along with the continuous stream. In this field the situation still is that these scattered seeds reach many people who may then go away after a public lecture and say, "What a lot of rubbish that man was talking!" Looked at the way we do in everyday life it is rather like all those fish embryos in the ocean being lost, but not if one takes a deeper look. The souls who came because of their karma and then went away saying, "What a lot of rubbish that man was talking!" are not yet ripe to take in the truth of the spirit. Their souls do, however, need to feel that the power that lies in the science of the spirit is coming up to them in this incarnation. And that feeling will go on living in their souls, however much they may complain about it; it lives on in their souls for their next incarnation, and so the seeds are not lost—they find ways. Existence in the spirit is subject to the same laws, irrespective of whether we study the spirit in the natural order or in the case which we have been able to cite as our own.

'But let us now assume that we intend to apply this also in everyday life, saying, "Well, this is also the way in which it is done in everyday life." It is indeed the case, my friends, that in doing what I will describe to you now we move towards a future where this will emerge more and more! People keep producing, building factories, and never ask, "How much is required?" You know there was once a tailor in a village who would only make a suit when it had been ordered. It was the consumer who determined how much was to be produced. Now people produce for the market, goods are piled up, as much as possible. Production exactly follows the principle which applies in the natural world. The natural order is also applied in the sphere of the social order. To begin with this will be more and more the case. But we are here entering into the sphere of material things. Being valid only for the spiritual world, the spiritual law does not apply in everyday life, and so something very peculiar arises. We are here amongst ourselves and so it is possible to say such things. The world, however, will not meet us with understanding.

'People are producing for the market today, taking no account of consumption, not in the sense of my essay *Anthroposophy and the Social Question*[52] but using storage facilities and the money markets to produce stacks of things and then waiting to see how much is bought. This trend will grow and grow until it will destroy itself—you'll see why from what I'm going to say next.'

This is the most important of the 'causes' of the present war; it must, however, be derived from spiritual life.

'With this kind of production in social life exactly the same develops in the social relationships of people on earth as in the organism when cancer develops. Exactly the same, a cancer, a cancer of civilization! Someone able to see through life from the spiritual point of view will see the dreadful beginnings of social cancers popping up everywhere. This is the dreadful thing, so depressing. Even if one could otherwise suppress all enthusiasm for spiritual science, if one could suppress the urge to open one's mouth and speak for spiritual science, to shout out to the world the remedy for something which is definitely coming and will be getting worse and worse. If something which should be the dissemination of spiritual truths in its proper field happens in a sphere where things happen as in nature, entering into civilization in the way I have described, this will cause cancer to develop.'

You find an exposition of everything that is taken from the ahrimanic and the luciferic worlds preceding this passage in the lecture. You will see there that one will not come to perceive the reality in the development of social cancers by simply comparing social life with the facts of nature. One has to look at the ahrimanic and the luciferic aspects to discover the real tendencies active in the present-day social order. Things that proceed in the social order must be looked for using spiritual methods. Using the methods of materialism will not produce anything but at most a comparison, an analogy to social processes with abstract facts in the natural world.

In those lectures, given in Vienna from 9 to 14 April 1914, I said that many cancerous tumours existed in the present-day social order, but merely said it to sum up something I have essentially spoken of in different ways in the years in which our anthroposophical movement has been developing. This was to prepare people for the time when the social cancer would be in a particular crisis, in 1914! A book has just been published, a rather foolish, worthless book dated 1918 and published by Max Rascher in Zurich. It is C.H. Meray's *Weltmutation* (world mutation).[53] I'll read you some passages from the book. The author has completely focused his mind on economic facts. And whereas the things said in those lectures on the inner nature of man were helpful in arriving at reality, this book encourages people to turn away from true reality, leads them into wrong ways of thinking. I'll quote you some passages from the book. The author endeavours to grasp the development of European and American civilization merely by comparison, analogy, with facts of nature. My lectures given in 1914 give you the reality, but here you get abstract monistic comparisons, mere analogies, that do not really say anything, Essentially, if one speaks just of facts of nature and then suggests that such things also exist in the social order, not understanding the social order but merely pointing out analogies, this obscures rather than illumines understanding. But what does it lead to? It is shown how from antiquity seeds of disintegration gradually entered into western civilization, gnawing away at it from within. Such an aperçu is then put in words like this:

'These pathological changes started in the early Renaissance cities as they came into flower, in the city republics of still purely productive middle classes when they had to feed their giant-cell cancer, adapted to the need and so had to become an apparatus for feeding a cancerous nodule...

'The development of this institution, this organization, which then became the structure of a modern state, went hand in hand with a transformation of the productive tissue, a tissue which must definitely not be considered to be part of their own life.'

He refers to civilization, the order of civilization, as a productive tissue, that is, he merely raises a tissue of natural facts and not the genuine spiritual fact.

'For foreign elements cannot normally be in contact with one another in bodies without causing inflammation—as initially such inflammations also occurred when the burgrave's soldiers came in contact with the burghers (think of the bells being rung to call the burghers together). Normally this would simply have meant cutting out the toxic nodule; people did start to do this, and efforts to do so may also be seen in later times. Yet the moment the two elements, the cancerous nodule and the tissue of work or trade, were able to tolerate one another without getting inflamed, an anomaly arose which could only maintain itself under pathological conditions.

'Such abnormalities are found everywhere in organisms where tumours, ulcers, in short foreign elements are encapsulated to avoid inflammation. The tissue which develops is a deformity and once healed serves no further purpose in the organism. *During the disease it does, however, serve to protect the organism. It is an arrangement which makes the poison harmless in the body, though it may on occasion hypertrophy, grow beyond all bounds* and then be a seriously morbid element itself.

'The modern state has thus also arisen as a deformity in a life of work or trade that was continually burrowed through. All the tissue needed to work together, however, to protect itself as the deformity developed and to paralyse the harmful nature of it and counteract the destructive toxic effects. *The state accordingly developed as a separate structure which whilst interlacing productive life never did itself become the structure, the apparatus, of productivity.* The system of the whole of modern economics developed separately, alongside the state...

'The richest people who required extensive protection for their commercial dealings had the most immediate relationship with the toxic nodule. Because of this they were also more eager and, being rich, also more able to offer more to the burgrave; they provided the money he needed, and he would turn to the patricians when he wanted to get somewhere with the city. It was very much in their interest that the prince be strong. Others, whose trading did not go beyond the city walls, had a regular, natural dislike of the burgrave (physiologically a negative chemotactic effect). They would really only tolerate him because of the protection given by the surrounding walls. The toxic effect did not, or only rarely, change the patrician's individual nature. They would only rarely become warring nobles for they did already belong too much to the antitoxic tissue of work or trade. Their wealth had come from this and was bound up with it. There would be a toxic effect not on the individual but on the protoplasm, meaning their *wealth*.

'In the past, wealth certainly did not serve or function as capital but merely as the reserves for life and prosperity. Now its role was changing. Wealth began to have work processes connected with it.'

At this point I'd ask you to recall that in 1908 I pointed out in lectures I gave in Nuremberg, which have now also appeared in print,[54] that the modern economic order is removed from direct personal influence and how money, capital as such, begins to work. I said: 'The present-day social order is under the ahrimanic influence working its way up in such a way that now one individual is on top and then another. The individual does not count any longer, what matters is that money as such runs things, casting an individual up and then throwing him down again. The shares, the piling up of capital and the credit system as its counter-pole, this impersonal and anti-personal way is the ahrimanic counter-image to the Spirit Self and intended to develop for the future social order.'

In the book all this is put in purely ahrimanic terms. There is, however, a danger that it will be considered with the greatest respect because page by page it presents extensive notes relating to natural science. This ahrimanic caricature of spiritual science has appeared years after reference was made to reality found through spiritual-scientific investigation; it is often using the same words for the same phenomenon. It will impress people in spite of being misleading, unless they want to build a bridge from the external, natural-scientific facts that are presented here and the purely spiritual-scientific processes which can only be found with the help of spiritual science. It will undoubtedly happen that something like this, like other things that have occurred and of which I have spoken in my lectures, will be accepted as genuine scientific knowledge, whilst the scientific validity of spiritual science will without doubt be denied and fought against most dreadfully in the immediate future, and this with an intensity which you cannot even image as yet.

One must be able to see through these things, all the more so as these facts are just below the irreality of outward reality. It does need good will to gain insight into such facts, the will to follow the spiritual-scientific investigations sensibly and with sound common sense.

Opposing streams, polarities, must be balanced out. This can only happen if new influences come all the time into events on earth, influences coming directly from the spiritual world, so that new facts concerning the world are continually revealed out of the spirit.

People once brought a Jesuit to me in Rome and I had a talk with him on this subject although I knew that it was pointless and that it really was a case of love's labour lost. The reasons behind it are, of course, different, for there, too, one must consider the genuine reality and not the outward appearance of things. I tried to explain to the Jesuit that in the first place he himself has to assume a revelation of the supersensible in the Mystery on Golgotha and what has been written about it in the inspired Gospels, and that the Roman Catholic Church does assume a continual development of spiritual life in the case of the saints. He replied, as one would expect, 'Yes, all that is correct, but it is over; one must not bring it about intentionally. In the present time it is a devilish thing to work one's way through to spiritual life. It is permissible to study the Mystery on Golgotha, the Gospels and the lives of the saints, but unless one wants to be in the power of demons it is not permissible in any way to seek to make a direct connection with the spiritual world.' It was to be expected that he would say this. I could give you many such examples.

There are those who are utterly against more and more new spiritual truths getting known. The Roman Catholic Church greatly fears even spiritism, which we are certainly not in sympathy with. They are afraid that it might happen that something from the spiritual world comes across through a medium, something which the Church cannot admit as it wants to stay within its old traditions. It fears spiritism because it is based on materialism and could easily—so the Church people have believed for decades—gain adherents when in some way or other something might be instilled into the world from the spiritual world, and the Church wants to rule the world.

You know that in 1879 the possibility arose for the spiritual world to have a tremendous, deep-reaching effect. I have said on several occasions[55] that the battle that had been fought among spirits in the spiritual world entered into the earthly order, the Michaelic order. Since then there have been occasions when things of the spirit were taken in by human beings who wished to do so. Please do not think that the initiates in the Roman Catholic Church do not know this! They know these things, of course, but build dams to keep them away. It is exactly in connection with this fact that spiritual life has been especially nurtured by the spiritual world since 1879 that the Roman Catholic Church has with foresight established the dogma of papal infallibility as a dam to hold back the possible influence of any spiritual truths. Now of course, if people are thanks to the infallibility dogma only permitted to work inwardly through things proclaimed *ex cathedra* [from the papal chair] as they seek to develop a philosophy of life, that is a mighty dam to block the inflow of spiritual truths directly from the spiritual world. This is the one, the Roman element which had its conditions pertaining to nature in the past and from these brought across the rigidity in its traditions, the rigidity in excluding any spiritual substance that might enter into human souls.

Another stream must be looked for at the centre which—at about the time when the infallibility dogma coming from Rome was in preparation—has to be taken serious note of for the peoples of the English-speaking world in England and America. We have spoken of this occult centre on various occasions. Traditional and falsely idealistic elements in the head allow Ahriman to make himself felt in the lower human being. As you have seen, materialism causes spiritual principles to develop in the lower human being. And of course, if it is not kept supplied from the head with the new spiritual truths which are revealed to the world from time to time it will be caught by luciferic powers, luciferic principles. The centre which has such a great influence on the Anglo-American peoples mainly seeks to reckon with the other pole. The occult Masonry rooted in this centre has a great influence on developments in the outward culture of the whole civilized world. It encourages materialism, being able to see through things, just as Rome has done with the papal infallibility dogma. Rome used infallibility to build a dam to prevent spiritual truths coming in from the spiritual worlds. Masonry seeks deliberately to encourage the spread of materialism in modern civilization, the spread of materialistic ideas in a lifestyle that is more or less materialistic. And the peculiar thing is that Anglo-American initiates are generally right when they speak of Rome. However much they vituperate about Rome, they are saying the right thing. They also know that there is spiritual life and the possibility of a continuous influence, though they keep this secret, only allowing it to flow into civilization though unknown channels. The non-English-speaking peoples in the civilized world have in recent decades—we can say in the last half-century—most extensively taken in the things that came from that centre. In the form which they take at present, other cultures are not really existing on their own but are in many ways fed by the materialistic tendency coming from that centre.

What Rome says of the centre, of that occult Freemasonry, the orders, is also right. We may say, therefore that what Rome says is right and what the occult Freemasons say is also right. This is indeed the problem, that in reality these things are most eminently able to throw people to the luciferic or the ahrimanic side but are not open to censure in what they say because what they are saying is quite right. They say the right thing when speaking about the others.

This fact merits thorough attention in the trends of modern civilization. People generally fail to look and see what becomes of something or other. They always look at things which are put into words for propaganda. But it is not the wording of any propaganda which matters. Materialism in the world of ideas was meant to make the lower human being, too, materialistic, but it actually makes it spiritual. It should be that by talking abstract idealism, talking of all kinds of beautiful moral ideals, we make human beings more moral; in fact we make them—forgive me, speaking metaphorically—fat, materialistic in their lower nature, dull and sleepy. On the one hand there is a marked tendency to make human beings ahrimanic and sclerotic, above all a Jesuitical way of doing things; on the other hand there is a marked tendency to make the luciferic spirits serve the materialistic world order so that materialism leads to spirituality, spiritualization, but with luciferic orientation. It really is not enough merely to consider only the surface appearance of things and take it literally. We have to consider true reality; as our examples have shown today, paradoxical though they may seem, often the opposite purpose is served from what a superficial view suggests. The present situation is that people are working in the world according to the principle of occult orders but keeping the matter secret. Rome is working according to the occult order and so is the other centre. Power lies in the fact that people are kept in the dark and not told what is really going on. This is the source of the hatred and enmity towards people who then come and tell them what is going on. The naivety of some people, a naivety where they keep thinking that something is achieved with the streams I have mentioned is particularly harmful when one shows them that our spiritual science leads to a beautiful view of Christ Jesus, or the like, when one shows them how the most profound truths of spiritual science may be found in genuine Christianity. It is naive to think one can gain the attention of certain groups if one shows them that one has a truth which they really ought to acknowledge considering the whole of their principles. This will actually provoke opposition! The more we show certain groups that we have the truth the greater will be their opposition, and the more this truth proves effective the more intense will the opposition be. In recent times people were merely waiting to see if the anthroposophical books were available in greater numbers, and thousands of people listen to anthroposophy after all before going into the attack, not because they think that anthroposophy is untrue but because they fear that anthroposophy will offer the truth. This has to be considered. There should be no naivety in our ranks but penetrating perception, looking at events without prejudice or bias.

It would please me if you were to take a sentiment, an impression, home with you from this lecture. Let me repeat once more what I said at the beginning of today's lecture. It is not so much the details which matter but a general impression, a sentience, of the whole spirit of this lecture. Gaining this we can make ourselves more and more capable of taking our place in our present civilization and in present-day life as it behoves someone who is truly awake and not asleep in the present time. We will continue with this the next time.

Lecture 10

4 October 1918

Today and in the next few days I want to draw some conclusions from the things said up to now, conclusions for human life itself. Let me say beforehand that in the world at large people have ideas about anthroposophy with regard to which we should really develop a view which we must then also stress. Things we want to assert for life in the spirit, for the spiritual order, are generally acknowledged today, but for the natural order. The anthroposophical view must inevitably be misunderstood if it is mixed up with any old-established errors or mysticism bordering on superstition. We must get in the habit of using terms like ahrimanic or luciferic, terms commonly used for the spiritual order, but at a higher level of existence. We may use them just as natural scientists use terms like positive and negative electricity, positive and negative magnetism or the like. But in contradistinction to common or garden-variety natural science with all its prejudices we must be clear in our minds that with regard to the spiritual order of the world terms which in natural science have a definite, and indeed abstract, meaning must be taken in a more concrete, distinctly more spiritual sense.

We know that human beings as we know them in the life between birth and death present one aspect which we have got in the habit of calling the physical body, then the principle we call the ether body, or in the endeavour to find a passable term the body of creative powers, then—and this already has spiritual character—the astral body, though it does not yet have the conscious-mind character that fills the present-day conscious mind which is closest to us. The principle which we call the subconscious, the term used by many people today, would be part of the astral body. Then there is our ordinary conscious awareness, as we call it, alternating between sleep and waking states. This sends only chaotic dreams into our sleep states, and in its waking states does not content itself with views or opinions but takes recourse to judgements and abstract concepts. All this we refer to as the human I. We might say that people of today only know where they are at when it comes to this last principle, the I as such. This I is mirrored by the conscious mind. It is where all thinking, feeling and will to act actually take place. Everything else—astral body, ether body and the physical body in its true configuration are below the level of consciousness and also of the I. Anything that can be said about the physical body in anatomy, physiology and so on is merely the outside; essentially it is nothing but the awareness of the human physical body we gain in the same way as we gain other information through the senses. It is the outer image of the physical body for the conscious mind but not the physical body itself.

The three parts of essential human nature which we call preearthly as far as their evolution is concerned—you know this evolution from my *Occult Science*—are initially outside the field of conscious awareness. You know that with regard to the spiritual order we speak of the spirits in hierarchies that are above man, whilst three worlds of nature—animal, vegetable and mineral—are below man. As soon as we consider the human being spiritually we can no longer speak of the details of the astral, etheric and physical bodies of which ordinary sciences or also anthroposophists speak when they are only concerned with human life as it is perceived through the senses. As I said in earlier lectures this autumn, the spirits of the individual hierarchies are connected with these 'lower' levels of essential human nature if we consider their true nature.

In the sense of what I said the other day when speaking of Goethe's philosophy of life[56] we can say that in so far as human beings develop in time with these three aspects of their nature, in so far as they go through the development which we can follow from birth to death, they relate to particular spiritual powers which are behind that development. I tried to explain this by saying that when we take this [see Fig. 9] to be the essential nature of modern man, we have to take a retrospective view and think of present-day human nature connected with the spiritual powers which we have identified as members of the higher hierarchies. As you know these spiritual powers do not have a direct influence on the I of normal individuals except for the Spirits of Form or Exusiai. Apart from the Exusiai, therefore, which give man his own original form, the other spiritual powers do not influence the present-day conscious mind of man. We get a limited but at least somewhat reasonable idea of the Spirits of Form if we turn our attention to the form—only a part of the general conformation—which human beings assume in their physical life. We are all born as more or less crawling creatures. The vertical is not within our power. A tremendous proportion of our general nature as human beings is connected with our uprightness—not exactly mathematical verticality but the power to be upright. If we consider the difference between human being and animal, purely in terms of external characteristics, we should not concern ourselves with the things which are usually considered—the number of bones and muscles and so on, which human beings essentially have in common with the animals—but indeed this power to be upright which gives developing human beings their form. This is merely a part of what is involved, but an important part. The power which intervenes in our physical development as power to be upright is of the same kind as all the powers which give us our form as earthly human beings. Only powers of this kind intervene in our I.

white

Fig. 9

Other powers do intervene. We call them the powers of cosmic movement, cosmic wisdom, cosmic will, referring to them as Dynameis, Kyriotetes, Thrones which are the old names for these entities now seen in modern terms. They intervene in something which does not come to human awareness, belonging to the astral body, ether or creative powers [etheric] body and physical body. If you observe these elements of essential human nature without the spiritual content of which I have been speaking you have really nothing but an illusion, a structure that merely seems to be something. In reality we are not in that outward, unreal body but in the spiritual powers to which I have been referring.

The two powers we called luciferic or ahrimanic influence human beings temporally, as it were, as I said the other day when referring to Goethe's philosophy of life though they do not relate directly to their development. We may say that the luciferic powers do so in a more mental and spiritual way [Fig. 10, red], and the ahrimanic powers more from the subconscious [mauve]. Human beings are thus cosmically placed in existence in a threefold way. We may say that there are spiritual powers in essential human nature which are directly connected with the stream of human development. Two

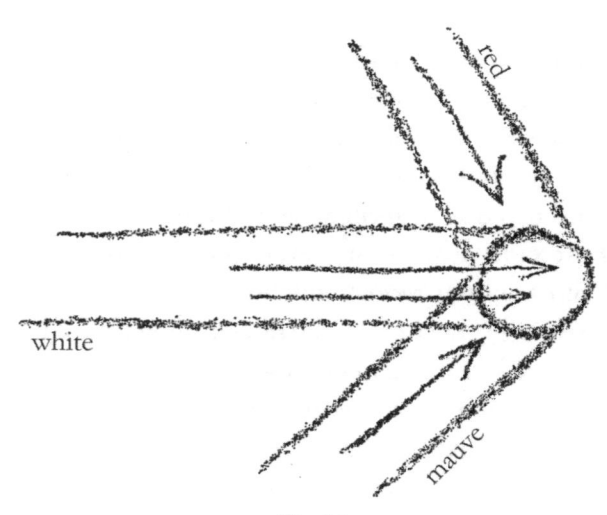

Fig. 10

other streams, the luciferic and the ahrimanic, are not connected with the immediate stream of development but influence human beings temporally, being additional to what really belongs to the human being.

Let us now look at life. When we do so we see not only the stream that belongs to us but always something in which the three streams have come together. Whatever we survey, be it the outside world perceived through the senses, or human history with its pleasure and pain, joy and sorrow, activity and inactivity, what we see is that the three streams have flowed one into the other. In ordinary life we do not do as a chemist does who does not simply accept water as the fluid which one sees but separates it into hydrogen and oxygen. Spiritual science has to do the separating and undertake this spiritual chemistry. Otherwise it will never be possible to penetrate human life completely.

We have been considering the particular nature of the spirit we call luciferic and the spirit we call ahrimanic from all kinds of different points of view. There is yet another point of view, human life itself, from which we may also look at them. We may ask: 'Where is the point in human life where the luciferic powers have a real influence, and where is the point where the ahrimanic powers gain particular access?'

If only human beings could just go through the steady development that is intrinsically theirs—but they cannot. You know from what I said on earlier occasions that they would only gain some self-knowledge in the second half of their life but this would only be if they were not exposed to luciferic and ahrimanic influences. In the real life which we have to live, however, human beings are exposed to them and must indeed reckon with those luciferic and ahrimanic powers. In real life, however, in the life which we must live, human beings are exposed to the temporal interventions of the luciferic and ahrimanic powers and do indeed have to reckon with those powers. In everything in us that belongs more to the sphere of the conscious mind, but in such a way that we do not merely come to it naturally but by going beyond the natural course—having self-knowledge already in the first half of life, for example—in everything human beings aim for by using the conscious mind there is something which we cannot call anything but hyperconscious awareness. Our conscious mind would be very different if there were not this hyperconscious element in it. The hyperconscious state of mind makes people put more into historical life than they would put into it if they gave themselves over to their purely physical development only. At the present time in human evolution on earth we would be in a civilization of a completely different kind if hyperconscious elements had not flowed into a conscious mind developed purely in the human way. But this hyperconsciousness does certainly make it possible for luciferic powers to intervene. We merely have to see in the right way how luciferic powers influence the conscious mind. People would never have occasion to develop a different way of thinking from the one which I characterized for you the other day as the ideal from the Goethean point of view if it were not for the intervention of luciferic powers. Because of the luciferic powers human beings develop fantasies about reality. They do not only take hold of reality but combine the hyperconscious with the conscious element. They get all kinds of ideas about reality, ideas which then enable them to grow more thoroughly together with this reality than they would grow together with it otherwise.

If we take the whole field of art, we have to stress that in art, where the hyperconscious element plays such a great role unless art is to degenerate into naturalism, the luciferic element has to prove effective to the highest degree. It will not do—and I have stressed this time and time again—just to say that people should keep away from the luciferic element in their lifetime. If they were to do so they would not be able to live a real life; they would be utterly philistine. Luciferic mental agility and intellectual liveliness are again and again acting like a leaven to save human beings, spurring them on to escape their philistinism.

But in a way, we might say, this luciferic agility and liveliness does also make people inclined to take a bird's-eye view of the world. Everything by way of programme, of really good ideas coming up which people always think will bring the golden age in some way or other—all this comes from the luciferic inclinations that flow into human beings. Everything which makes people endeavour to escape from being together with reality, every means by which they would seek to raise their wings above the situation in which they have been placed as human beings, all this suggests a luciferic element. The luciferic principle in human nature is the drive which makes us again and again grow less interested in others. If we were to follow our own inherent human nature, that is the powers of development that belong to the actual human stream, our interest in others would be much, much greater than it actually is. The luciferic spirit which is part of human nature leads to a certain lack of interest in others. We should attach considerable value to this very point in studying the essential nature of the human being. Many things would be different in this world if we were to acknowledge this real urge we have to be much too interested in anything we concoct ourselves, and take far too little interest in anything which other people think and feel and do. We only gain true insight into human nature if we let a question illuminate our view of the human being and that is 'What drives me away from developing an interest in others?' It will have to be a task set for future human civilization to develop exactly this insight into human nature. Today we often still call it knowledge of human nature when someone says that what he imagines to be human nature is or ought to be such and such. To take people as they are and be clear in one's mind that people as they are—even if criminals, which is something that also has to be said—will tell us something about the world that is more important than the fantasies we have about essential human nature, however great our ideas on the subject. To say this to oneself is to give the luciferic element the right degree of equality in us. Such endeavour to understand human nature would tell us infinitely much. The present age is really further removed from the nature of human evolution on earth than any other. Do not confuse what I mean here with being uncritical about human nature. Of course, anyone who makes it his rule to say, 'You must consider everyone to be good and love everyone equally,' will make things nice and easy for himself in a luciferic way, for he is really and truly basing himself on fantasy. To consider everyone to be equal is really and truly a luciferic fantasy. It is not a question of cherishing a general idea but exactly of taking each individual in real terms and developing understanding that is full of love, or perhaps better put 'full of interest'.

Now you may ask, 'What is the point of all this luciferic power in us if it prevents us from being tolerant of human nature in a way full of wisdom and developing an interest in it?' That power has its justifiable place in the human mind and spirit. This luciferic power does have to be there as well, for if we were only in the ongoing stream, developing the inclination to gain insight into every human being, we would simply drown quite miserably in our knowledge of the human being. We would drown, we would not be fully ourselves. It is connected with many of the secrets of existence that there is really nothing to be found in it which if consistently followed, its consequences taken to their extreme, will not then turn into evil, into misfortune. The principle which really and truly unites us with others, which lets us find the other person in ourselves, would make us drown in our knowledge of humanity if that luciferic element were not always there, again and again picking us up, away from drowning, again and again taking us to the surface, to find ourselves and develop our interest in ourselves again. In our relationship to others we are constantly alternating between our own inherent power and the luciferic power. And anyone who says that it would make more sense for people to follow only their own inherent power and not be touched by the luciferic power at all would be the kind of person who, seeing a balance with its beam and two scales, would consider it better to take away one scale and weigh things only on the one single scale. Life proceeds in states of balance, not in absolutes. Speaking of the luciferic influence initially with regard to human life, we may say that it takes hold of the conscious mind but in such a way that hyperconscious elements enter into it.

The ahrimanic influence is initially on subconscious human life. The ahrimanic powers enter into all the subconscious, often most artful drives which are part of human nature. To characterize Ahriman and Lucifer as persons, let us say, we might say: 'Lucifer is an arrogant spirit which prefers to flip up into bird's-eye view, getting a great overview; Ahriman is a morally isolated spirit which does not easily show itself, active in the human subconscious, influencing the subconscious mind, conjuring up judgements from this subconscious sphere.' People then think that they form judgements in the conscious mind when in fact they are often conjuring them up from their artful subconscious impulses or also let them be conjured up by ahrimanic powers.

As we know, religious references often originate in ancient spiritual-scientific views, and Peter was not wrong in referring to Ahriman as the lion who walks about, seeking whom he might devour. Peter called Ahriman this because Ahriman does indeed prowl about secretly, in the subconscious mind, and seeks to achieve his goal in the world by drawing the subconscious power of the human being to himself, using it to achieve goals in world evolution that differ from those which are reached by following the straight line of human evolution.

With regard to historical life, it is always the luciferic powers which make us think up great cosmic dreams which, however, are not in accord with human nature. Think of all the great utopian ideas people have thought up! This happens because such luciferic thinking has the bird's-eye view perspective, ignoring all the lesser life down below. People then think that the world can be organized along the lines which our thoughts take from the bird's-eye view. Such ideas about creating an ideal world are luciferic by nature. Dreams of world power arising from human spheres that are set apart are ahrimanic by nature. They evolve from the subconscious mind. It is ahrimanic to take a certain sphere of human existence and aim to encompass and embrace the whole world in that sphere. Anything connected with the desire to gain power over others, everything which goes against sound social aims is ahrimanic by nature. Anyone of whom we are able to say that he is possessed by Lucifer—now not in a superstitious but in our sense—is losing interest in others. Someone who is possessed by Ahriman wants to have power over as many people as possible and if he is clever will use their weaknesses to gain power over them. For it is ahrimanic to look for human weaknesses in the underground sphere, in the subconscious, and so gain control over people.

We now have to ask where all this comes from. The question which has to be of the greatest interest to us is 'Where does all this come from? What is the nature of spiritual powers such as the ahrimanic and luciferic ones?' You'll agree that we know our earth to be a metamorphosis—to use the Goethean term—of earlier cosmic bodies, the fourth metamorphosis. To be able to put names to them we spoke of Earth's first embodiment as Saturn, then Sun, then Moon. It is now embodied as the planet earth. We know, therefore, that this earth is the fourth embodiment of its cosmic nature, the fourth metamorphosis. It will go through further metamorphoses. We have to consider all this when we now want to ask 'What significance do the ahrimanic and the luciferic powers have in the whole cosmic setting in which man finds himself?' We know that the Spirits of Form are connected with the configuration of our earth, the part of the cosmos with which we are in immediate contact. When we consider the special characteristic of the earth's configuration we find that it is identical with the quality which—as I said earlier—is found in the way in which we overcome gravity in our power to be upright. This may be just a very small part of it all, but still, it is there. The Spirits of Form are, as it were, the ruling powers in earthly existence, in the present metamorphosis of our planet. And we know that they act through other spirits to which in our modern way we give the ancient names of Archai, Archangeloi and Angeloi.

The first of these to interest us are the Archai, the Prime Origins or Powers. We know that in the ranking order of the hierarchies the Spirits of Form come, as it were, immediately above the Archai. In the course of evolution intrinsic to man {shown as simple white chalk lines in Figs. 9 and 10} the powers of the Archai are, as it were, serving the Spirits of Form. Archai and Exusiai influence our human nature, spirits which we call the Prime Origins, the Spirits of Form.

But apart from this the following is also always the case. Some Spirits of Form disguise themselves as Prime Origins, as Archai. They could be Exusiai but do not show themselves as such but as Archai. They are in disguise.

As a consequence anything which is part of the outward form of earth may be as dependent on them as it is on the actual Spirits of Form. The important point is, however, that in our earthly existence everything connected with space, taking form in space, configures itself out of something which is non-spatial. We will only fully understand the spatial principle if in its image nature we trace it back to archetypes which are non-spatial. It is most difficult for western minds to envisage the non-spatial, but the situation is that everything connected with our own intrinsic human nature, everything arising from the Spirits of Form and assuming configuration in space results from the non-spatial. In real terms this means that as an individual human being who first went on all fours we come upright, overcoming gravity in erect configuration in space. The power which is behind this enters into space from a non-spatial sphere. So if we were merely subject to the Spirits of Form which belong to us we would in every way in which we occupied space bring the non-spatial to realization in space; for the Spirits of Form do not live in space. You will not find the divine if you look for it in space; of course not. Any configuration appearing in space is a realization of the non-spatial.

The spirits which really are Spirits of Form but disguise themselves as Archai, as Prime Origins, would by their nature have been destined for the non-spatial sphere. But they enter into space, they are active in space. And that is the actual ahrimanic quality. Spirits which are designed to be non-spatial have preferred to be active in space. This makes it possible to configure things in space in such a way that the configuring does not shine in directly from the non-spatial sphere but that the spatial is reproduced in space, the one by the other in space.

To give you an instance. We all differ from one another because all of us are placed in life from the non-spatial sphere. Our originals are in the non-spatial sphere. Everything is altogether different. You'll know the instructions Leibniz[57] gave to princesses—sometimes they don't have anything else to do—to look for two leaves that were exactly alike. They did not find any, for there truly are no two leaves that are exactly like one another. In a sense, therefore, we are all of us configurations that come from the non-spatial, for none of us are like anyone else. Yet we are also like one another, especially if related by blood. We are like one another because there are spirits which shape spatial according to spatial, shaping the spatial not only according to the non-spatial but also the spatial according to the spatial. We are alike because there are ahrimanic powers in us. People have to admit this to themselves, otherwise they'll go on speaking ill of ahrimanic and luciferic powers without ever wanting to understand them.

This example shows most clearly how Ahriman plays into life. In so far as you have the nerve to say, 'I am a unique human being in my configuration and not like anyone else,' you are in the straight line of evolution. And if this alone did apply in the world, if the ahrimanic stream were not to come in from the side, no mother would take pleasure in having a daughter who looks so much like her for she would notice that every human being is a reproduction in space of something non-spatial, with no spatial form resembling another. The entry of some Spirits of Form into space was the occasion that gave rise to the ahrimanic principle. That principle is not, of course, limited to human forms being alike; it applies to many things, but we were able to give it as an example.

I would now ask you to remember what I added—not to cheer you up but as part of our subject matter—when I said that human beings are really only intelligent enough for self-knowledge in the second half of their life. I said that in so far as our life proceeds in time, and if it did only this, with nothing else influencing us, we would indeed only gain self-knowledge in the second half of life. However, I said that luciferic powers were active in the first half of life and produced a self-knowledge that does not arise from our own inherent human nature. But I juxtaposed what human life would be if it followed only its own inherent trend with the realm of eternity, as I called it. With regard to everything which is part of our essential human nature we are a different person at 50 from the one we were at 20; we develop. With regard to everything where we do not develop we belong not to our physical body but to the element of spirit and soul and are connected with the realm of eternity, the realm where time does not play a role. Just as something non-spatial is behind everything spatial, so something timeless is behind everything that exists in time. We would be completely different human beings if we did not have the connection with the realm of eternity. We would only wake up from a kind of dream life, as I said some time ago, when we were 17 or 18. But we live in the realm of eternity and this balances out the half-asleep state in the first half and the terrible cleverness in the second half of life.

All the spirits of the higher hierarchies that we know belong to this realm of eternity, the only exception being the Spirits of Form. They play into the realm where things evolve in time. However, their life is spatial and non-spatial for they live, as it were, between non-space and space, and so they bring the forms from non-space into space. This is subject to a time process; their life plays into time. But the other spirits that are above the Spirits of Form in the hierarchies belong purely to eternity. We can only speak of them as spirits in time by way of analogy. To take it as real would make it nonsense. It really is difficult to speak of these things, the simple reason being that in the present evolution of time only very few people have a lively awareness of the concepts and ideas which one develops when stepping out of space and out of time. Most people today would anyway declare anything non-spatial to be sheer fantasy, as they would things that are timeless, eternal and imperishable and then also anything unchanging.

Yet beyond the order of Exusiai all spirits belong to the realm of eternity. There are, however, those among them which disguise themselves as spirits in time, entering into time. Just as the ahrimanic spirits enter into space, so do other spirits enter into time. These are luciferic spirits which in the hierarchic order really belong to the Spirits of Wisdom but act as Spirits of Form because they are doing so in time. They move the elements which otherwise would be timeless in the human soul into time. Because of this some things which would be there for ever if we were able to follow solely the realm of eternity are also subject to time. We may forget them, for instance, or recall them to a greater or lesser degree, which happens because of our body-and-soul nature and not our spirit-and-soul nature—recall, memory.

The luciferic powers are spirits of eternity disguised as spirits of time. They are really spirits, spiritual powers of a most elevated nature in the cosmic order, ranking above those of which some parsons who consider themselves well versed in theology speak when speaking of the divine principle. In fact they are talking about much less sublime powers, as we have mentioned earlier here in this place.

These luciferic powers have the potential to translate into time, as it were, things which otherwise from our human point of view would seem to us to be purely spiritual and eternal. They make it appear to progress in time. And it is this apparent progress of certain phenomena in time which solely and only makes people say that their mental and spiritual activity is connected with processes of a material kind. If our souls were not filled with luciferic spirit, as it were, our mental and spiritual activities would be immediately evident as being spiritual by nature. We would never even think that mental and spiritual activity could be attached to matter. We would be aware that the only image which I often use is also the only correct one— that anyone who thinks his mental and spiritual activity has a material basis is like someone who stands in front of a mirror and thinks that the image in the mirror comes from an entity that is behind the mirror. Yes, the image does depend on the form of the mirror; in that way our thinking also depends on our bodily nature. But in this respect the body functions in much the same way as a mirror. This would be immediately apparent to the beholder if it were not for the luciferic illusion that the mental and spiritual activity is configured on the basis of physical matter. To the degree to which Lucifer enters into the hyperconscious he is again producing the illusion which fools us much in the way in which we may be misled to shatter a mirror in order to see what the person behind it is like.

The illusion that something non-physical can derive from physical matter is essentially luciferic. We may say that anyone who says that things of the mind and spirit are the product of matter is making Lucifer his god even though he may not actually say so. To say that anything mental or spiritual arises from physical matter is exactly the same as saying that the mirror produces the mirror images as if the entities were behind it. To say such a thing is wholly identical with saying, though not in explicit terms, that Lucifer is God.

We may also enquire into the opposite pole. It is a luciferic notion that the mirror, physical matter, lets something flow from it that is non-physical by nature. The opposite pole is that human beings are also under the illusion that things in the world which we perceive through the senses could ever really have an influence on our inner life. If it were not for the ahrimanic illusion created by powers that enter from non-space into space, people would realize that powers which are anchored in the sphere of matter can never influence essential human nature. To say that powers, energies anchored in matter can take effect in human beings is purely ahrimanic. Those who say this declare Ahriman to be their god, even if they do not explicitly say so.

However, human beings float between these two illusions, one which again and again makes them think that the mirror lets images flow from it that are real entities, as if matter could generate mental and spiritual activities. The other illusion is that the external existence we perceive through the senses contains energies which can lead to human activities if converted in some way. One is the luciferic, the other the ahrimanic illusion.

It is a characteristic of our time that people have no inclination to concern themselves with things of the spirit the way they do with the natural order. It is of course easier to talk about the spirit from a point of view of nebulous mysticism or of abstract concepts relating to nature than it is to enter into spiritual processes and spiritual impulses in a truly scientific way, the way one does for the natural world. We do live in an age when people must start to enlighten themselves about the principle which is active in their soul sphere. We know why the time has passed when people could find the impulses that would take them further in their unconscious. Today we must start to enter consciously into the field in which the soul lives and generates conscious awareness.

We may say, therefore, that human beings would really be very different from the way they are now if they followed just their own inherent nature and the good spiritual powers in the world as they develop. The fact is that they follow this original development and are at the same time also under the influence of luciferic and ahrimanic powers which are active in time. The question is, how can equilibrium arise between the three powers? To establish this equilibrium, or at least discover how it can be established, we have to pay attention to the following.

People take things easy in external natural science, for in certain areas they base themselves on the principle 'One needs a knife to eat, so one takes a razor from its case and uses it to cut up the food on the table'. Many scientific views are developed in this way, for instance the one about death. In modern natural science people tend to use not much more of the concepts at hand for the phenomenon of death but the cessation of an organism. That is simple, and one can speak in the same terms of plant death, animal death and human death, which is what some who call themselves scientists do in a really grotesque way. This does not really differ from putting a table knife and a razor in one and the same category when speaking of a knife. In reality the principle which we may call death is different for plants, different for animals and different for human beings. Generalization comes in because one sees the cessation of functions in all three cases.

If we study death as part of human nature—we have spoken of the phenomenon of human death on several occasions—the nature of death is such that in a way we may see it as the power that balances out the luciferic powers. Death, after all, is not a once-only phenomenon, for human beings actually begin to die as soon as they are born; the impulses for dying are in them, and death ensues at a particular point in time. All the impulses that lead to death are also the powers which establish equilibrium with the luciferic powers. For with death human beings are taken from the realm of time into that of eternity.

We know the nature of the luciferic powers to be such that they actually belong to the realm of eternity and take the things they should be doing in that realm into the realm of time. This could not be balanced out if death were not part of the realm of time; it takes human beings from the realm of time into the realm of eternity. Death balances out the luciferic. The luciferic element takes eternity into time; death takes time into eternity. That is putting it in an abstract way, but there is a vast amount of reality in this abstract notion.

What was it that we had to say of Ahriman? He makes the similar similar. I gave the example of similarity in human nature which is connected with the ahrimanic principle. A counterbalance has to be created or must have been created—we can't be teleological about this, hence 'have been created'—for this state of being similar. There has to be this counterweight which acts against the similarity. Oddly enough, people often use one of the confusing ideas which one gets if one does not enter into deeper connections in ascribing this similarity to the very counterbalance. The counterbalance for similarity actually is the power of heredity. We are similar not only in the form which leads to our configuration but also have inner powers of heredity in us. With these inner powers we actually counter that similarity of form. A science must be confused if it puts similarity and heredity together. We look like our parents but at the same time our parents have passed on certain powers which we have in our inner being, powers that seek to take us back again to the original image of man. Our inheritance really lies in fighting that similarity. A more subtle study of human life can indeed show this, even without supersensible observation, in purely external terms. Do try to ask life in the right way, do try to study people who are particularly similar in appearance to their parents, grandparents and so on in some form element or other, and then consider the inherited moral impulses.

You will find that the inherited moral impulses do as a rule counteract the similarities of form.

Study the more outstanding historical figures, looking at portraits which show their outward appearance to be similar to an ancestor, and you'll everywhere find qualities of soul in the biography which have been inherited and go against those that have produced those similarities in appearance, in form. In essence this is one of the secrets of life. Ancestors would understand their descendants, parents their children very much better if they were able to accept such a fact without prejudice. So for example—please forgive me saying such things, but we are not, after all, a community of philistines—if a mother has a young son who looks very much like her she may be pleased that he looks like her, but for his upbringing it might be a good thing if she now said to herself, 'What kind of qualities is he about to develop which are rather like those that cause me to be in frequent clashes with my husband?' We need to pay attention to such real impulses that have tremendous significance in life. For bringing up children in future, for future human evolution, it will be most important to gain insight into such impulses. For, in future, education cannot be based on abstract principles. One will have to look for foundations, empirical, real foundations. And these cannot be found unless one is able to read life. We must be able to read it, which means we must know the letters. In real terms, as you know, there are many more, but to spell out what is needed for the immediate future it will be sufficient to know three letters—normal development, and the ahrimanic and the luciferic principle. Those who do not know them cannot read, just as someone who does not know the alphabet is unable to read a book. They simply are the letters through which we come to know life, to read life. And the utopian spirit which is so widespread can only be overcome if we learn to read life. It means, however, that we must study the powers that play a role in life.

Someone may, of course, say, 'You speak here of something which you say is original human nature, yet this is nowhere to be found.' That is obvious, but the objection is the same as when someone says,

'You are telling me that the water flowing in the river contains hydrogen and oxygen; I do not find them there.' You see, we have to go into these things and above all get a real idea of what form is. I have made the following comparison before and would like to repeat it now.

You may go to Koblenz in Rhineland-Palatinate, or also to Basel, and admire the river Rhine, and the thought may come to you: 'This Rhine, there it flows, no one knows for how long it has been flowing, for centuries no doubt, and perhaps even for time immemorial. How old this river Rhine is!' What does 'old' really mean? The water you see there will be somewhere entirely different in a few days' time; it will have gone. It certainly is not old, for a few days before it simply was not there but somewhere entirely different. What you see there certainly is not old, you should not think of it as centuries old. And when you speak of the Rhine you will probably not be speaking of the channel in the ground in which the water is flowing. You are actually speaking of something which actually is not there at all. For speaking of reality you cannot speak of something which is there in front of you, for what you have there in front of you is a coming together of currents that are active throughout the world, and it is merely that they are in equilibrium. Wherever you look you see states of equilibrium. The realities are something which you need to penetrate. Spelling out life is only possible if we penetrate into the realities.

Tomorrow I'll talk about the way the luciferic and ahrimanic impulse is connected with the Christ-Yahweh impulse so that you may see how this Christ-Yahweh impulse really relates to these streams.

LECTURE 11

5 OCTOBER 1918

You will have been able to learn from the many things I said about the Christ mystery that we must make distinction between the general progress of evolution at the time of this Mystery on Golgotha and the new elements that came into human evolution through that Mystery. You have learned that this is a continuous flow of powers that come from the spirits of the higher hierarchies and are part of man's original inherent nature, and that there are also two lateral streams—one luciferic, the other ahrimanic.

The luciferic and ahrimanic streams came to a peak within human evolution exactly at the time of the Mystery on Golgotha. In a sense, if one may put it like this, humanity faced the danger then of development going beyond this peak, which could upset the balance between ahrimanic and luciferic activities for the whole of human evolution as it progressed. For the following had emerged in the course of this evolution. If we make progressing human evolution a straight line [Fig. 11], we can say that this evolution has gone through—let us begin with the Lemurian age—the Lemurian age, the Atlantean age and our own age, the fifth, post-Atlantean age, as we may call it. Now I add the strength of the luciferic influence as a red line, say something like this. We may say that there was a certain strength to it in the Lemurian age, and it grew, then became less, and this luciferic strength diminished greatly and was then lost altogether in the Atlantean age, to rise again in post-Atlantean times. During

Fig. 11

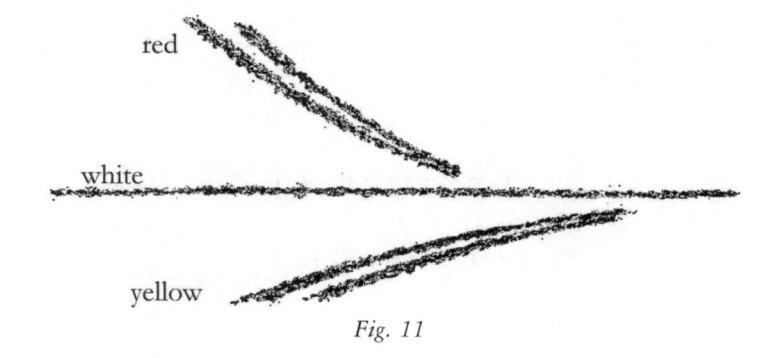

the Atlantean age—I am speaking not of individual human beings but of the evolution of humanity—essentially there was little direct luciferic influence [Fig. 12, red].

But ahrimanic evolution—I'll put it in yellow—was particularly strong in the Atlantean age, growing weaker here, in the post-Atlantean age. I am speaking of historical development and we have to be clear in our minds that when we characterize anything like this we must always take account of what I said the other day: 'When Lucifer is particularly powerful he calls up Ahriman in the subconscious.' So if the luciferic curve is a strong one in our fifth age, this does not mean that Ahriman is outside our sphere; quite the contrary, with Lucifer most active among the historical powers, Ahriman is particularly active in the subconscious regions of human beings.

You see that there is a kind of wavy line for ahrimanic activity and for luciferic activity in the course of human evolution on earth. A balance must be established between the strengths of the ahrimanic

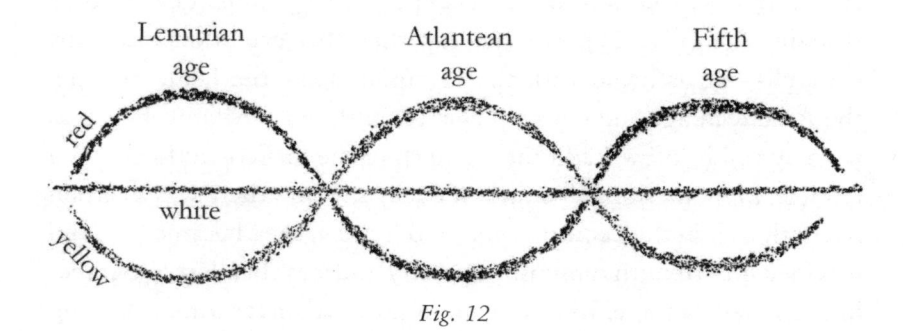

Fig. 12

and luciferic elements. This state of balance has never been a perfect one in the course of historical evolution. There were times when the luciferic activities were most powerful, and times when the ahrimanic influence was really marked.

If we consider the period of human evolution when humanity was approaching the Mystery on Golgotha we find that the state of balance between the luciferic and ahrimanic powers was extraordinarily unstable, fluctuating, and there was no real balance. On the one hand there was the stream of humanity moving towards the Mystery on Golgotha, historically presented in the evolution of Semitic peoples. This stream of human evolution was particularly open to luciferic principles, with the result that powerful ahrimanic influences were generated in the subconscious.

Greek nature, on the other hand, was very open to the historical ahrimanic powers, with the result that powerful luciferic influences were generated in the subconscious. We will only understand Semitic and Greek civilization, which were polar opposites, if we really take note of this fluctuation between ahrimanic and luciferic influences in human world evolution. For the western peoples, the influence of Greek civilization was of the greatest significance at the time when the Mystery entered into Earth evolution from outside. This Greek influence was, however, already getting less, having passed its peak. Greek civilization was about to go into decline. We are able to say: 'The Greeks developed sublime wisdom exactly because of the ahrimanic influence which became evident as a luciferic element in their art.' This wisdom assumed a highly individual, humanly individual character, as we also said on other occasions. Basically, however, it was greatest where the things which the spirits themselves had taught human beings shone into Greek wisdom from very early times.

We know that in very early times the teachers of humanity were inspired, initiated directly from the spiritual world. The spirits of the world themselves spoke through them and looking back to most ancient times in human evolution we can, even at the beginning of the fifth age, still discern a marvellous original wisdom. Its concepts and ideas had been purified to such effect that it had adapted itself to essential human nature. In earlier times it had been presented more in the form of pictures, of images by the great initiates, but the Greeks put it in ideas and concepts, adapting it to human nature. The most admirable thing about the Greeks, however, is the original wisdom which humanity had received from the lips, we might say, of the gods themselves, a wisdom still to be found in Plato's philosophy. Now, however, humanity was in danger of losing this wisdom.

Looking back to the time when the Greek spirit evolved, an age which Nietzsche[58] referred to as tragic, we look back on the great Greek philosophers, on Anaxagoras,[59] Heraclitus,[60] and one sees, I'd say, the last to have that divine wisdom, though already changed into ideas and concepts. Thales[61] was the first, in a way, to base himself wholly on natural concepts; he no longer had a connection to the direct, living impression made by humanity's original wisdom which one can still see in the work of Anaxagoras. That original wisdom was in the process of being lost to humanity. Yet the human ability in early times to know anything at all about the human being, insight into human nature, had come from that original wisdom. That wisdom was meant to imbue Greek and all original wisdom. The mysteries were meant to provide insight into human nature. 'Come to know yourself' was one precept. But that ancient insight into human nature was conveyed in a roundabout way, through Lucifer, and human beings gained it with the help of ahrimanic powers. It was entirely bound up with the state of balance between ahrimanic and luciferic powers.

At the time when the old world was coming to an end, and the Mystery on Golgotha was approaching from the other side, ahrimanic powers were slightly in excess. They were particularly strong at that time. The strength of the ahrimanic powers above all caused the inner life of human beings to drift towards abstraction, even the high degree of abstraction we see in the Romans. We have to ask ourselves what would have happened to humanity if evolution had proceeded solely in the stream which I have just characterized and there had been no Mystery on Golgotha. What would have happened is that people would no longer have a notion, an idea, sentience of the nature of the individual human being.

This is an extraordinarily important statement. Humanity was threatened by this because they could no longer be told anything in the way that had come from the gods, because even the tradition of that way had been lost, and they were becoming more and more of a riddle to themselves. We need to get a strong feeling for the truth of this. If it had not been for the Mystery on Golgotha human beings would have been in danger of becoming more and more a riddle to themselves. They would have been able to gain wisdom but only about nature, not about themselves. And they would have been forced gradually to forget that they were born of the spirit. They would have had to lose that knowledge completely.

Then came the Mystery on Golgotha. It can be considered from many points of view, including the one that with the coming of the Mystery humanity was made able again to grasp themselves as individuals* from the spiritual heights which in the earthly field had been lost. The Christ impulse made it possible for people to see themselves again as individuals, but now doing so with powers that come from within.

Today it is extraordinarily difficult for people to imagine how those early people gained their awareness of individual nature, for modern people won't believe one how very different the external philosophy of life was in those days. One cannot understand the whole significance in world history of Julian the Apostate[62] unless one knows that he was one of the last people who still saw the sun in a different way from the way we do today. Today we see the sun as a

---

*In Rudolf Steiner's day the German term *Persönlichkeit* meant 'individual' or 'individual nature' in English and the German *Individualität* would refer to a 'person'. Decades of translation by people not trained in translation (particularly in the field of psychology) led to *Persönlichkeit* being translated as 'personality' and *Individualität* as 'individuality', in spite of the fact that 'personality' and 'individuality' are qualities which people *have* in English and not people as such. In this volume, I am translating the terms as they would have been translated in Rudolf Steiner's day. AM.

physical body. The influence of the moon as a natural phenomenon has stayed with us for a longer time. Lovers still walk in the moonlight today, rapturous and dreaming. Fantasy grows and flourishes in the moon; in the twilight the poetry of the moon, both true and false, continues to be familiar to many. The people of old had much more intense feelings when on waking up they saw the sun than some people still have in the moonlight today. When those early people woke up and saw the sun they would not just talk of the sunlight; they were sentient that something enters into us like a ray from this entity in the heavens to fill us with warmth and light and that this made us into individuals.

Julian the Apostate still felt this. He believed that it might be retained for humanity, though here he was in error, and this was the great tragedy. Their individual nature no longer came to developing humanity from the physical sunray. This insight into individual nature was now coming to them in a spiritual way. Something which the sun out there in space could no longer give to human beings, which could no longer come to them from outside, now had to rise up from deep down inside them. The Christ had to connect his world destiny with humanity so that they would not drop out of the stream of evolution that took them forward because the scales are continually moving up and down between Ahriman and Lucifer. We have to accept in all seriousness that the Christ came down from spiritual heights to human beings and linked his destiny with theirs. How is that? The strange thing is that when human beings looked into the world perceptible to the senses before the Mystery on Golgotha they would at the same time also see something spiritual. I have just made this clear to you by telling you how the sun was seen. This was gradually lost. People had to be given something else instead; they had to be given something spiritual, the spirituality of which would at the same time give them the impression of reality as it is perceived through the senses. That is what is notable about the Mystery on Golgotha and the way it relates to human powers of gaining insight.

This Mystery on Golgotha, which had given Earth evolution its true meaning, took place in a small corner of the world, practically unnoticed by the Romans. Tacitus[63] did not really know about it when he produced his excellent study of Roman history a hundred years later. Nothing is really said about the Mystery on Golgotha in history, for the Gospels are not history; they were written in the way I have described in my *Christianity as Mystical Fact*[64] and are really mystery books applied to life. Whatever efforts theologians make, there will never be history about the Mystery on Golgotha the way there is history concerning other events. This is indeed meant to be the characteristic of the Mystery on Golgotha, that nothing should be known of it historically, by way of external, factual history. Anyone who wants to know something about it must believe in the supersensible. The Mystery on Golgotha cannot be proved to have happened as a historical, sense-perceptible event.

Where the people of earlier times looked into the sense-perceptible world and also perceived supersensible truths, modern people who do not want to lose their insight into individual nature must look on the Mystery on Golgotha as something that was supersensible. Looking at the supersensible they will gain the conviction that this, too, was a historical event, though there is no mention of it in history.

Those who do not consider that throughout the evolution of human history there has been no external record made of the most important historical event will not understand the whole relationship of the Mystery on Golgotha to modern humanity. For modern people are meant to learn from the Mystery on Golgotha to turn to the factual reality of something about which there are no historical documents. And this factual element is meant to have an effect. What did we say yesterday did really come from Ahriman and Lucifer? We said that Lucifer detracts human hearts and minds from taking an interest in others. If only luciferic principles were active in humanity we would progressively lose interest in others. It would mean little to us how one person or another thinks. You actually get a good indication of how much luciferic nature there is in someone if you ask, 'Does this person take an interest in others, objectively tolerant, or is he or she really only interested in himself or herself?' Luciferic natures take little interest in others, are rigid, obdurate within themselves, only considering the things to be right which they have thought up themselves, of which they are sentient, and are not open to the opinions of others. If the luciferic principle had continued to act in the same way in human evolution as it did before the Mystery on Golgotha, humanity would gradually have taken a course which would have to be characterized as people being inwardly obdurate and uncommunicative, with everyone only considering their own concerns, only considering the things they have thought up for themselves to be true and not inclined to look into the hearts of others. This, however, is nothing but the opposite side to losing individual nature. For in losing the possibility of seeing the human being as an individual we also lose understanding for the individual nature of another. There were a great many people— many more than you'd think, especially at the time when the Mystery on Golgotha was approaching—in the Greek and the Roman world, in Africa, in western Asia, who went about as, well, we can't say oddballs but as arrogant, isolated people who wanted to be on their own. There were many such, and there were also people who made it into a philosophy not to care about others but to follow only what they had within themselves. This happened because the luciferic principle had dropped out of the state of balance.

The ahrimanic principle was present to excess at the time. This is most clearly evident when we look at the early Roman emperors, the Julio-Claudian Dynasty. Only the first of them, Augustus,[65] had been initiated, though in a somewhat questionable way. Among the others were at most those who enforced their own initiation, but all of them considered themselves to be the sons of gods, initiates, descended from the gods. For the ahrimanic principle shows itself particularly in that people do not wish to live among other people as one individual among others, but to have power, as I said yesterday, that they want to be in power by making use of the weaknesses of others.

Those were the two great dangers for humanity at the time of the

Mystery on Golgotha; humanity would have succumbed to them if the Mystery had not come. Lack of interest in others, every individual lusting for power. The Christ connected his destiny with that of humanity and in doing so implanted something in human beings that was extraordinarily profound. You may perhaps understand this best if I tell you in a schematic way what the Christ actually implanted in human beings. I have told you that we human beings have powers which we develop out of our own inherent nature. As you know, that inherent nature really only lets us grow intelligent in the second half of life. I have told you this in every detail and on several occasions. There is more to this, however. Essentially everything I have told you about people growing more intelligent between birth and death only applies to Earth evolution, and we are meant to grow even more intelligent in the course of the Jupiter, Venus and Vulcan evolutions. The powers which we are meant to develop in the course of Jupiter and Venus evolution are already in us.

What happened was this. You know that human beings cannot gain any of the self-knowledge which they are able to gain in the first half of life by their inherent nature. They need Lucifer to gain it. Their inherent original nature progresses. Luciferic principles coming in during the first half of life give them self-knowledge; in the second half of life Ahriman dampens down this brilliant self-perception. Another stream came into human evolution with the Christ impulse. The impulse that came with the Mystery on Golgotha addresses the inmost depths of human beings. If humanity were to gain the insights which have entered into Earth evolution through the Christ entirely by their own inherent powers they would only be able to do so during the Venus evolution. However intelligent human beings might have grown by the time they die they would not be able to achieve of their own accord what they do achieve because the Christ impulse has connected its destiny with Earth evolution.

We live our life on earth, therefore, but will not be able to understand the Christ impulse by the time we die if we purely follow our own inherent course of development. Surely this tells you that the Christ had contemporaries, his pupils. The tradition of original wisdom enabled them to gain so much wisdom about him that they were later able to write the Gospels, though they did not really understand them. They certainly could not gain insight into the Christ impulse in their lifetime. So when could they gain it? After death, in the time after death. If we assume that, let us say, Peter or James were contemporaries of the Christ, when were they ready to understand the Christ? Only in the third century after the Mystery on Golgotha. They were not ready for this in their lifetime but only in the third century.

Here we touch on a highly significant secret. Let us take a careful look at it. The contemporaries of the Christ had to go through death and live in the spiritual world until the second or third century; only then did they gain insight into the Christ in their life after death, and were then able to inspire those who towards the end of the second or from the third century onwards wrote about the Christ impulse. As it was a matter of the Church Fathers being more or less clearly inspired, the works written about the Christ impulse had a specific character, but only from the third century onwards. It is because of this that Augustine, essentially so important for the Middle Ages, came at that time. You can see from this what was needed for understanding the Christ impulse, Venus wisdom, if I may put it like this, which even now human beings cannot experience in their lifetime but only after death—and indeed only centuries later—to have the inspiration of this Venus wisdom come to the earth. I wish the way of putting it were not quite so silly, but there is no other term really that meets the case, it was 'lucky' that inspiration could come in the second and third centuries, that it could begin then, for if one had waited for longer than that, beyond the year 333, humanity would have grown more and more obdurate against the spiritual world and not prepared to accept inspiration.

You see that the influence of the Christ impulse on humanity through the centuries of Christian evolution is connected with all kinds of secrets. Anyone wishing to look for them again today will find the most important parts of insight into the Christ impulse only by seeking supersensible insight. Essentially it was the dead who were the first genuine teachers of the Christ impulse and I think this is evident from what I have just been saying. They had been contemporaries of the Christ and were not ready to gain full understanding until the third century. Understanding was then able to grow in the fourth century, but it was also getting more difficult to inspire people. The difficulty was even greater in the sixth century until finally the time came when Rome created order in the way spiritual secrets were given as inspiration for humanity through the Christ Mystery, with an obdurate humanity resisting. Rome finally established order in the ninth century, in 869, at the Council of Constantinople, where they finally got rid of the spirit. All this inspiring ultimately got too much for Rome and the dogma was established that human beings have something in their soul that is spiritual by nature but that it is heresy to believe in the spirit. People were to be drawn away from the spirit. This essentially is the dogma connected with the eighth Ecumenical Council held in Constantinople. I have referred to this on several occasions. It is simply a consequence of this removal of the spirit when Jesuits tell one today (I spoke of this the other day), 'Well, there were inspirations in the past, but today inspiration is devilish. One must not seek supersensible insight, for then you get the devil.'

These things are connected with the most profound thing which must interest us if we truly want to enter into spiritual science. They are connected with a form of recognition given to the wisdom character which many so-called 'spiritual sciences', especially those which have come together in secret societies, do not recognize. I'd say that there is a kind of deception which is brought into humanity over and over again by the people who know spiritual secrets. This deception comes under the cover of a false polarity. Surely you have heard people say that there is Lucifer, and his opponent is the Christ. People establish polar opposition between Lucifer and the Christ. I have shown that even Goethe's Faust concept suffers from Ahriman and Lucifer being confounded, that Goethe could not tell ahrimanic principles apart from luciferic principles. This is also the subject of the second essay in my small volume entitled *Goethe's Standard of the Soul*.[66]

This is something of extraordinary importance. The true opposition, as those who would speak truth from the spiritual world have made known to human beings, is between Ahriman and Lucifer. The Christ impulse brings something else and has nothing to do with the polar opposition between Ahriman and Lucifer. The Christ impulse moves in the line of equilibrium, of balance. Something of tremendous importance rests on the recognition of this fact. We will take this further tomorrow.

LECTURE 12

6 OCTOBER 1918

Basing myself on the science which we must call the science of initiation I made two remarks yesterday which I want you to call to mind again, for we need to take them further. In the first place, I said with reference to the Mystery on Golgotha that the most profound truths relating to this Mystery on Golgotha must, according to the nature of the matter, be truths that cannot be established by means of sense-perceptible historical evidence. Anyone looking for external, historical evidence that the Mystery on Golgotha did in fact take place, doing so in the way in which one looks for evidence for other historical facts, will not be able to find it. The Mystery on Golgotha is intended to assume a place in humanity where access to its truths is ultimately mediated in a supersensible way. In a way, people are meant to get used to having the most important thing in earthly existence in such a way that they cannot approach it through evidence of the senses but only in a supersensible way.

The second thing I said yesterday was that the kind of understanding given to them as earthly creatures up to the time of their death—note well, literally up to the time of their death—will not take them so far that they might be able to grasp the Mystery on Golgotha with the understanding which is their own, an understanding which develops in the world perceived through the senses. I said that it is only after death, *post mortem*, when they are in the supersensible world, that human beings develop the understanding, or the powers to develop understanding, for the Mystery on Golgotha. Because of this I said something yesterday which the outside world will inevitably consider to be absurd, wholly paradoxical. I said that even the contemporaries of the Christ were only able to understand the Mystery on Golgotha in the second or third century after the event, and only in their other life, and that the things written about the Mystery on Golgotha were inspired by those contemporaries, who inspired the actual writers in the second and third centuries from the supersensible world.

The seeming contradiction is that the Gospels—which after all are inspired works, as you can see from what I have said in *Christianity as Mystical Fact*, are works to inspire Christianity. The inspired Gospels could only say the truth about Christianity because, as I have also stressed on a number of occasions, they were written not out of inherent original human nature but with the last remnant of atavistic clairvoyant wisdom concerning the Mystery on Golgotha.

The things which I have been saying about the way in which human beings relate to the Mystery on Golgotha were taken from the science of initiation itself. Having reconnoitred something like this from such supersensible insight, one may well ask, 'What does such a thing look like when one compares the facts of external historical life with it?' Today I will therefore begin by taking one particular ecclesiastical writer from the second century, initially more as a question, with the answer coming to us at the end of today's discussions. I might just as well have taken Clement of Alexandria,[67] Origen,[68] or any other ecclesiastical writer, though the whole would then, of course, have to be in a different form. I am taking one who is often mentioned—Tertullian. Referring to him I would like to pose the question: 'How does the external progress of Christian life relate to the supersensible facts of which I spoke yesterday and the most important aspects of which I have recapitulated for you today?'

Tertullian is a most unusual figure. Hearing the things usually said about him one does not gain more than essentially the knowledge that it is said to have been Tertullian who justified belief in the

Christ spirit, in the sacrificial death, in the resurrection by saying *Credo, quia absurdum est*—I believe exactly because it is absurd, because it goes against common sense. Those words actually are not to be found anywhere in his works. Nor are they to be found in the writings of any of the other Church Fathers; they are pure invention, but it is through them that the view taken of Tertullian to this day is often made into dogma. Yet if one takes the actual Tertullian—no need to become an adherent—the more one comes to the man himself the more one does develop respect for this strange man. Above all one feels respect for the way in which Tertullian handled the Latin language, a language which reflects the most abstract way of human thinking and had already in his day become a language used by other writers to reflect utterly prosaic Roman culture. Tertullian used the language with a real spirit of fire; he brought temperament, mobility, sentience and a sacred passion into his way of putting things. He was a typical Roman who put things in an abstract way like any Roman when it came to the things one often says are real. People of that time with Greek education would not even have considered him to be a particularly erudite person, but he wrote with great intensity, with inner strength; he wrote in such a way that using the abstract language of Rome he actually became the creator of the Christian way of speaking. The way he spoke, this Tertullian, is indeed intense. In a kind of protective declaration for the Christians he did, we may say, put things in such a way that the effect of the written word was like hearing it said in words directly by someone in the throes of a sacred passion. There are passages where Tertullian becomes the defender of the accused Christians who would during a procedure that was very much like torture not deny but confess that they were Christians, and say what they believed in. Tertullian wrote:[69] 'Everywhere else those under torture are accused of denying the truth. It is done the other way round with the Christians. They are declared to be mentally deranged when they confess what lives in their souls. The torture is not meant to force them to tell the truth, which alone would make sense. The aim is to force them to say things that are untrue but in fact they are telling the truth. And when they confess the truth from their hearts they are said to be evil-doers.'

In short, Tertullian was someone who had a real sense for absurdity in life. He was someone who had grown together with such Christian awareness and Christian wisdom as had developed, a sensitive observer of life. It does therefore mean something when he writes, 'You have sayings, you do very often in life say from immediate sentience: in God's hands, God willing, and so forth. And that is Christian faith—the soul professes itself when it expresses itself as a Christian, doing so unconsciously.' Tertullian was also an independent spirit, someone who told the Romans, being a Roman himself: 'Look at the God of the Christians and consider if the things you give to the world as Romans are truly religious, or if the things which the Christians want reflect true religiosity. You bring war, trouble and strife into the world, and this is exactly what the Christians do not want to do. The things that are sacred to you are blasphemous, for they are victory signs, and victory signs are not something sacred but signs for the desecration of sacred places.' This is what Tertullian said to his Romans! He had a sense of independence, and seeing the things that went on in Rome he said, 'Is one praying when one looks up quite naturally to heaven, or when one turns one's eyes to the Capitol?' Tertullian certainly was not someone who was wholly given up to abstract Roman civilization, for he was deeply conscious of the supersensible, the spirit, being present in the world. Someone who is on the one hand speaking so independently and freely and at the same time so much out of the supersensible as Tertullian did had to be sought out, even in those past times, when the supersensible was still closer to human beings than it would be later. Tertullian did not only say in a rationalist way, 'The Christians tell the truth; you declare them to be evildoers when in fact we should only call those people evildoers who do not tell the truth under torture.' This was certainly rationalistic, but it was also courageous, and Tertullian said other things as well. He said, for instance, 'If you Romans take a real look at your gods, who are demons, and genuinely ask them, you will learn the truth. But you do not want to learn the truth from the demons. If one brings someone possessed by a demon face to face with a Christian and lets the Christian ask him the right questions, the demon will show itself to be a demon. And it will be afraid but will say of the god whom the Christians acknowledge: That is the god who now has a rightful place in the world.' Tertullian referred to the evidence not only of the Christians but also that of the demons by saying that the demons will also profess themselves demons if we merely ask them, doing so fearlessly, and that they acknowledge Christ Jesus as the true Christ Jesus, as it also says in the Gospels.

It was at any rate a strange character who faced the Romans as a Roman in the second century. He attracts our attention when we note his attitude to the Mystery on Golgotha. He spoke about the Mystery in about the following words: 'The Son of God has been crucified. We do not feel shame because it is ignominious. The Son of God has died; it is utterly believable because it is inept.' The actual words are *Prorsus credibile est, quia ineptum est*. It is credible, wholly credible, because it is inept. So he said that the Son of God had died; it was utterly believable because it was inept. And he had been buried, had risen from the grave, and that was certain because it was impossible. The words *Prorsus credibile est, quia ineptum est* became the other, untrue statement: *Credo, quia absurdum est*.

We must rightly understand the words Tertullian said about the Mystery on Golgotha. He said: 'The Son of God has been crucified. When as human beings we consider this crucifixion we do not feel shame because it is ignominious.' What did he mean? He meant that the best thing to happen on earth must be ignominious because it is human nature to do things that are ignominious and not those that are outstandingly good. If something were to be presented as a good deed, so said Tertullian, the best deed to be done by human beings, it could not be the most outstanding for events on earth. The most outstanding deed for events on earth will no doubt be the one which brings disgrace on man and does not mean glory; this was what he meant.

To go on. The Son of God died. This was wholly believable

because it was inept. The Son of God died. It was wholly believable because common sense finds it inept, senseless. If common sense were to consider it intelligent, it would not be believable, for things human sense finds intelligent cannot be the most sublime, cannot be the most sublime on earth. For human sense is not at a level in its intelligence where it comes to the most sublime. It comes to the most sublime when it grows inept.

He was buried, rose again. This was certain because it was impossible. It is impossible as a natural phenomenon that the dead rise again; but it was Tertullian's view that the Mystery on Golgotha had nothing to do with natural phenomena. If one had to refer to something as a natural phenomenon it would not be the most valuable thing on earth. The most valuable thing on earth must not be a natural phenomenon, which means that it had to be impossible in the sphere of natural phenomena. It was exactly because of this that he was buried and rose again, and it was certain because it was impossible.

In the first place I want Tertullian to stand before us as a question, especially in the words I have quoted which are taken from his *De carne Christi*. I have tried to characterize him, firstly as an independent free spirit, secondly as a spirit who also saw the demonic and supersensible in man's immediate surroundings. At the same time I quoted three sentences he wrote and because of which all intelligent people must really consider Tertullian to have been a nincompoop.

It really is always a strange thing with matters of this kind that people are biased in their judgement. In also producing the wrong notion such as *Credo, quia absurdum est*, they are sitting in judgement on a whole human being. It is important, however, to consider the three sentences which do not make immediate sense—Tertullian certainly also did not want to make immediate sense—together firstly with the independent spirit of Tertullian, and then with his complete awareness of the supersensible world being involved in our human environment.

Let us now consider something which can cast light on the Mystery on Golgotha from a different angle, as it were. These are two phenomena in human life to which I did already refer the day before yesterday. One is death, the other heredity. Death is connected with the end of life, heredity with birth. With regard to death and heredity it is important that we have a clear understanding when it comes to human life and human knowledge. Considering everything I have been telling you, for weeks now, you can see that when human beings use their senses to consider their environment and want to use their intellect to understand the world perceived through the senses, the phenomena of heredity also present themselves, with the characteristics of the ancestors popping up in their descendants in a sense and people acting out of the subconscious aspect of these inherited powers. We are often studying all these different inherited traits connected with the mystery of birth even without thinking of them directly. When we study ethnology, for instance, we always speak of inherited traits without being aware of doing so. One cannot really study an ethnic group without seeing everything really in terms of inherited traits. Speaking of any nation—Russians, English people, Germans and so on—you speak of characteristics which belong in the sphere of heredity, traits which the son has from his father, his father from his grandfather and so on. The field of heredity, which is connected with the mystery of birth, is vast indeed, and speaking of the external life into which the human being is placed, we often speak of the facts, the powers of heredity without always being aware of doing so.

The mystery of death enters into the life we live in the senses, a fact which is frequently apparent to us, so we need not waste words on this. However, something else emerges when we look back into human powers of insight. We find that our human powers of insight can grasp much in the natural order, but this human power of insight declares itself to be sovereign, wanting to grasp *everything* to be found in this natural order. Yet this human power of insight will never serve to grasp the fact of heredity, which is connected with the mystery of birth, nor the fact of death. Then the strange phenomenon arises in human life where the whole of human understanding is filled with the wrong concepts. This is because we consider phenomena to be part of the world perceived through the senses which make themselves known in that world but are by nature utterly spiritual. We consider human death—it is a bit different for the death of animals and of plants, as I said the day before yesterday—to be a phenomenon in the world perceived through the senses because that is what appears to be the case. This does not help us, however, to learn about human death. No natural science could ever say anything about human death; all we achieve with it is that we transform our wholly human view into a pseudo-view, mixing the facts of death into everything. We only learn the truth about nature if we leave death aside and leave the hereditary traits aside. The peculiar thing about human insight is that it is ruined—if I may put it like this—and made into a pseudo-image because people think it could cover everything in the world perceived through the senses, including death and birth, and as death and birth are mixed into the view taken of nature, human perception ruins all views on the world that are perceived through the senses. One will never gain a view of the human being as a creature perceptible through the senses if one includes the qualities of heredity, which are, of course, connected with birth, in the sense-perceptible world. One ruins the whole image of man for oneself—I have spoken of three streams, the straight line, normal evolution, the lateral luciferic and the lateral ahrimanic stream—the whole of human evolution which proceeds in a straight line if one counts birth and death as part of essential human nature in so far as man belongs to the sense-perceptible world.

That is the strange situation when it comes to human powers of perception. Guided by nature herself, these powers are driven to think the wrong things; for if they were actually able to think, an image would emerge from nature in which there was no heredity and no death in human life. One would need to abstract from death and heredity; one would also have to think nothing of death and birth and develop an image which does not include them. This would give us an image of nature. There is no room for inherited traits and for death in the Goethean philosophy of life. They do not fit into it. That is the peculiar thing especially with the Goethean philosophy of life—you cannot do anything with death and heredity in it. This is what makes it so good, and because of this we can take it to be a true nature image which is real, for there is no room in it for death and heredity.

Up to the time of the Mystery on Golgotha people did on a certain spiritual basis still think in a more natural way about death and heredity. The Semitic population considered inherited traits to be due to the continuing direct influence of the god Yahweh; one needs to know this to understand the Yahweh point of view. It put anything relating to heredity—at least in places where the Yahweh view was still well understood—outside of mere nature and saw in it a continued direct influence of Yahweh. The god of Abraham, of Isaac, of Jacob—that was nothing but the inherited traits continuing. And in Greek philosophy people sought to grasp something in human nature—though decadence meant that it was with little success—which lives in man also between birth and death but has nothing to do with death; they sought to pick something out from the sum of phenomena where death cannot interfere. The Greeks had a certain fear of understanding death; their philosophy focused on the sense-perceptible and so they did not want to understand death, instinctively feeling that if one focuses purely on the world perceived through the senses—as Goethe also did—death is an alien element. Death has no place in the sense-perceptible world; it is alien to it.

Then other views evolved from this, and it was particularly characteristic of the nations and people which were in the lead at the time when the Mystery on Golgotha was approaching that certain old views began to change. People were progressively losing the ability to look into the spiritual world. They therefore came to think more and more that birth and death or heredity and death were also part of the sense-perceptible world. After all, heredity and death move around in that world, doing so in a truly tangible way. People came to think more and more that heredity and death were part of the sense-perceptible world. This came to be part of the whole human view. Centuries before the Mystery on Golgotha the other view had thus been invaded by belief that heredity and death had something to do with the sense-perceptible world. The result was that something most strange developed. You'll only be able to grasp it if you let the spirit of what I have been saying here in recent days influence you in the right way.

The fact of heredity was seen by moving it into the sphere of natural phenomena. People came to see it more and more as a natural phenomenon. Any fact of this kind calls forth its polar opposite when it comes up in life. You simply cannot accept a fact in human life without it calling forth its opposite. Human life proceeds with opposites kept in balance. It is a fundamental condition for all insight gained that one acknowledges that life proceeds in opposites and the state of balance between opposites must be sought. So what was the consequence of believing that heredity was a natural phenomenon? The consequence was the most dreadful disparagement of the human will. A fact from ancient times, which in spiritual science is known as the influence of luciferic and ahrimanic spirits, entered into the human will as the opposite evolved, and a fact which people were really looking for in the field of nature was acting so powerfully in the human soul that it drove people to a moral philosophy of life. Heredity was included among natural phenomena and therefore misunderstood, so that the opposite evolved—belief that the human will had once brought it about that original sin ['hereditary sin' in German] continues on in the world. The wrong inclusion of heredity among natural phenomena created the fundamental evil that original sin has shifted to the moral field.

This meant that human thinking was also ruined for it did not get to the point of taking up the right belief that the whole idea, the whole way in which people usually see original sin is blasphemy, a terrible blasphemy. A god who, purely from ambition, permits the things usually told about paradise to happen in paradise, which is what most people think, doing it not because of the intentions described in *Occult Science, an Outline*, but the way it is usually described, really and truly would not be a sublime god. And to ascribe such an ambition to the god is blasphemy.

One will only arrive at the reality in this field if one does not consider the inherited traits which pass from ancestors to descendants in moral terms, but sees them in supersensible terms even though perceptible through the senses, looking to the supersensible without first giving a moral interpretation, and seeing in supersensible light the things one should not with rabbinical theology make into a moral interpretation of the world. Rabbinical theology will always intellectually reinterpret the powers of heredity that are spread out through the sense-perceptible world. We should train ourselves to see the spirit in things and so discover the spirit also in the inherited traits we see in the sense-perceptible world. That is the crux of the matter. My main concern is to have you realize that without this Mystery on Golgotha humanity would at that time have denied the spirit, having learned to deny the spirit in the hereditary traits which were evident in the sense-perceptible world, and people would have come more and more to use rabbinical and socialist interpretations instead of taking the spiritual view. Tremendously much depends on it that we know it to be necessary to say, 'You'll not comprehend anything in the sense-perceptible world unless you equip yourself to deal with something which is indeed a supersensible stranger in the sense-perceptible world because it has spiritual connections.' Things connected with heredity must be considered by taking the spiritual, the supersensible view. The intellect which has made spiritual into something which is sense-perceptible although it is indeed something supersensible, making it into something moral that is grasped with the intellect, is the spirit which opposes the spirit of the Christ, the spirit of the Mystery on Golgotha. So much about heredity and about death.

Yes, the Church Fathers themselves were able to establish that among pagans too there were many people who were convinced of immortality. But what was that about? Well, in early times people did realize that death is a supersensible phenomenon even in the world perceived through the senses. By the time of the Mystery on Golgotha people had ruined their philosophy of life by taking death to be a sense-perceptible phenomenon, and thus spreading the powers of death also through the rest of the sense-perceptible world. Death must be considered a stranger to that world. This alone will make it possible to have a pure science of the natural order.

Added to this were the things which some philosophers of antiquity in decline thought about immortality. They considered the immortal principle in man, rightly so, for they said to themselves that death is present in the sense-perceptible world. They did however say this from a corrupted philosophy of life, for if it had not been corrupted they would have had to say that death is not present in the sense-perceptible world; it only appears to enter into that world. They gradually came to think of a sense-perceptible world where death had a place. In doing so, one does, however, ruin everything else for oneself. Of course, you also do so if you generally think that death has its place in it. But when they did so from a corrupt philosophy of life they also had to say something else to themselves, and that was: 'We have to turn to something or other which contradicts death, something supersensible which contradicts death.' In the decline of antiquity people had a corrupted philosophy as they turned to the impersonal spiritual principle that this immortal spiritual world—which they did actually call something else—was the luciferic world. What matters is not what we call things but what is truly powering in our ideas, and so it was the luciferic world. Although different words were used, the philosophers of paganism in decline really said nothing else in all their interpretations but: 'As souls escaping death we want to flee to Lucifer who will take us in and we shall then be immortal. We die into the realm of Lucifer.' That was the true meaning.

Today we still see the last remnants of the powers at work which reign in human insight from all the preconditions of which I spoke today. What do you really have to say to yourselves if you take the words which I have spoken from initiation science today seriously? You have to say: 'There is man's origin and his end. These two must not be grasped with the intellect we have as human beings, an intellect which is fit for the natural world. One arrives at a wrong view of both the supersensible and the sense-perceptible if one mixes birth and death in with the sense-perceptible; they do not belong there, being strangers to it. One ruins both one's understanding of the spirit and one's understanding of nature.' And the consequence? One consequence is this, for instance. There is an anthropology in which the origin of man is ascribed to very lowly creatures, doing this in a very natural-scientific and very clever way. Go through all the anthropologies where the origin of man is said to go back to lowly creatures which are envisaged as if something which is said to be found among indigenous people had been there at the beginning of the human race! Such notions are a perfectly correct judgement in natural science. But the conclusion to be drawn is the following. It is wrong exactly because it is scientifically correct, correct in the light of a natural science where birth and death are believed to be part of the sense-perceptible world. Things were not like that at the true origin of man. When Kant and Laplace developed their theory they did so on the basis of natural science. It seems that no objection can be raised to their theory, but it was exactly because the theory was developed on the basis of natural science that the situation was different. You will arrive at the right knowledge if for both the origin and the goal of man and for the origin and goal of the earth you accept the opposite to be true of what is considered right today in natural science. Anthroposophy will provide the right information about the earth's origin the more it is contradictory to what can be said in the natural science which is considered to be correct today. Anthroposophy does not contradict natural science! It lets it stand but instead of broadening it beyond its limits it draws attention to the points where a supersensible view must come in. The more logical anthroposophy is, the more correct is it with regard to the natural order which is necessary to and inherent in present-day human beings, the more will it *not* say what was *not* at the beginning of human and earth existence. And natural science will be less correct about death the more people fantasize on the basis of the ideas it provides.

Without the Mystery on Golgotha it would have been the fate of human beings on earth that exactly the most important things would have had to be considered on the basis of a corrupt philosophy of life. For it absolutely did not depend on a human failing but merely on human evolution. It simply happened in the course of that evolution that people came to consider themselves to be this combination of flesh, blood and bone. An ancient Egyptian would have found it utterly comical if someone had said that the figure going about on two legs, consisting of blood, flesh and bone was a human being. But these things do not depend on theoretical reflections. We cannot dream them up nor dream them away. No, it gradually came to be an accepted thing to consider oneself to be the form which is made of flesh and blood and bone though in fact one is the image of all the hierarchies. So much error spread about this that oddly enough some individuals who came upon the error stumbled into an even greater error.

Yes, some did come upon it but they did so in an ahrimanic and luciferic way—that human beings are not the combination of flesh and blood and bone. They would say: 'If we are something better than this combination of flesh and blood and bone, let us above all despise all flesh and see the human being as something more sublime. Let us then cast aside the sense-perceptible human being.' Yet this image made of flesh and blood and bone together with ether body and astral body, as we see it before us, is a sham. In reality man is the absolute image of the deity. It is not that we want to see the devil in the world (as I said, that is an error); it is because we want to and should see the god in our own world within us that it is an error to identify with sense-perceptible nature. It is also quite wrong to say to oneself, 'Yes, I am a most sublime being, terribly sublime, and there [Fig. 13] is this inferior, horrid environment.' That is not how it is, but rather like this. There we have the realms of the higher hierarchies, all the divine

Fig. 13

spirits [Fig. 14]. They considered it their divine goal to join forces in creating a form. This form has the outer appearance of the human body. Into this form, which is calumniated, miserably calumniated when people consider it inferior, the Spirits of Form have placed the human I, the present-day soul, which is the baby among the different levels of human existence, as I have often said [dot in the blue circle].

So if there had been no Mystery on Golgotha human beings could only have developed wrong ideas about heredity and about death, and those wrong ideas would have got worse and worse. They do sometimes come up in an atavistic way today—in some socialist bodies a philosophy of life is promulgated today which is atavistic— in views where death and birth are included among the phenomena of the physical world. As humanity continues to evolve it would have to happen that the gate to the supersensible world would close for the human being and anything he found in the physical world of the supersensible; heredity and death would lead him astray, would be

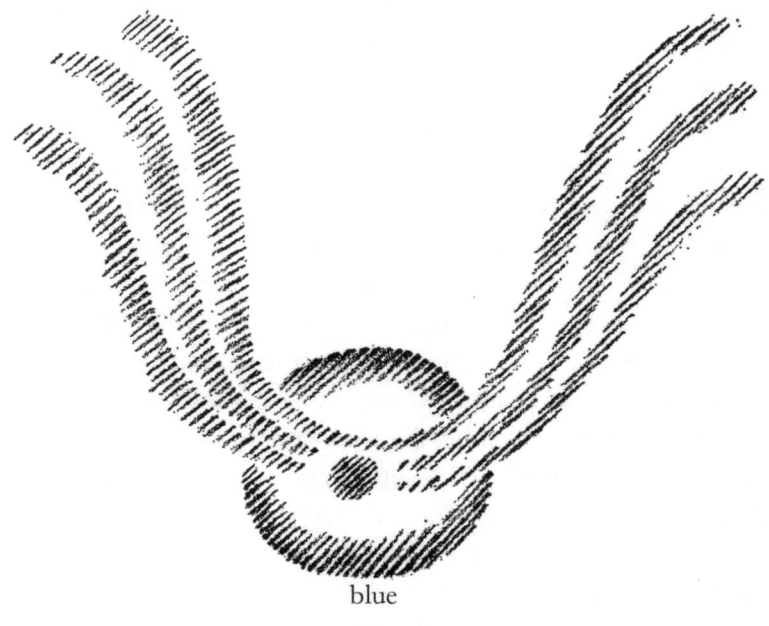

blue

Fig. 14

tempters who would come and say, 'We are part of the physical world,' when in fact they were not. We will only come to the truth if we do not believe in a natural world which pulls the wool over our eyes concerning death and birth. Man's position in the world is that paradoxical.

Something had to be implanted in human beings that would maintain the balance and guide them away from the idea that heredity and death were physical phenomena in human life. To do this, something had to be put before them which made it evident that death and heredity are supersensible and not sensible phenomena. The event which showed humanity the truth again about these things had to be beyond the reach of ordinary human powers, for those were getting corrupted and needed a strong nudge in the opposite direction to correct them. That nudge was the Mystery on Golgotha. It entered into human evolution as something supersensible so that people would have the choice of either believing in this supersensible element, in which case you could only gain insight into it in a supersensible way, or accepted the views which would inevitably result if they considered death and inherited traits to belong to the sense-perceptible world. Hence the ingredients of a true view of the Mystery on Golgotha are the two borderline facts of the Mystery—resurrection, which cannot be thought of without its link to the immaculate conception, but not in the way in which the wool is pulled over people's eyes, pretending it is a fact, but in the supersensible way, and going through death in a supersensible way. These are the two basic facts that must be the boundaries of the life of Christ Jesus. No one understands the resurrection which is meant to be the concept that is presented as the true concept instead of the false idea that death belongs to the physical world, no one understands this resurrection unless he also accepts its correlate, immaculate conception, birth as a supersensible fact. People want to understand this—resurrection and immaculate conception—and today's Protestant theologians actually want to grasp this fact in theology, using ordinary human common sense, but that common sense is but a pupil of the sense-perceptible world, of the corrupt view gained through the senses which has evolved since the Mystery on Golgotha. And when they cannot grasp it they become followers of Harnack or the like, denying resurrection, producing all kinds of phrases about it. As to the immaculate conception, they consider this to be altogether something no one who has any sense would talk about.

Yet it is closely connected with the Mystery on Golgotha that it holds within it the metamorphosis of death, that is, its metamorphosis from a sensible fact into a supersensible fact, and the metamorphosis of heredity, that is, that where the physical world pulls the wool over our eyes about heredity, which is connected with the mystery of birth, birth is transposed into the supersensible with the immaculate conception.

Whatever may have been said in error or inadequately about these things, humanity's task is not to accept these things without understanding but to develop the supersensible insights that will let them grasp these things which cannot be grasped by sensible means. When you think of the lecture courses where I spoke about these things and particularly also of the lectures on the Fifth Gospel,[70] you will find a number of ways for understanding these two things, though only by supersensible means. For it is the case that for as long as common sense continues to be a pupil of the senses, which is how it has to seem to people today in their philosophy of life, humankind will not be able to grasp this fact. It is exactly where the most sublime facts in earthly life are such that the mind, being a pupil of life in the senses, cannot grasp them that they are indeed true. It is not surprising, therefore, that external science is fighting against initiation science for this is about things which quite naturally, exactly because they do not contradict genuine natural science, must contradict a natural order which originates in a corrupt view of the natural world. Theology, too, has often taken the wrong direction, albeit a different one from that of corrupt naturalism.

If you consider what I said yesterday, that human beings can only arrive at the right view of the Mystery on Golgotha after death, you will no longer find it incomprehensible, if you think about it, that on dying, going through the gate of death, human beings enter into a world where they can no longer be told the fable that death is part of the physical world, for they then see death from the other side—I have often spoken of this—and they learn more and more to consider death from the other side. This will prepare them more and more to consider the Mystery on Golgotha, too, in its true form. We have to say, therefore: If the Mystery on Golgotha had not come about—but anything we say in this way can only be grasped supersensibly—humanity would die. There would also be evil in the world, there would be wisdom in the world. But human evolution made people succumb to a corrupt view of the natural world, and so they had to have the wrong idea about death. Wanting to turn to immortality they therefore turn to Lucifer and succumb to Lucifer exactly because they want to turn to the spirit. They are like animals if they do not turn to the spirit, and they succumb to Lucifer if they do turn to the spirit. To see the world looking ahead—one wants to be immortal in Lucifer. To see it looking back—one interprets the world by changing the element which is supersensible even as a hereditary trait into something moral and thus fabricates the medieval blasphemy of original sin.

Genuine devotion to the Mystery on Golgotha will save one from all this. It provides the world with a true, supersensibly gained view of birth and death. Such a true view should cure humanity of the wrong, corrupt view. This makes Christ Jesus also the healer, the saviour. Because of this and because human beings chose the path that led to a corrupt philosophy of life not because they were good for nothing but in the course of their evolution, their essential nature, the Christ is also a healer, truly not only the teacher but also the physician for humanity.

These things have to be considered, but, as I said—and I have repeated it again and again, and it needs supersensible insight to see this—when we ask ourselves, 'What insights would the souls have gained which in the second century inspired an individual such as Tertullian?' we have to look to the dead who may have been contemporaries of Christ Jesus and in the second century inspired such a man as Tertullian. As there was much corruption of insights in the world some things would of course be wrong, obscure, having one touch or another of obscurity. But if we hear the contemporaries of the Christ in Tertullian's words, contemporaries who were dead at the time but inspired the writer, we can understand how he was able to say such a thing as, 'The Son of God has been crucified. We do not feel shame because it is ignominious.' People had to arrive at seeing a thing as ignominious because views had become corrupt. The event which is the meaning of the earth in the highest degree would show itself to be an ignominious act in human life. The Son of God has died. It is wholly credible because it is inept. *Prorsus credibile est, quia ineptum est.* Being foolish ineptitude for anything which human beings can grasp throughout life using ordinary common sense, it is exactly a true fact in the sense in which I have put it to you today. He was buried and rose again, and this is certain because it is impossible—because there is no such thing in the corrupt way of looking at nature.

If you take Tertullian's words in a supersensible sense as inspired by contemporaries of the Christ who had then been dead for a long time, you might say to yourself: 'Yes, certainly, Tertullian took it in the way he was able to take it in with the state of soul he was in.' You will, however, be able to sense their inspired origin. Only someone who was so thoroughly in the supersensible with his knowledge that he would speak of the demons as witnesses of the divine as if they were human witnesses would, of course, have had access to such an origin. Tertullian wrote that the demons themselves said that they were demons and that they acknowledged the Christ. That was the precondition for Tertullian being able to perceive anything of what was inspired into him.

For those who want to be Christians in the wrong sense this is a most uncomfortable business. Just consider, if even the demons speak the truth and point to the true Christ, those demons might at some point be questioned by a Jesuit! The demons might engage someone of whom the Jesuit says that he is in touch with demons in conversation about the real origin of the Jesuits' Christ, and the demon might then say: 'Yours is not the Christ; it is the one of which the other speaks who is the Christ.' You understand the Jesuit's fear of the spiritual world. You understand that it is profoundly upsetting if one fears being exposed to the danger of being disavowed from some corner of the spiritual world! One might then produce Tertullian as one's principal witness and say: 'Well, dear Jesuit, the demon itself is saying that yours is the false god, and Tertullian, who you must acknowledge was a proper Church Father, says that it is the very demons which speak the truth about themselves and about the Christ, which is also what it says in the Bible.' In short, the matter is getting most precarious as soon as it is admitted by the supersensible world, albeit in an unjustifiable form, that demons bear witness to the truth. Even if one were to call on Lucifer, he would not speak untruthfully of the Christ! But it might become evident that something else is untruth concerning the Christ.

Initiation truths sometimes sound different from the things which people are comfortable with. This does mean that all kinds of chaos arise when people attempt to introduce initiation truths to the external world today, especially when such initiation truths have to be introduced into the immediate reality. Yes, as soon as the field opens up where things are made known from the supersensible sphere, conflicts arise, some of them quite extraordinary if considered in relation to the things that do not well forth from the supersensible.

We can often apply this to everyday life. I did feel a certain satisfaction when a suggestion I had made just for myself in my teaching—and things I say in my teaching I say from a personal conviction that is not meant to be binding for anyone—was taken up and this building was in accord with our experience of the times called the Goetheanum. Even if we include some supersensible impulses it seems to me to be right and good. If, however, someone demanded that I provided a list of all the reasons, counting them out on my thumb and all other fingers, for something that is felt out of a profound need, all the pros and cons, this would feel like a real sham wisdom to me. One often finds oneself in this situation, particularly when bringing supersensible impulses into play that are meant for the will. People often say, 'I don't understand this, I cannot grasp it.' Well, does it matter so very much whether another person or oneself is able to grasp something? What does 'grasp' mean? It means nothing else but to put the matter in the light where the thoughts are at ease, thoughts which one has comfortably found to suit one for decades. Otherwise 'understand', as people call it, does not mean much compared to the truths revealed from the supersensible world. When the supersensible spheres are not just something one is teaching but are meant to intervene directly in the will, in the sphere of actions, it is always bad if people ask questions intellectually: 'Why, why, why is this or that so?' or 'How can one understand this and this and this?' With regard to this one should get used to seeing certain things of the supersensible world in parallel to things one is continually accepting for facts of the natural world, but only in parallel. I don't know—if you go outside and Rover or Wolf or whatever name the dog has bites you and you had not been bitten before but have now been bitten—do you then ask, 'Why did the dog bite me?' or, 'How can I understand this?' What connection is there to make sense? You have to let the facts tell you. In the same way certain supersensible things just have to be told. There are many of them, as you can tell from what I hinted at today, that two seeming things hide their true nature in the sense-perceptible world—human death and birth. They are really bringing something supersensible into the world of the senses, are strangers to that world but wear masks, pretending to be part of it and in doing so also spreading their false mask over the rest of nature. Modern man therefore has to see the rest of nature, too, in the wrong light.

To understand things thoroughly, taking them thoroughly into one's search for insight—this will be asked of man in the future, asked especially by the Spirits of the Age of those who want to seek insight for the future and unfold their will in a particular sphere. The demand should apply particularly to the academic fields of theology, medicine, law, philosophy, natural science, technology itself and social life, and indeed politics—politics, yes indeed, truly, even this strange construct! Those who understand the age ought to introduce the knowledge gained through spiritual science into all of these.

LECTURE 13

11 OCTOBER 1918

By now you know from all kinds of different angles that the evolution of modern humanity went through a crucial point in the fifteenth century, at the beginning of the fifth post-Atlantean civilization. We know that this was the time when humanity entered into evolution through the spiritual soul. In the preceding Graeco-Roman period evolution proceeded mainly in the region of the rational or mind soul. It is important not to be merely theoretical, abstract, about the fact that we entered into the age of the spiritual soul in the fifteenth century. We must accept it in all seriousness, having the will, as it were, to consider all the time: 'What should be our state of soul, what should we do to this state of soul so that we do justice to the fact that we are now in the age of spiritual soul evolution?'

Above all it is a matter of humanity being given cause in this age of the spiritual soul to make every conscious effort to arrive at certain views which were not consciously striven for in previous ages. We know that among the many more or less important things affected by what has just been said there was also the most important of all events in earthly life—the event on Golgotha. As I have stressed on many occasions, when the event on Golgotha first entered into human evolution, human souls were not yet able to grasp its significance fully. Full conscious awareness of the event can only come gradually. I have also stressed on several occasions that the powers of which we are aware made human beings develop the tendency to lag behind in their development on the one hand and to overshoot their goal on the other. In the cultural sphere we therefore see numerous endeavours to hold on to the unconscious way of grasping the event on Golgotha and use humanity's conscious development as little as possible with regard to the event. We had an instance recently of the struggle between those who want people as far as possible to accept only the old established, unconscious knowledge of the Mystery on Golgotha, whilst in modern Roman Catholic endeavours,[71] as they are called, efforts were made, though the means were inadequate, to advance in understanding also the Mystery on Golgotha in a more conscious way than has been done so far. Resistance to making the effort to gain insight in spiritual science into the Mystery on Golgotha merely represents an effort made by those who would prefer to keep this Mystery on Golgotha in the unconscious sphere in human souls.

In a fruitful way of moving towards an understanding that is particularly necessary for the spiritual soul's development, we must above all try and get a clear idea of the human being's essential nature from many different angles, not a lot of talk but getting our bearings from the facts. Let us consider the present age as far as possible in its facts. Let us first of all draw attention to facts which are particularly significant for evolution in the age of the spiritual soul.

In recent times people have been referring to the 'age of science' with great pride if not arrogance. In a sense they are right, for it is not only people who have studied natural science who live in this age of science but practically all educated people live in the natural-scientific stream of the present age. You see, it is not a question of whether one thinks the way modern botanists do about plants, zoologists about animals, anthropologists about human beings in this age of science. It is not a question of knowing anthropology, botany or zoology but of having given one's thoughts an orientation along natural-scientific lines. The orientation of natural-scientific thinking is that of most people today who have had even just something to do with education in schools, and thus are not illiterate or almost illiterate. The people who count today therefore think in the natural-scientific way. Some of them may also be regular churchgoers, listening to the sermons, and be religious, pious. You know, just ask yourselves how much influence this religious piety still has on life in general, even if one believes oneself to be faithful or that one ought to be faithful. The religious sentiments developed within one religious confession or another have extraordinarily little power or influence on people's thinking about the world. In the whole of external life, among the majority of the population, people think along natural-scientific lines. For most people today the religious element is merely an added extra. It is reasonable to say, therefore, that the more recent age of the spiritual soul is proud, indeed arrogant, about scientific achievements and the natural-scientific way of thinking connected with this. People today show a certain arrogance when looking at earlier ages.

Consider the sentiments, the self-satisfied, middle-class sentiments proper people of today have about their ancestors, saying that they believed in ghosts. One need not say anything much against their saying that their ancestors believed in ghosts, for they did so. Today we'll not so much consider the subject matter of 'our ancestors believed in ghosts, and we are so intelligent that we no longer believe in ghosts', but concentrate more on the feelings we have when we consider the people of today, how they think about their stupid ancestors who believed in ghosts and how mankind has finally grown out of this and does no longer believe in ghosts. The opinion that the ancestors believed in ghosts is in itself a half-truth and therefore an extraordinarily dangerous truth; half-truths are often worse than complete errors, for the latter are easily spotted, whilst half-truths haunt the world like ghosts themselves.

It is true enough that when we go back to earlier ages, to the time before and after the Mystery on Golgotha and even earlier times, we mainly find that people believed in ghosts, in demons. I spoke about this the other day in connection with the great Tertullian. That is correct. But this age was preceded by another one where people would also speak of ghosts but not in the way in which they did in the times I have just been characterizing. In the second and in the first post-Atlantean eras people would talk of ghosts knowing that this was the fruit of their powers of imagination. This would only enable them to imagine ghosts. But behind those ghosts which they imagined were images of the spiritual world.

So there was a long period when people would imagine ghosts but know that behind the ghosts which they saw in images was the spiritual world. In a way they were creating an image of the spiritual world in their minds, a world of spectres. Then the spiritual world came to be more or less forgotten, or rather lost from view. Mere images remained and were then taken for real, and belief in ghosts came from this, though it was merely the ruins of what had gone before.

We are thus able to say: 'The ancients developed a state of mind by developing the given powers, instinctively limiting themselves to having nothing but ghosts before the mind's eye.' In those early times they envisaged the gods in the form of those ghosts, and later they took the ghosts for real. It is not that the ghosts were untrue but people's views of them became untrue.

Well, modern man admits that the ancestors imagined ghosts and that it is superstition to imagine ghosts; pleased with himself and self-satisfied he thinks he is a clever man. He'll not accept that the people of early times used ghosts to gain a picture of the spiritual world, for the spiritual world does not hold much interest for him today, only the natural world. He thus feels infinitely superior to those ancestors as he develops ideas about the natural world in his mind. The age of the spiritual soul does, however, call for something which is different from the things our ancestors were able to do. We have to gain enlightenment about what our view of nature really is.

We are also developing ideas in our mind as modern, self-satisfied, enlightened and intelligent people; we develop ideas about nature. But when we examine our ideas about the natural world without prejudice we find that we do have those ideas but that we cannot encompass nature in forming those ideas. There are always limits to our understanding, as people tend to say. I have repeatedly spoken of a modern philosopher, someone who has not become widely known as an author but has divulged things which others do not divulge, not having gone into them so deeply. Richard Wahle[72] has written two major and a number of smaller books. He may be considered to be an exponent of modern man; we might say that everyone orientated towards the natural world really thinks the way Richard Wahle does. He has considered all the consequences, however, and this means that he became a professor of philosophy and immediately wrote a great tome on the end of philosophy, trying to prove on the basis of natural science that there should be no such thing as philosophy. In this tome, *Ueber den Mechanismus des geistigen Lebens* (on the mechanism of intellectual life), this professor of philosophy and philosophical author says strange things about his colleagues, the philosophers. He has said more or less that philosophers are and philosophy is like a restaurant. Before, chefs and waiters would be standing around and produce inedible meals for the guests; now they were standing around with nothing to do.[73] This one chef or waiter or philosopher says, therefore, that philosophy can be compared to a restaurant where chefs and waiters—his philosopher colleagues—produced nothing but unhealthy food in the past, and things had gone so far that now the chefs and waiters were not even producing unhealthy food but were just standing around. Being such a chef, waiter or philosopher himself it must of course seem to him that he is really quite useless as he stands there. He therefore set himself a final task, as he sees it, in his two books; after this there'll be no more philosophers, he'd be the last of them. That, approximately, is the deeper meaning of his books. He's to be the last, for he has set himself the task—well, how can I characterize it? Richard Wahle as one waiter or chef among others, who used to produce unhealthy meals of philosophy and now are left with nothing to do at all, is busily producing a poison among these chefs and waiters that will kill them all! That is an extraordinarily interesting scene! If one is used to looking at the evolution of history symptomatically this is a serious and highly remarkable symptom of the present time. For this philosopher shows great acuity, going deeply into the problems of thinking in the natural-scientific way.

I am convinced that, having picked up one of these books, most of you will soon put it down again for these books are written in modern philosophers' academic language which, as you know, is a terminology that cannot be understood unless one has studied it. Anyone who knows how to handle this language can see that there is a vast amount of acuity in them, the kind of acuity people are able to show today, and that behind the pitiful circumscriptions found in the books is an intuitive insight which must however be defined with a different kind of precision from the one used by Richard Wahle. One might say, however, that this peculiar passionate element, this peculiar passion he has to set about producing the poison I spoke of for the other chefs and waiters, a passion which shows that insight throbs in him, for otherwise he, a well-established professor of philosophy, would not have said that human beings had no more wisdom than do animals,[74] and differed from animals only in that the animals at least were not so sensible as to seek wisdom, whereas human beings do seek wisdom, which means they are sensible enough to have an inkling of something which actually cannot exist for them.

An important insight is throbbing there, though it is more or less negative by nature—in there insight is throbbing concerning present-day knowledge of nature. This knowledge of nature is meant to bring to mind nature in the form of ideas for the modern mind. Yet when we really look into the ideas developed about nature, developed in highly academic circles, we find that oddly enough the human mind thinks up nothing but ghosts. In earlier times people thought up ghosts for their gods; modern people think up ghosts for facts of nature. The ideas people have and consider to be natural science relate to nature the way a ghost does to reality. Someone like Richard Wahle sensed that in the age of the spiritual soul we will have to realize that we are not really superior to our ancestors. They used their powers of mind to develop ideas of ghosts, and we are also developing ideas of ghosts. The only difference is that our ancestors had better looking ghosts than those produced by modern thinkers in natural science. Essentially these are horrific tissues of abstract concepts. And they are ghosts, just as the ghosts of our ancestors were ghosts. The relationship of these ghosts of natural science, this ghostly natural science itself, relate to reality just as the old ghosts related to divine realities.

In the age of the spiritual soul it is right for us to be aware of the fact that living in ideas one is indeed living in ghosts. It is extraordinarily important to realize this important fact in the age of the spiritual soul. The ancients did not live in the age of the spiritual soul and therefore were not obliged to gain awareness of the fact that their ideas were ghosts. Our natural scientists are also imagining ghosts; but in the age of the spiritual soul it is our task to know that we are also imagining ghosts, that we are having ideas not about nature but merely about nature ghosts. Our ancestors had developed from their ancestors who had not taken the ghosts for real but for images of divine influences, images of supersensible intelligences. And in the age of the spiritual soul we must rise to the point where we admit that our natural-scientific ghosts are not reality—though natural scientists believe them to be—but point to realities which we are meant to look for through them. If we are deceived about the ghostly nature of natural science we also cannot gain enlightenment about the human being. We can look at the natural world with our ghostly ideas, and it will nevertheless be there in front of us in its true form. In the age of the spiritual soul we must gain conscious, living experience of the human being. In that case it will not do to apply ghostly ideas, for in that way we make ourselves into ghosts. And much of that has certainly been happening.

Goethe's theory of evolution is not wrong. It goes in the right direction because the aim is to understand the real human being. According to the materialist Darwinian theory of evolution man is descended from the animals. But although something in us does stem from the animals, or at least has a common origin with them, that is not the human being as such; it is the ghost of us which is known in natural science. In that science, the human being is first made into a ghost as well, for all one knows is his appearance as a ghost. Then people ask: 'Where does this ghost come from?' We will only arrive at the truth when we discover that not the human being but his ghost can be treated in the way in which it is done in natural science. One has to live, however, and you will unhesitatingly admit that you would not have gone here, come here, if you had not come yourself but sent the homunculus, the ghost which according to natural science you are meant to think. If only the homunculi which live in your self-awareness were sitting here I also would not be able to speak to these homunculi. You do bring your real human being here, but not in your conscious awareness. In the age of the spiritual soul it will, however, be necessary to have conscious awareness of the real human being. We must advance from homunculus to homo. If that were not to happen, human beings would also come to experience the polar opposite of being ghosts. If one does not take oneself for a ghost but for real, as the ancients did—they did see themselves as ghosts but because they had atavistic powers in them reality was still able to enter into them, whilst nothing enters into modern human beings except what comes through the spiritual soul—and if one has only the ghost of the human being in one's spiritual soul, then moral and spiritual impulses cannot come in through this spiritual soul. Look at the things that come with the ghostly science of nature and you will find that in these more recent times, when we have a ghostly science of nature, it is really never accepted that impulses for acting morally come to us from the spiritual world itself. The moral impulses that govern human actions today are most ancient, coming from atavistic ages, for modern humanity does not want to ask the spirit when impulses to act emerge but ask nature instead. They want to ask: 'What is the nature of man? What drives are there in human nature?'

It is terrible how humanity of more recent times really only wants to question nature, though they know only a ghost of nature. Because of this, reality lies and is powering unconsciously in modern human beings, asking to come in via the conscious mind, the human spirit, because we are living in the age of the spiritual soul.

I have now explained something which is important in the present-day situation. I have sought to show that in the present situation matters are such that on the one hand people develop ghostly ideas about nature, turning into experimenting naturalists in every field; people then approach nature as she really is and consider the human being as he really is. But the ghostly concepts of natural science are inadequate means. Those people therefore do not become observers of humanity but merely observers of the human ghost—psychoanalysts. Psychoanalysis is very much the offspring of ghostly natural science and I therefore always call psychoanalysis something which is using inadequate means.

We may ask what has brought it about? The situation has arisen because the constellation which has arisen in Earth evolution had led to a quite specific relationship between mainstream human evolution and the ahrimanic and luciferic lateral streams. I have been referring in various ways to the mainstream and then also to the two lateral streams, the luciferic which came in Lemurian times and the ahrimanic which came in Atlantean times. These three streams are there in human evolution and whatever happens in human evolution is under the influence of these three streams.

Everything in these streams caused an important nodal point to come about in a particular year of human evolution. In that year, a nodal point came in human evolution where the three streams came together. This is merely covered over by chaotic external conditions, so that one does not see exactly what happens but only the chaos. This important nodal point came around the year 666 after the Mystery on Golgotha. At that time, in AD 666, something that should have happened and could have happened did not happen. You will hear why that was so in a minute.

A significant spirit might have come in 666—visible to external humanity, especially in the Occident—though it would not have appeared on the physical plane. But it would have been clearly perceptible to humanity, also externally, so that people would have become subject to it. If this spirit had appeared in the configuration which it had planned, we would not have the year 1918 now but—

minus 666—only 1252. For this spirit would have inspired people to have based their calendar on it as well. If this spirit could have appeared as planned, it would have brought about something unusual. The point is that 333 years earlier, in AD 333, came the midpoint of the fourth post-Atlantean age, of the Graeco-Roman period. You can work it out for yourselves. It began in 747 and ended in 1413, making it 2160 years, which is as it should be. One half of 2160 years is 1080 years, and that many years had passed by the middle of that post-Atlantean age. Take away 747 years and you have 333; AD 333 was the middle of the Graeco-Roman age. This midpoint did not come before the Mystery on Golgotha but really only after it. It signifies the greatest possible though in fact not external reality, for the other streams also came into it in external reality. If evolution had continued in a straight line and there had not been the lateral streams, that would have been the proper midpoint, and it would have been the high point in the age of the rational or mind soul. In that case, the rational or mind soul would have had to come to its utmost, highest degree of development. This did not happen because the serpent had already got in, as it were, proposing to undertake a particular procedure with human evolution 333 years later, in 666.

The procedure to which human evolution was to be subjected by this spirit, Sorat, the beast, the dragon, was to be that having fully developed its spiritual soul at a time when human beings had only come as far as the rational or mind soul it would give human beings all the achievements in soul and spirit which they did not have through their rational or mind soul and would only be able to make their own when they developed the spiritual soul, which would be at a later time. The culture of the spiritual soul was to be given to humanity prematurely. The situation in the world was such that 666 would have been the best time for this; the spirit would then have had such an influence on the earth that it might have said: 'I will now teach human beings everything they will ever be able to find with their spiritual soul. I will now, in the age of the rational or mind soul, instil in human beings something which the gods whose enemy I am only want to give them in the next period of civilization.' Its aim was to mix the rational or mind soul together with the spiritual soul in a way that was not justifiable.

Anyway, it would hardly have been possible to get the whole human race, who are after all at different stages of evolution, to take the content of the spiritual soul into their rational or mind souls. It might, however, have been possible with a large number of human beings. It could have succeeded so that if this spirit achieved its aim there would have been a number of geniuses in the world, especially among the educated people of the western world. For they would indeed have been geniuses. Something that people would not have been able entirely to go along with, people who were still lagging behind in evolution, and will normally only know in 2493—remember, in the middle of the age which started in 1413; for if you add half a period of civilization, which would be 1080 years, to 1413 this will give you 2493—could have bubbled over at that time (not the way it would later have been but through powers of foresighted fantasy) and reveal itself to an unsuspecting humanity in the western world.

Strange phenomena were planned. If you consider the ideals of present-day natural science and hear people speak of the great advances made in recent decades—just imagine the ideas which the same people might have as to what humanity on earth would be like in 2493, considering how clever they are already in 1918! They would not have produced machines and so on, experimented, done things the hard way, but with powers of genius they would have had an idea of things in advance and would also have done much. The year 666 was meant to flood humanity with insight and a civilization which the right and original gods have planned for man in the third millennium. You cannot imagine, need not imagine, the situation in which the educated world, as it is called, would have been if it had been flooded in this way with this knowledge of 666. Lacking the necessary self-discipline, people would have grown depraved. For if you look up the histories, which of course tell only one side of the state of soul people had in 666, you will certainly discover how those people would have behaved if they had had geniuses among them in this way. They had made such great advances by 1914; think where they would have got to if they had been flooded with all that wisdom of the beast! But that had been the plan of certain higher spirits, particularly one that was ahrimanic by nature and intended to be the leader of these spirits. This would have appeared, though not on the physical plane, but it would definitely have appeared.

It had to be prevented. However many people may think that nothing should be withheld from humanity when it is possible to give such a thing, it had to be prevented because it was not in line in the spiritual sense with human evolution. It was possible to prevent it by counterbalancing it. Consider—333 was the midpoint of the fourth post-Atlantean age, and 333 years later came the year 666. Then the ahrimanic powers would have taken arrogance of the materialistic kind to tremendous heights, though with powers of genius. The only way of counterbalancing this was for the spirit to come on the scene 333 years earlier, that is at the beginning of our chronology, to appear and put its own substance into human evolution to maintain the balance and prevent that 333 years after 333 this spirit would appear of which I have spoken.

Here you have the beam of the balance [Fig. 15]. It is 333 years from 333 to 666. And there's the other beam which maintains the balance—from 333 back to the Mystery on Golgotha. This creates a state of balance. Something happened which took place behind the

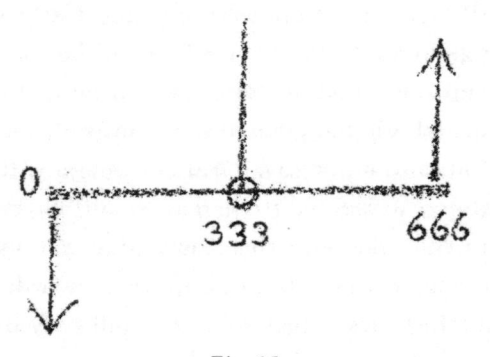

Fig. 15

scenes of external profane history, as it were. Something that could have happened was prevented by something else which did indeed happen, but can also only be grasped with supersensible powers, as I said the other day, for the whole process of supersensible significance serves the evolution of the earth.

What would have happened from 666 onwards if the beast had been able to intervene in human evolution and there had not been the Mystery on Golgotha? You can get an idea of what might have happened if you consider the things I characterized earlier. People were hastening towards the fifteenth century; if the beast of 666 had done its mischief until the fifteenth century then it would have got complete hold of what was coming. It was the ghostly natural-scientific view of the world which was coming and with it the emancipation of human drives. The spiritual soul was meant only to grasp the ghost of the human being, which meant that the real human being was left behind; he could not grasp himself. Human beings can only become truly human in the age of the spiritual soul by doing so consciously. Otherwise they will continue to be animals, lagging behind in their evolution as human beings.

The spirit which intended to intervene in 666 wanted to make itself into a god. It said: 'There will be people who will no longer turn their attention to the spirit; the spirit will be of no interest to them. I will see to it'—and this is something this spirit did still achieve—'that a council will be held in Constantinople in 869 where the spirit will be abolished. People will take no further interest in the spirit; they will turn their attention to the natural world, developing ghostly ideas about it. Then, with human beings not noticing because they will not perceive themselves to be real human beings but ghosts, I shall have the spiritual soul completely in my power. I shall deceive human beings about themselves; I will let them see themselves only as ghosts, and then pour all the wisdom of the spiritual soul prematurely into their rational or mind soul. Then I'll have them, I'll have taken hold of them.'

What would have been achieved? If human beings developed more or less normally, with that spirit not intervening, they would advance to Spirit Self, Life Spirit and Spirit Man. But they would be utterly deprived of this. The intention was that they would stay with the spiritual soul, being given what earth has to give and no more, and not move on to Jupiter, Venus and Vulcan evolution. If human beings received the contents of the spiritual soul at the right time and through their own inherent powers, then the normal evolution they would have gone through would have given them the ability to advance to Spirit Self and so on. But the aim was to prevent this. Human beings were to have the spiritual soul and its contents instilled prematurely into their rational or mind soul. Their development would then have stopped at the spiritual soul; there would be an absurdity of knowledge handed over to them from the sixth era onwards. But that would put an end to them; they would not develop further but incorporate it all in their spiritual soul, in their utmost egotism, at the service of the spiritual soul.

It was the intention of the spirit that wanted to appear in 666 to cut off future evolution on earth, see to it that it would be cut off—to conclude evolution when it had gone through the Saturn, Sun, Moon and Earth stages, with humanity not taking the road which the spirits from the higher hierarchies wanted to take with them, spirits who had from the beginning taken normal evolution in hand.

The only way of preventing this was that this balance, this state of equilibrium, that entered into the cosmic evolution of man with the intervention of the Christ, the Mystery on Golgotha, was made to come as far back from the midpoint of the fourth post-Atlantean age as the time when the beast intended to intervene lay ahead.

You see how things are connected behind the scenes, the facts, of outward maya. In the age of the spiritual soul, the only possible way is for people to gain insight into such things. For we need to be aware and not go on unawares. Consider, we are all of us in the situation which could only come about—as it says in a certain 'general epistle' in the New Testament[75]—because the beast was bound in fetters by Christ Jesus. This is a most strange fact in the epistle of James,[76] considered to be genuine in some of the original Gospels, but said by the western Church to be apocryphal—exactly that Christ Jesus kept the beast in balance. In certain circles people knew what should not get out among the people in the western world if one wanted to prevent insight into the secrets of the Christ from entering more and more into the spiritual soul.

If you consider what I have been saying today you also will not be surprised that the writer of the Book of Revelation[77] spoke of this with a degree of temperament. You will find it easy to connect the things I am saying about the temporal today with what I have said from other points of view about the beast. These things are always considered again from a different point of view, and you know we have to do this. The writer of the Book of Revelation expressed himself with some temperament at the point where he spoke of the appearance of the beast, saying more or less, 'The number of the beast is six hundred threescore and six, and it is the number of a man.' Better put, it is the number of the man who wants to resist saying, 'Not I but the Christ in me.' Human beings must grow more and more aware, seeing that they have entered the age of the spiritual soul.

But take the facts the way they still are today. Do not make them into the 'everything was better in the past' kind of criticism but a challenge to really do something, taking things as they are. If one were to speak of such things to the very clever people of today—imagine you are sitting down with someone who is particularly clever in some field, a leading person, and you tell them such a thing as this. Imagine what opinion that person will develop! However, if you are taking the picture in your mind in all seriousness, you'll have to say to yourself, 'We have indeed entered into the age in human evolution when we are least understood as we speak of present-day spiritual science though this is the science most appropriate to this age.'

I'd say no two parties have ever understood one another less in the world than the spiritual and the non-spiritual do today. The spiritual scientists can understand the non-spiritual ones, of course, and this is not particularly difficult. But the non-spiritual scientists fight with every fibre of their being and particularly with their tongues against any understanding of the spiritual that is of a different kind.

Well, we should not be surprised at this, for other things also do not fit well together today, and our age is the age of the great discrepancies and the great disharmonies, with opposites in direct collision. When one of those clever people sees an article about the kind of things we have been considering today, he will say, 'Strange to see such things in this day and age; it is out of place!' He believes that only his way of thinking fits in with this age, and considers anything else to be out of place. Tomorrow and the day after tomorrow we'll talk about the way it fits in supersensibly if not sensibly.

But there are also other things at the present time that are not in harmony. Just look at the reflections on life that have been published, how marvellously far humanity has come in the twentieth century in humanitarianism, and mutual understanding among nations! You'll find essays, whole books written at the beginning of the twentieth century that go in this direction, full of butter and sweetness. Such an advanced individual of the present age found that the description of his own era was like honey on his tongue. There are many such descriptions, saying how far humanity has advanced. And then compare this with the present, with the last four years. Does it really fit together?

But all arises from the fear of entering into the age of the spiritual soul. For if we truly enter into this, quite a lot of truths must emerge about human evolution. A lot of nonsense is produced today because people are afraid, because they should all speak in full conscious awareness and yet do not want to do so.[78] We'll say more about this tomorrow.

Lecture 14

12 October 1918

Yesterday we attempted to characterize the inner nature of an extraordinarily important fact in human evolution, doing so from a different point of view than on other occasions, a point of view which is, however, extraordinarily significant. Let us briefly call this to mind again. What I tried to show yesterday was that a kind of balance was achieved in the evolution of European humanity by counterbalancing the event which should have happened in the year 666 with the other one which we call the event on Golgotha. I said that humanity is subject to a course of evolution which was, as it were, predestined for it by the powers that rule the world, powers in whom humanity had its origin. If one follows this human evolution in detail one comes to see how the soul is able to find its place in whatever age it is born into. We are living in the fifth post-Atlantean age which had its beginnings in the fifteenth century and will extend as far as the beginning of the fourth millennium or the end of the third millennium. Humanity is meant to develop the spiritual soul, as we call it. Painful and joyful events, ordeals for humanity and events which we call a divine blessing, all the light and all the shadows we encounter in this age are meant to enlighten human beings more and more about themselves and their connection with the world. To take our place in full conscious awareness in the world and with this to gain insights which in earlier times and to this day have been the subject of much fantasy, never seen in the right light—to gain this, doing so with self-discipline, as independent human individuals, with real control of the will gained by self-education—this lies ahead as humanity's mission for this age. Putting it in popular terms we may say that it is the decision of the divine spirits with whom humanity has been connected from the very beginning, spirits who guided them from stage to stage. Other powers have gone against them, however, powers coming from two sides which we usually call the ahrimanic and the luciferic powers.

I also said that if we set up the hypothesis that the event on Golgotha had not taken place, if no Christ had decided to link his divine destiny with that of humanity on earth—what would then have happened? We cannot get to know history if we consider only what is in evidence, for we will never arrive at a real, proper view of events if we look only at the outer evidence. So if for example we were to be prevented by something from doing something which we would have done if it had not been for that something—perhaps being prevented from appearing somewhere or other tomorrow where we might have died in a railway accident—we cannot say that we give the right value to the event today by merely taking note of it. Seen by itself, the event could definitely be something utterly insignificant, merely stopping us from being in a place the next day where we would have died; we could not understand the event which prevented us today if we merely considered it in isolation. It is exactly because people pursue only a sense-perceptible, rational science, never asking what might have happened, that they do not gain insight into the true reality and value of such events.

So our question is: 'If we were to assume that the Christ would not have linked his divine destiny with that of humanity in the event on Golgotha, what would then have happened?' Yesterday I told you that in 666, when certain measures would have become possible, human beings would have gone through a very different point in their evolution. Certain geniuses appearing among them would have gained a vast sum of great wisdom, slightly bizarre, but a vast sum of it. This wisdom would have been of enormous significance for humanity because in the natural course of evolution human beings would evolve slowly towards such wisdom, as predestined for them by the divine spirits who are connected with their origin. They would have had to wait for it through millennia, as I said. They would in that case also gain it in a different way, because it would have to depend on their own efforts.

The intention was, therefore, to pre-empt something which humanity would only be able to gain by their own effort over long, long periods of time. Humanity would have gained it when still immature. It is hardly possible to imagine today what the history of 'civilized' humanity would have been if this event had happened. Humanity would have gained immature knowledge as if by instinct, but an instinct of genius. A tremendous chaos would have developed. And something else—people would have been stunned as all that knowledge was poured over them and their future evolution would have been cut short. They would have had the spiritual soul inoculated in the seventh century and not, as predestined in the natural way, from the fifteenth century onwards; but there would have been no further development into Spirit Self, Life Spirit and Spirit Man. People would have been extraordinarily perfect as human beings on earth, but their development to higher levels would have been taken away. This is hinted at so vividly—I am using the terms 'temperament' and 'vividly' in all seriousness and not as generally used—in the Book of Revelation when speaking of the beast or dragon. The figure six hundred, three score and six is given there, which has given much trouble to scholars. All of them have more or less guessed wrongly.

Before that—to make sure that this did not happen and provide humanity with a counterweight—the event on Golgotha had to enter into human evolution when humanity was able to take in what did then enter with the coming of Christ Jesus.

This is yet another point of view for forming the right opinion about the event on Golgotha and human evolution. It gives the whole of evolution on earth its proper meaning. As I have always been saying, to give just an indication of the true nature of the event on Golgotha, if an entity of the same rank as the human being on earth which happened to be on another planet in our solar system, an entity not belonging to that other planet, were to come down to earth one day, many things on earth would, of course, be new to it; suddenly arriving on earth, such an entity would not be able to understand all kinds of things, but there is one thing which it would understand. If you were to take such an entity, wherever it might have come from, to see Leonardo da Vinci's *Last Supper* and the Christ among his disciples, this entity would have an inkling in its own way of the meaning of our earth. You might show it all the products of nature on earth, all the works of art on earth—the only thing it would understand would be that the destiny of the Christ is in some way interlinked with Earth evolution. Yesterday I spoke of things arising purely from the spiritual point of view—I said the same for something else a week ago. This spiritual point of view is the only possible guide for present-day humanity, showing the way to facts that are important in life. Looking at events in the course of time with supersensible senses will show this contrast between the year of Christ Jesus' birth and the year 666. Let us look at external history with this in mind, however. Let us ask: 'Does that history confirm in any way that something did actually happen?'

Well, since the academic world does not know much about these things, they have also never been very much recorded. But when one knows the truth then it is indeed the case that one will also in external history find the events which can then provide information about things of the greatest importance. You see, certain things happen here in life. There is a spiritual world behind them. Someone who knows the situation will know how to relate the one thing or the other which happens to its spiritual background. Looking at the way humanity of more recent times has developed from the ancient Graeco-Roman era, the evolution of Greek and Roman civilization, one will find many, many things puzzling if one considers only the outward aspects of history. But the inner connections make them clear to us.

Take an event which is of little interest to the world at large but which is nevertheless of extraordinary significance. Take the fact that in 529 the Emperor Justinian[79] faced Greek schools of philosophy with legislation that they should cease to function, not permitting the schools, which were the glory of antiquity, to continue. Justinian's edict of 529 got rid of the scholarship which from time immemorial had influenced the Greek schools of philosophy, giving rise to an Anaxagoras, a Heraclitus, later a Socrates,[80] Plato and Aristotle.[81] We can, of course, develop ideas from what history tells us as to why the Emperor Justinian swept the old knowledge away in Europe, as it were; but if we are honest in thinking about these things we find that none of the details offered satisfy. We sense that unknown powers are at work in this. Strangely, this event coincided—not entirely, but historical facts which may sometimes even be a few decades apart do appear to go together when considered at a later time—with the expulsion of philosophers also from Edessa, which was done by Zeno the Isaurian.[82] Learned people were thus driven out from some of the most important places in the world at that time. And these learned people, who still had the ancient knowledge in so far as it had not yet been influenced by Christianity—this was in the fifth and sixth centuries of the Christian era—had to emigrate. They emigrated to Persia and established the Academy of Gondishapur or Gundeshapur.[83]

Even philosophers do not refer much to this Academy. Yet one must be aware of the nature of Gondishapur which was established by such ancient scholars as remained, or one will have no idea of the whole evolution of humanity in more recent times. For the ancient wisdom of the sages who had been driven out by Justinian and Zeno the Isaurian provided the basis for tremendously important teaching which was given to the students in Gondishapur in the seventh century. It was there that Aristotle, the Greek philosopher, was translated. And the strange thing which happened was this. Aristotle—otherwise his work would probably have been lost completely—was first translated into Syrian in Edessa by the scholars who had been driven out by Zeno the Isaurian. The translation into Syrian was taken to Gondishapur where it was then translated into Arabic. Something rather strange may be found in this translation of

Aristotle from Greek to Arabic via Syrian. Anyone who gains some insight into the changes which thoughts undergo when translated properly from one language into another, when one attempts to translate them, will be able to understand that there may have been something—well, let me put it hypothetically—like intention to take not the Greek Aristotle but the Aristotle which had gone through Syrian to Arabic. The Arab soul, a strange soul at that time, combined great acuity of thought with something that had an element of fantasy to it, though it was along logical lines and would rise even to the level of vision. And with the translation of Aristotle a basis was created of Aristotelian concepts seen in the light of that Arab soul. And a mighty philosophy of life developed at Gondishapur in the light of this particular way of seeing things. It was at Gondishapur that the event to which I was referring happened in the seventh century.

The event to which I was referring was not out of the ordinary, not even something that did not exist already on earth; at Gondishapur they were indeed teaching what I spoke of yesterday, taken in its essence the greatest contrast one can imagine to everything that has evolved from the event on Golgotha. The learned people at Gondishapur had a particular aim. This was—and it was exactly what I told you yesterday and have also just referred to—a comprehensive body of knowledge which was intended to replace the efforts of the spiritual soul. It would have made human beings into nothing but earthly creatures, closing them off from the evolution which man's creators intended for him, with Spirit Self, Life Spirit and Spirit Man. Anyone who has an idea of the wisdom of Gondishapur will consider it to be extremely dangerous for humanity, but at the same time also a tremendous phenomenon. The intention was to flood the whole known civilized world of that time, everywhere in Asia and Europe, with this scholarly knowledge.

A beginning was made. But the knowledge that was to flow from Gondishapur was held back, in a way, by spiritual powers which retard, powers which were after all connected—in spite of also being a kind of opposite—with the elements that were influenced by the

Christ impulse. The wisdom that was to flow from Gondishapur was in the first place blunted by the coming of Muhammad.[84] He taught a fairly imaginative religion particularly in the areas where the gnostic wisdom of Gondishapur was meant to be taught, taking the ground away, as it were, from under the feet of Gondishapur wisdom. He skimmed off the cream, as it were and when the wisdom of Gondishapur came sailing along it could not get through the things done by Muhammad. This may be seen as the wisdom of world history; we will also only know Islam properly when apart from other things we know that Islam was destined to blunt the gnostic wisdom coming from Gondishapur, taking away the great ahrimanic powers of temptation which would otherwise have been addressed to humanity.

The wisdom of Gondishapur has not completely disappeared. To understand what happened in connection with the gnostic movement of Gondishapur we must carefully follow developments from the seventh century to the present day. The things which the great teacher there—his name has remained unknown but he was the greatest opponent of Christ Jesus—taught his students have been lost, but something else has been achieved. It does, however, need careful study to perceive it. We may ask, 'What has really led to modern natural science, this peculiar natural-scientific way of thinking?' What I am going to say now is actually not unknown to careful historians. The present-day natural-scientific way of thinking—I characterized it for you yesterday—has not developed by something evolving in a straight line from Christianity; we may say that in reality it has nothing at all to do with Christianity. We can trace step by step, from decade to decade, how gnostic Gondishapur wisdom, even if blunted, spread via southern Europe and Africa to Spain, France and England and then across the Continent, especially via the monasteries, and we see how the supersensible was driven out and only the sensible retained, the tendency, as it were, the intention. Natural-scientific thinking in the western world thus arose from the blunted gnostic wisdom of Gondishapur.

It is particularly interesting to study how the gnostic wisdom of

Gondishapur flowed into Roger Bacon[85]—not Francis Bacon, Baron Verulam, but Roger Bacon who as a monk was not greatly respected by his colleagues. People know so little today of the origins of things that influence their souls. They believe their thinking to be natural-scientific and without bias when it has actually come from the Academy of Gondishapur.

Thus it is not the case that knowledge gained from spiritual vision cannot be substantiated; we must merely use the right method so that we can also show in life as we experience it how something gathered from the spiritual realm has really happened. Studies like this will be of tremendous importance for the immediate future of humanity. For humanity will have to get orientation about its past if it wants to find a way out of today's confusion, the chaos of recent years. Today people tend to look at everything from the natural-scientific point of view and this does not really have anything to do with Christianity as such. It is the outcome arising from preconditions which I have been characterizing. We therefore do truly have these two streams, two forces in evolving western civilization—on the one hand the Christian stream, on the other the element which has so profoundly influenced western thinking, an element we can study by looking at the cultural life in medieval times.

The cultural life of the Middle Ages is studied in a rather biased way. But go and look at the work of the painters which shows how medieval scholastics behaved towards Arab philosophers.[86] See how in the western Christian tradition they showed the scholastic who stands there with his Christian teaching and with this teaching made occasion to trample those Arab scholars underfoot. Again and again this passionate theme—using the powers of the Christ to trample the Arab scholars underfoot. See this in the paintings produced under the influence of Christian tradition in the West, and realize that it is all the passion of the Middle Ages which lives in those paintings to oppose with the Christian ethos the elements which originally arose from opposition to the Christ at the Academy of Gondishapur, oppose Arab scholarship coming across to Europe. Those who know the situation will see echoes of what I have been telling you about in

Maimonides Rambam,[87] Avicenna[88] and everywhere. Consider, man was intended, with the Mystery on Golgotha to help him in this, to find the spiritual soul out of his own individual nature, and then ascend further to Spirit Self, Life Spirit and Spirit Man. At that time, however, the intention was to give him direct revelation out of the genius of gnostic scholarship of the wisdom which he would otherwise have to find by his own individual effort and skill, which was the intention of the divine spirits who determined his fate, Christ Jesus being one of these spirits.

This still lived in the thoughts of those who, like Averroes,[89] still had the gnostic wisdom of Gondishapur, even if it had been blunted. Reading the foolish notes referring to Averroes that appear in modern textbooks and are out of context, how is one to understand why Averroes, Andalusian polymath of Arab extraction, said, 'When we die, only the soul's substance flows out into general spirituality; human beings have no personal individuality, but everything the individual has by way of soul is but mirroring the one universal soul'? Why did Averroes say this? Because it is a branch of the wisdom coming from Gondishapur which has made it clear to people not that every individual was to develop the spiritual soul but that the wisdom of the spiritual soul was to be given to them as a revelation from above. It would have been an ahrimanic revelation. Humanity would in that case truly have had a spiritual soul with monistic content, and individual minds would essentially have been but maya. Everything that lives in western civilization becomes clear when we look at things from a spiritual point of view. We do, however, have to ask ourselves over and over again: 'How can this development leading to the spiritual soul take place?' It will after all have to take place. Secondly we must ask: 'What prevents people today from turning to spiritual science, which alone can show the way to the spiritual soul?'

Yesterday I told you that the natural science, which modern humanity is so proud of, really leads to ideas which do not reflect nature but contain a ghost. The things people know about nature are not the truth of nature but a ghost, relating to real nature the way a ghost does to something that is absolutely real. It is merely that scientists do not know that theirs is a ghostly knowledge, that their knowledge of the human being is not of homo but of homunculus. The kind of progress in human evolution, which started in the fifteenth century and will continue to the end of the third millennium, will be such that people will have to realize more and more what they are gaining with insight into nature for instance, how they come closer to reality with this insight into nature. People will have to seek insight; they will have to avoid the obstacles they meet when they develop their desire for insight. The major obstacles—we have already characterized them from one particular point of view and will bring them back to mind now—arise because in the age of natural science, which is the offspring of Gondishapur Academy, people gain only ghostly knowledge for there is nothing spiritual in their ideas of nature. We might ask: 'Why do human beings do this in this day and age?' Because it will give us an idea of what we have to overcome. Why do human beings unconsciously want to have a ghostly knowledge of nature, and are actually proud and in high spirits with their ghostly knowledge of nature? Why?

Well, the moment one realizes fully that this knowledge of nature gives us only a spectre of nature one also feels the need to penetrate to the true reality that is behind the spectre. One then wants to have the reality of nature. We might also characterize our natural-scientific philosophy from the following point of view. We might say: 'This natural-scientific philosophy comes with ghostly ideas, settles down with them, thinking that these were ideas about real nature, and one then develops all kinds of concepts—atoms, molecules and so on which, as you know, simply do not exist but are pure invention—invents all kinds of laws such as the conservation of energy, conservation of matter, which do not actually exist.' People look for all kinds of hypothetical aspects behind something which does not exist, behind their ideas which are ghosts acting according to ghostly laws. Why do they do this? Well, because deep down the fear I mentioned earlier makes itself felt. It is just that people do not know they have this fear, seeing that it is unconscious. I might also call it cowardice. For what would happen if people had the courage to confess: 'You want a concept of nature and not a ghost nature. You must therefore penetrate to the reality!' Then you won't find atoms, nor molecules, nor concepts developed by Ostwald or by Haeckel. You will find Ahriman and his hordes! Things get spiritual then. Someone who truly penetrates to reality with a proper science of nature will find Ahriman. But that is what people are afraid of, for they think they will fall into the abyss when they find the spirit where they were merely looking for matter which in fact does not exist. Initially the spirit shows itself which one cannot worship but against which one must protect oneself. One has to be fully clear in one's mind about this spirit.

In the sculptured group next door there is nothing arbitrary about putting the Christ together with Ahriman and Lucifer. The composition reflects the most profound vital issues of our time and humanity must become aware of such things. Our knowledge of nature is ghostly, has to be ghostly for as long as people do not have the courage to look for the spiritual aspect; there they will, however, find Ahriman. Our knowledge of the soul does not give us the true soul but merely an image of it. Essentially the psychology taught at academies and universities today gives merely an image of the soul. And this image blinds us to the real soul, for if one were to continue one's investigations in the same way as that which has produced the image it would be Lucifer who appeared. That is the next spiritual element which one would find.

Yes, anyone who is truly able to penetrate through the historically blunted wisdom which still remains of what was to be established in Gondishapur will find that this approach provides very exact knowledge of Lucifer and Ahriman. But it was intended to lead to Lucifer and Ahriman only and not to the guidance which Christ Jesus gives to humanity.

The medieval scholastics who wanted to tread the Arab scholars underfoot did have a feeling for this, always finding themselves in this situation, and they felt it because it is connected with humanity's most profound developmental impulses. The wisdom which was to have been revealed to humanity with the help of Ahriman, instead of being gained by people's own efforts through centuries, would have been most dangerous. Humanity is in the process of gaining this wisdom, which has to do with three things, through the spiritual soul today; but at that time, in the seventh century, it was to come to them in the way I have indicated. This wisdom relates to three things. It is not that humanity is not meant to gain it, but they are meant to do so under the guidance of the Christ impulse. The three things are—firstly the nature of birth and death. We have often spoken of this and you know from the way in which we have spoken of birth and death that human beings can only master them with supersensible insights. As the human being is born and as he dies, the supersensible shines into the sense-perceptible world. Birth and death continue to be riddles for those who would only grasp them outwardly, through the senses, for they are not sense-perceptible phenomena. The sense-perceptible phenomena of birth and death are unreal; in reality these are supersensible events. When one attempts to explore the secrets of birth and death supersensibly, using real observation, secondary phenomena will appear to the enquiring mind. Above all one comes to see that in life here in the sense-perceptible world one has only an apparent inner life. In the western world people have refused to accept this truth for centuries. You can follow the history of this refusal in my book *The Case for Anthroposophy*,[90] where I discuss this right at the beginning. I had to be careful how I put things, however, for one cannot yet present these things to the outside world; people find them paradoxical. You know very well that the words of Descartes,[91] which are still ascribed to Augustine, are known throughout the western world: *Cogito ergo sum*, 'I think, therefore I exist'. People believed that they could grasp the soul's reality by thinking. The words should really be different if one wanted to speak of the truth of man living in the sense-perceptible world. We would have to say, 'I think, therefore I do not exist!' For we cease to exist the moment we start just to think, when we develop inner thinking only. What is then within us? A highly complex phenomenon, but we will get a clear idea of it today and tomorrow.

Let us assume that this [Fig. 16] is human life and here is what a

Lecture 14 * 245

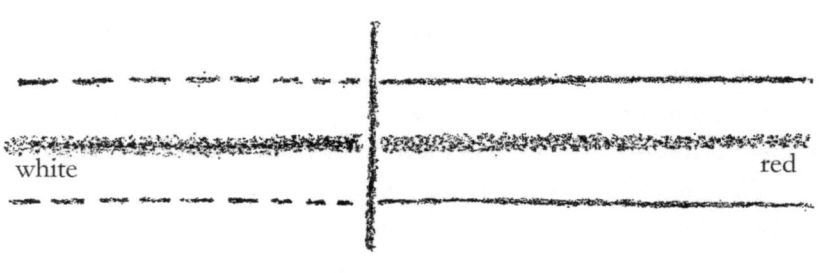

white | red

Fig. 16

thinking human being, forming ideas, inwardly experiences throughout life. This would then be merely an apparent structure, really like a tube running from birth to death [red], for the reality came before this, before birth, or let us say conception [white]. There we are real in the spiritual world, in the supersensible, and at the border, where we enter into the sense-perceptible world, only an image is allowed to pass through. We are but an image of our life before birth or conception. The truth is not that something which lives now is speaking as I speak to you, but only images which have been allowed to come through. In truth, it is something which has been in the spiritual world which still speaks today. We are not eternal because we endure but because today we still are what we have in truth been before birth or conception. This speaks into our present time. By entering into our bodily nature we have really become an image of our essential nature for the period of a life on earth. I think, therefore I do not exist—from Augustine to Descartes, philosophers have obscured this profound truth. We shall never fathom the secrets of birth and death in such darkness. For you ask: 'When did the soul begin?' At birth. 'When does it cease?' At death. Knowing supersensible truth we should put the question differently: 'When did the soul cease to unfold its life as soul?' When we were born, or conceived. 'When will it start to unfold its life as a supersensible entity again?' When we die. Here on earth we interrupt it so that not only the supersensible is active in our life and we'll be able to take in the achievements of the sense-perceptible world, taking them with us in our life as a whole. This is no rapturous asceticism but the fact that earth is an absolute necessity in human life as a whole. Our life on earth has great significance exactly because of this and is apparently material because our actual human life as a supersensible human being ceases as we enter into life on earth, and starts again as we continue to live having gone through death.

The secrets of birth and death only begin to reveal themselves when we know ourselves as supersensible entities and know that we are but an image of what we were before birth and will be as a soul entity after death. But we must have the courage to look and see what there is in us. If that [Fig. 16] is merely a hollow tube, an image, we must have the courage to say to ourselves: 'Let us not be blinded by the image but face up to Lucifer in our search for insight. It takes courage, inner courage to gather insight which is truly fruitful for life.' This is something to be emphasized again and again. So the one thing is the knowledge which relates to birth and death.

The second knowledge relates to our biography. We see our relationship as a soul to the body in the wrong light, justifiably so for the reasons which you will find in my *Occult Science, an Outline*. Human beings therefore also see their biography in the wrong light. Their idea of it matches the image of Father Rhine which I presented a few days ago. You'll remember how I spoke of the image. Someone stands there, looks down from the bridge in Basel and says, 'I see the old Rhine.' The old Rhine—oh yes. I then ask, 'What is this old Rhine? The water flowing down there is definitely not old. In a few hours it will be a long way downstream and in a few days somewhere in the wide ocean. It definitely is not old. And this old Rhine you speak of does not seem to me to be the mere channel which extends from the Swiss mountains to the North Sea.' So what is Father Rhine, the old Rhine, of which people speak so often? In material terms it is nothing; nothing of substance remains when you take the Father Rhine concept. Nor does anything remain in truth if you take your own bodily nature. This body of yours is a flowing river—destruction, renewal of the fluids. Nothing remains but the form which is a product of the spirit. Into this form pours something that appears to have substance, pours in, is destroyed, just like the water in Father Rhine.

What external maya, illusion, is actually creating prevents us from seeing the river of steady dissolution and renewal which is the truth with regard to external life in the senses. We are looking at something which is said to have been born, lumps of flesh with blood and bones in them which is meant to grow and increase in size until fully grown and then stays like that until death. That is more or less the same idea as when we think of Father Rhine as a piece of water—which, of course, does not exist—extending from the Swiss mountains to the North Sea and, what is more, see it as a quiet piece of water lying in its river bed; that is how we imagine the human body. It is in constant flow but we think that it is something static—one cannot even find the right word for it—between birth and death. If we were to see ourselves as we really are it would be as being in constant flow and we'd be quite unable to get the idea that this has anything to do with our true nature, for it is in continuous flow. If we were able to see what is behind the constant process of dissolution and renewal, the powers behind it, we would have a science of medicine, the spiritual medical science which would indeed be different in form from the medical science which we have today. You would not be able to say of that science of medicine, 'Ah well, it is used to cure diseases.' Diseases are not cured because there can be no question of curing diseases the way people want this to be done today. With a genuine spiritual medicine one can only maintain the totality of health-giving powers. A true medicine would consist in organizing life in such a way that human beings govern the powers which effect constant elimination, dissolution and renewal. One would then need no pharmaceutical products, with individuals not only knowing how to apply this in their own case but living together with others in such a way that this could find its way to the whole human race. I have spoken of this before. It is the second thing.

The third thing connected with this insight is a true science of nature. What is a true science of nature? I have stressed on several occasions that occult science does not go against natural science the way it is today but one knows that this natural science does present nature not as she is but as a ghost. It is not a matter of fighting that ghost. Our human constitution being what it is, we have to accept the ghost. There is no question—I referred to this when speaking of the philosopher Richard Wahle yesterday — of thinking up a poison, even if a poison for philosophy, a philosophical and not a physical poison, to rid the world of all the people who may be thinking in a natural-scientific way. It is a matter exactly of finding out where they are right. We should say to natural scientists, 'If you were to say that you are using the right methods of investigation we would fully agree, but you also have to admit that using these methods which are the right ones for natural science you arrive merely at ideas of a spectre of nature and not its reality.' We have to see through it, however. It is indeed the task we are set for the age of the spiritual soul that we see through things as they really are.

The natural scientist will say, 'Yes, I have various reasons why I will not have made my knowledge of nature into a ghost.' The spiritual scientist will have to reply, 'But you are quite right to have a ghostly knowledge of nature. You would be wrong to look for any natural substance outside the spectre. You are only right when you look for all kinds of ahrimanic elements behind the spectre, when you look for something spiritual behind it. But you do right in looking for ghostly knowledge.' The things I told you about the human being's bodily nature do indeed have very much a ghostly character. And someone who penetrates nature from a higher point of view considers a very different natural phenomenon to be true and not deceptive than the robust natural phenomena which are normally presented to us. The strange thing—I will also speak of this tomorrow—is that in spite of it all the world will everywhere point firmly to the right thing at one point or another. A pointer to the right thing will be found somewhere or other when one wants to know what to think of the reality of the natural phenomena which surround our senses. What should we really consider? Is there something in nature herself that will enlighten us?

Yes, there is. The rainbow, for example. The rainbow is the perfect image of a natural phenomenon. Just think—you know this yourself—if you were to get up to where the rainbow is you would be able to walk straight through it, for it is merely the result of certain processes coming together. All natural processes are as spectral as the rainbow, are ghosts just like the rainbow; we merely do not notice this. They are not what they are to the eye or the ear or the other senses but a coming together of other processes, and these are non-physical. We put our feet down on what we think is solid matter; in reality it is merely something we perceive as a power or force, just like the rainbow, and when we think we are putting our feet on solid ground it is Ahriman who sends up the power or force from below.

As soon as we go beyond the merely spectral or ghostly aspect of natural phenomena we come upon things of the spirit. This means that all exploration looking for 'crude matter' is fairly senseless. Once humanity gives up the search for crude matter as the basis of nature—and they will do so before the fourth millennium—they will arrive at something completely different. They will find rhythms everywhere in nature, rhythmic systems or orders. These exist, but are generally laughed at in the materialistic science of today. We have created an image of these rhythmic orders in the seven pillars, in the whole configuration of our building here. But you also find it everywhere in the natural world. One leaf rhythmically follows another in the plant; petals show rhythm in their arrangement, all is rhythm. Temperatures rise rhythmically when you are sick and then go down again; all life has rhythm. To penetrate the rhythms of nature, that will be a true science of nature.

Penetrating the rhythms of nature also induces us to make use of rhythms in technology. It is to be the aim of future technology to generate harmonious waves or oscillations on a small scale and then transfer them to the large scale. This means that simple harmonization makes it possible to do tremendous work.

Tomorrow I am going to show you in detail why it is truly wise in the Christian world order, which in this sense is the wise divine world order, to let humanity mature through centuries for the insights to which I have been referring, whereas the Academy of Gondishapur intended simply to throw them at people. Humanity must strive for something else if these insights are to come to them. These insights must only come for humanity when in the first place, and together with evolution towards such insights, there is a completely selfless social order for the third point, widespread among humanity. You cannot develop rhythmical technology without bringing more disaster upon humanity unless a selfless social order is striven for at the same time. An egotistical humanity would see disastrous consequences from developing rhythmic technology. It also is not possible to provide human beings without further ado with the second power I mentioned, which is identical with human healing powers, powers in evidence where one sees processes of dissolution and renewal, elimination and uptake. This power cannot simply be given to humanity (as I have said from other points of view) unless one does at the same time breed absolute conscientiousness in human beings, when it comes to their attitude not only to things that are outwardly perceptible but also to things that are not outwardly perceptible—when human beings deny themselves not only things that are outwardly visible but follow a certain rule of conscience and deny themselves also things that are not outwardly visible: thinking and feeling. This power is hidden from us because we see the stream of life from birth to death as a rigid body. If we were to gain insight into and learn to control this power we would be capable of doing enormous harm unless the power were to develop in the light of absolute conscientiousness also with regard to things not evident to the senses.

The third thing would be corresponding to my first point, insight into the secrets of birth and death. Yes, these secrets of birth and death require that human beings first go through a certain state of maturity. They require that human beings can face Ahriman and Lucifer in full awareness. Anyone fully able to work out what is meant with this first point will know the following, which I am now going to consider in conclusion. More details will follow tomorrow.

Such a person knows that one can gain knowledge of nature that is entirely spectral, not knowing that it is merely the ghost of knowledge. It helps us, it really does, for we do not then face the danger of getting close to Ahriman. You can make Ahriman invisible but in that case you have to gain insights into nature merely in the present-day sense, and that is untrue. It makes a good barrier against Ahriman to stick with insight into nature that is untrue. You merely have a choice between wanting the truth—in which case you will also have to acquaint yourself with supersensible ahrimanic influences in the world—or taking untruth. Breed untruth. Say, 'The ghostly knowledge of nature gives us real nature.' Well and good, in that case you stay with the things that suit Ahriman. Ahriman wants the lie, he lives on it. And he'll manage to live particularly well on this hidden lie; there is nothing he likes better than to have this lie prevail, the view being: ghostly knowledge of nature is real knowledge of nature.

I have again spoken of something which is but a maya of what exists in the supersensible realm, referring to it as the image that was allowed to pass through. You then also have the choice. You can penetrate to the supersensible—good, in that case you must also come face to face, supersensibly of course, with Lucifer. Or you stay with untruth and consider the maya of the psyche to be reality—you will, however, never find out about birth and death in that case and about immortality since you'll not be considering the soul, which is immortal, but just a mere image. This is what I wanted to speak about today. Tomorrow we'll take it further.

It is an important thought—on earth, human beings have the option now, in the age of the spiritual soul, to strive for the truth. They must then also face the spiritual sphere with courage. Or they may choose to avoid the spiritual, in which case they can stay with the illusion, the non-truth. The Academy of Gondishapur wanted to spare people the effort of seeking the truth, wanted to spare them the effort of further development, wanted to reveal to them what had been revealed to them themselves in ahrimanic ways. The last shadow, the ghost, of the Academy of Gondishapur is the natural-scientific illusion of today. The aim of the Academy was to make man into a wholly earthly being. It was overcome in its endeavours by something which was made part of humanity even before it came to exist—the Mystery on Golgotha. More of this tomorrow.

Lecture 15

13 October 1918

YESTERDAY we saw how the state of mind we must aim for in the age of the spiritual soul evolved historically, as it were. Let us be clear in our minds about the external world situation in respect of this. We can say, as it were, that the year AD 333 represents a certain state of equilibrium [Fig. 17] that was clearly evident in historical evolution though little is made of it in formal history. The simple reason for this is that it was a kind of pivot, I'd say, and a pivoting point does not in itself form part of a moving mechanical system, though things do move around it. Take a balance. You see the pans and the beam move, but the pivoting point is ideal and not physical. It is, of course, the most important element and must above all be supported.

Above all we must understand what came to pass, unnoticed by the outside world, in the important year 333, like the pivoting point of a balance. Well, the year 333 was the central point in the fourth post-Atlantean age, the midpoint of that important period which extended from 747 before the Mystery on Golgotha, when Rome was founded, to about AD 1413 when the Graeco-Roman period came to an end and the age of the spiritual soul began which will continue to the end of the fourth millennium. This central point in 333 does not stand out much when we study historical events, no more than the pivoting point does on a balance. More was however in evidence 333 years later, in 666. That was the year of which we were able to say: 'The natural-scientific way of thinking which humanity developed

Mystery
on Golgotha   AD 333   AD 666

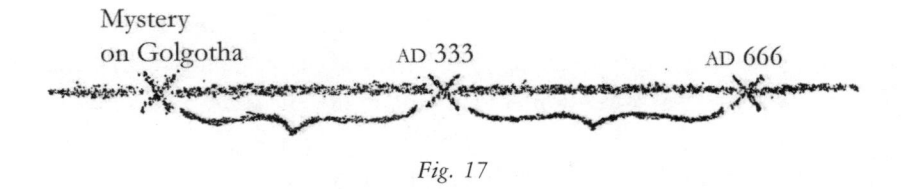

Fig. 17

later is seen here as having been undertakings of the Academy of Gondishapur, undertakings which had been blunted by Islam.' Yesterday we saw how a particular state of mind spread through southern Europe, later becoming the particular scientific attitude which we really still have today in natural science and which is widespread also in modern thinking. So that was 333 years after the time when one was really only looking back, as it were, on earlier times, as Julian the Apostate did. It was 333 years to 666; going back 333 years along the other side of the balance, we come to the Mystery which was in preparation with the birth of Christ Jesus.

Essentially we said about all these events: 'What would have happened in human evolution if it had not been for the Mystery on Golgotha?' The establishment of the Academy of Gondishapur and everything it did bring about happened independently of the Mystery on Golgotha. The Athenian philosophers' schools did in a way relate to Christianity. Justinian closed them down in 529, however. Pure Greek wisdom passed through Syria to Gondishapur in the Neo-Persian Empire. Everything connected with this, if not blunted, was the true aim of Gondishapur, excluding Christianity, excluding the Mystery on Golgotha. The real situation is that nothing happened without the impulse of the Mystery on Golgotha taking effect from the year zero of our calendar onwards; many things were, however, intended.

We may now say that the things which at the pivoting point, in the fourth century, were influencing human souls that did not incline towards Christianity can only be considered in their pure form if we first of all ask ourselves: 'How would western humanity have developed if it had not been for the Mystery on Golgotha?' One can study, even in historical terms, what would have become of the evolution of western humanity, by looking at Augustine, for instance, who presents both aspects for the study of people who came later. At first he was quite independent of Christianity, trying to solve the tough riddles in his philosophy of life with the Manichaeans, and only came to Christianity after this.

We can go further back, however, and then an important question arises: 'What would be the case if we were to look at evolution specifically at the time of the Mystery on Golgotha, asking ourselves what did things look like at the time when the Mystery on Golgotha took place in Palestine in all the regions that were untouched by the event?' With the exception of the most immediate sphere where the Christ lived and worked those were all other parts of the globe. What were things like all around the globe? What were things like especially in Rome, with the impulse of the Mystery on Golgotha spreading to it later and being a particularly great influence?

This question is particularly relevant for us, and it is not just theoretical in our day and age: 'What were things like in Rome when the Mystery on Golgotha was enacted in Palestine?' For we shall see later on how much our present age is similar, though in a slightly different sphere, to the time which we may consider to have been the time of the Mystery on Golgotha. We should never forget, though we easily do, something connected with the Mystery on Golgotha. We must again and again—feeling an inner need to do so—enter in sheer sentience into the civilization of ancient Rome where people had no idea that a single individual with a handful of adherents had appeared over yonder, lived a particular life, suffered death on the cross, and that the insights concerning birth and death which are so important for human beings born after this were connected with that individual. We have to enter again and again into the idea that although this event, which today is the full sun shining out over human history, happened at the beginning of our era, all inner and outward life across the globe evolved without people taking note of this Mystery on Golgotha in Palestine. Because of this we have to ask: 'What were things like then, especially in Rome?'

We'll understand one another more easily if we start with the aims which the people who had created the Academy of Gondishapur had particularly in mind later on, in 666. As I said yesterday, their aim was to give the knowledge they had themselves gained by ahrimanic methods to humanity as a revelation, when human beings were actually meant to develop the spiritual soul at a later time and by their own efforts. The year 666 was still in the age of the rational or mind soul; human beings were not able to think of their own accord in a way that would have given them spiritual awareness of everything. And the aim was to give them this: something that was to come thousands of years later was to be given to humanity right then. The opposite situation applied in the year zero, in the age in which the Mystery on Golgotha itself took place. Three hundred and thirty-three years after the year 333 the aim was to give humanity something belonging to the future, something predestined for future times; 333 years before that, around the time of the Mystery on Golgotha, the aim was to force humanity back to something which in the normal course of human evolution entered into that evolution thousands of years before.

It is extremely difficult to speak of these things, the reason being that history, which also has its own history, evolved in such a way that where these things were concerned humanity was really always driven into error by history. Things that actually happened in the southern regions of Europe were obscured so that human beings would not know of them. Historians do speak of the personality of the Emperor Augustus, for instance. But no effort is made to help people understand the crucial role played by that individual, deliberately so by some and inadvertently by most. The Emperor Augustus was the focus for Roman endeavours to bring about, quite deliberately, a world civilization that was to obscure for human eyes everything the rational or mind soul had provided, obscuring the things human beings had been able to gain by their own efforts from 747 BC onwards. People were above all to be limited to what had been gained before the age of the rational or mind soul, in the age of the sentient soul, the Egypto-Chaldaean civilization.

At a later time, in 666, the scholars of the Academy of Gondishapur wanted to bring something destined to come later at an earlier time. In the days of the Emperor Augustus anything which human beings were able to gain at that particular time was to be wiped out. Instead they were to have the full glory of old, something which humanity had had in Egypto-Chaldaean times, the age of ancient Persia, and they were to have it in its old meaning. Looking back on the reality under the brushwood piled up on top which calls itself history one may ask oneself: 'What exactly did Rome deliberately wish to preserve at that time, the preservation of which was then prevented as the impulse of the Mystery on Golgotha spread? What did Christianity prevent from being preserved?' And one would realize the following.

Well, it was essentially twofold. In the first place they wanted to preserve the feeling, the sentient feeling, for the old rites, the rites which had been the usual practice for centuries—among the Egyptians and in Asia Minor, and also deeper into Asia. They wanted to eliminate the rational mind, the intelligence of people, making it ineffective, and let only sentience develop by presenting all the significant, the magnificent and tremendous rites meant to be effective and, being effective in olden times, effective at a time when human beings had not yet developed intelligence, effective at the time when the rituals for the gods were meant to evolve from the sentient soul so that human beings would not be without gods. Those great, significant rituals were to take the place of reflective thought, were meant to stimulate awareness of the godhead and a state of being in harmony with the gods in human souls, in something of a hypnotic state, according to old, atavistic custom. Rome intended to revive sentience of this.

You only get to know the specific difference between Roman and Greek civilization, the latter going into decline at that time, if you look at these more subtle differences. The sentience which the Emperor Augustus in particular wanted to introduce in Rome, being a man with a tremendous retrospective initiation impulse, such impulses were not known in Greece. The Greeks did not want to reach back to olden times. They wanted to have things before them which they could understand themselves, things they could relate to. If the Christian impulse had not come later on, very soon after, if the Christian impulse had not taken rapid effect against the intentions of Augustus and his successors, rituals of much, much greater brilliance would have sprung up in Rome than those which did spring up.

So the first thing to remember is that it was the aim of Augustus and his adherents to have a powerful ritual go out from Rome (just as later on a prophetic wisdom was to go out from the Academy of Gondishapur), that would cloud the whole world. It was to deprive the world of the potential of the rational soul and later also the spiritual soul. The aim of Gondishapur had been to give humanity the spiritual soul and so cut off later development, cutting off the development of Spirit Self, Life Spirit and Spiritual Man because the spiritual soul had come too early. The event intended to happen in Rome was meant to prevent the spiritual soul from coming to human beings at all, and also to eliminate the rational or mind soul, even 333 years before the turning point, presenting them with mighty rites for the soul that would give them awareness of the gods. This was one thing which Augustus, an initiate, wanted to introduce.

There are always two aspects to the rational or mind soul. One is essentially inclined downwards to the sentient soul. You know that when we differentiate we have sentient soul, rational or mind soul and spiritual soul. The sentient soul was the first to develop, and its development came to a conclusion in 747 BC. The rational developed from 747 BC until about AD 1413—the figures are approximate—and this was followed by the age of the spiritual soul. The one in the middle, the rational or mind soul, tends towards the sentient soul on the one hand [Fig. 18, arrow] when it wants to imbue itself with what has gone before, as I have just shown. Augustus wanted to revive the state of mind which is gained out of the sentient soul. If you take the rational or mind soul back, as it were, to the standpoint of the sentient soul, what becomes of the part which inclines—it has not yet developed, of course, but it is there—towards the spiritual soul, of the more intelligent state of mind? We have to ask, and at the time of Augustus this was a major question relating to civiliza-

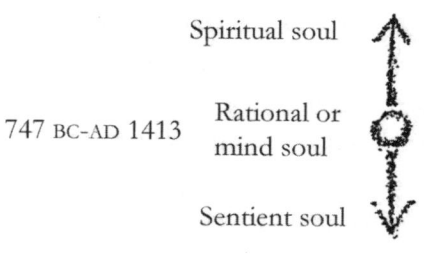

```
                Spiritual soul      ↑
                                    |
   747 BC–AD 1413   Rational or     O
                    mind soul       |
                                    ↓
                Sentient soul
```
Fig. 18

tion: 'What happens with the part that wants to develop in the direction of the spiritual soul if development is curtailed and one does not allow development of the rational or mind soul? What does then become of the element in the human soul that seeks to strive towards the spiritual soul?' The element which strives towards the sentient soul is satisfied, more so than the degree of normal human evolution would permit, with the revived ritual. But what does one give to the element which strives towards the spiritual soul? There is a word which one always avoided mentioning in this situation, so that the right light would not fall on a fact in human evolution from those times. We only have to mention this word and understanding will come. On the other hand one gives rhetoric to the soul when one aims to deal with it in its sentient aspect. Instead of giving the soul substance, inner content, rhetoric provides only an outer shell which strives for the configuration of the words, the sentence structure, rather than concepts full of life.

Under the influence of Augustus, life in Rome became something very different from life as it had been in Greece. The garment worn by a Roman may have looked similar to that worn by a Greek, but looking at it you'd no longer see how a Greek felt himself to be within its folds, but see it from the outside as something meant to be decorative. An echo of Roman rites of veneration still survives in the folds of a Roman toga as distinct from the Greek garment. One would sense a tremendous difference if one were prepared to be sentient of it between Demosthenes,[92] who stammered and in spite of his outward stammering appearance was to reflect the Greek spirit—not with rhetoric!—and the Roman rhetors to whom it mattered that there was not a stammerer among them but only someone who knew how to formulate the sequence of words and structure of sentences really well.

The aim that came from the Augustinian age was on the one hand to give humanity the ancient rites that were not understood. The whole point was that people should not take to the ritual with understanding, and certainly should not ask: 'What do the elements of the rite mean?' This attitude still persists in many different areas today. There are Freemasons today who'll tell you something really odd. You tell those Freemasons, for example, 'Yes, you have an extensive symbolism and there is much in it. But present-day Freemasons don't care at all about the meaning of those symbols.' If you tell them this, their answer is: 'That is exactly what is so good about present-day Freemasonry. Every individual can have his own ideas about the symbols.' Such a person will usually think whatever his simple mind suggests, and that is far, far removed from the profound meaning of the symbols, from the profound meaning which takes one into human brains and human hearts.

This was the deliberate intention in Rome at that time—ritual and no one asking about the meaning of the ritual, not using intelligence and will to tackle the ritual. The other pole, which is necessarily connected with this, is empty rhetoric, a rhetoric used not only to make speeches but one that has as rhetoric entered fully into Justinian's *corpus iuris*, flooding the western world with Roman law, as it is called. This Roman law relates to the quality that was meant to be alive in souls as they moved towards spiritual soul development as rhetoric relates to things said from warmth of heart. The chill which Roman law has cast upon the world is due to the fact that Roman law relates to warmth of heart as rhetoric does to things said, however haltingly, from the heart's warmth and light.

This Roman Catholic ritual truly is something sacred, something great, for it brings the sacred spirit which has been there for humanity for times immemorial. (Everything has its great, tremendous sides, and we must never take just a biased view.) The only right way of looking at its focal point, for instance, at the Sacrifice of the Mass, which reflects the most sublime mysteries of all times, is to give new life to something which has become dead and was to be made accessible only to the sentient soul. We give new life to it with the things which spiritual science with anthroposophical orientation now has to say about the Mystery on Golgotha. We can bring the rediscoveries made in spiritual-scientific investigation in the normal course of human evolution into the Augustinian thinking preserved in Roman Catholicism, just as we can bring everything spiritual science can gain from the spiritual worlds into what remains of the intentions of the Academy of Gondishapur, blunted and reduced as they are to the sensual. The spirit must enter into natural science. Only those who are able to feel—and those who have worked with the science of the spirit for some time can feel this—and sense the whole and great significance of what I have been saying will be able to see how much our age resembles the time when the Mystery on Golgotha was approaching for humanity with regard to what lives in our souls, though largely unconsciously so. I have said on several occasions, and you also find it presented in the first of my Mystery Plays, *The Portal of Initiation*, that today we are about to come to an important turning point just as a point had been reached at that time which led to a turning point, and at the relevant time in the past, the time of the Mystery on Golgotha, humanity faced that turning point that was to come in the fourth post-Atlantean age in 333. The time interval is a bit shorter because the speed at which the higher spirits move changes. One cannot calculate it to say that today, too, one is to face it in 333 years time. Things like this change in the course of time. The speed at which individual spirits in the higher hierarchies move changes. Today, in the first third of the twentieth century, we have important events approaching. And all upheavals, all disasters are nothing but the earthquake-like upheavals preceding a major spiritual event in the twentieth century. This will not be an event in the physical world but one which will come to people as a kind of enlightenment. It will have come before the first third of the twentieth century has ended. Taking the word in the right sense we may call it the second coming of Christ Jesus. He will not appear in a physical body as at the time of the Mystery on Golgotha but as something at work in human beings, and people will be supersensibly sentient of him. He is present in the ether body. Those who are prepared can be sentient of him at all times in visions, be all the time counselled by him, entering into a direct personal relationship with him, as it were. Everything which thus lies before us is comparable to what the Romans were sentient of as the physically real Mystery on Golgotha as it was approaching in the days of Augustus.

One needs the right sentience for such things. Looking at various outer events that took place, ultimately leading to this terrible world catastrophe, one has to be aware of how humanity once again felt a great need for ritual. Consider—but please with your senses fully alert—how this urgent need has been felt for more than a century by those who are most perceptive, seeking to find the way to ritual again and escape from the dry, sober Protestantism of the intellect. Note how the very people among the Romantics who could have some idea of the whole significance which ritual has in the soul were moving towards Catholicity. Not yet able to let the light of spiritual science show them what was striving to come sacramentally into the world they inclined towards Roman Catholicism. Individuals such as Novalis—whose particularly profound spirituality, which arose in him from relatively early youth, made him a particularly characteristic individual—were not content in prosaic Protestantism but inclined towards the forms of Roman Catholicism; they were, of course, sane enough to preserve them from becoming Roman Catholics. They reflected what our age must reflect if it wants to be sound and sane—the desire to feel something sacramental, ritual in the world again, but not something intended just to drag along old ritual. That is something which many do today there where the invalids of spiritual life are to be found, invalids of spiritual life, among whom I must number Hermann Bahr,[93] known to me for many years, and very much a friend in earlier times. We see how these invalids of life in the psyche tend towards Catholicism. We see this inclination towards a misunderstood Roman Catholicism also in the present time, in Hermann Bahr, in Scheler,[94] in Boerries von

Muenchhausen,[95] in all these people—it is a great number, and I know many of them personally—who strive out of the infirmity of their inner life towards Catholicism. It is a state of soul we know very well. It develops because people cannot make the effort to live an active inner life, to a genuine, courageous, active inner life, for as I said, they have become invalids of the inner life and look for things that present themselves ready-made. This is evident in all of Scheler's Romanticist works, which are quite brilliant, all of Hermann Bahr's recent Romanticist treatises, and so on. In a sense this is invalidism of the soul. It is the easygoing attitude where one does not want to make the soul yield up what the age demands, which is to find in the age of the spiritual soul what is needed to rise to a natural science where a sacramental quality is seen in all nature, with the whole of nature reflecting the divine and spiritual world order.

Yes, in the age of the spiritual soul we must very soon be people who are able to have not only the dry, abstract natural science which petrifies the whole human being yet is considered to be the world's salvation today, but the natural science which goes deeper and becomes a prayerful beholding of the sacred symbols which the godhead spreads out over the whole world in all the deeds that satisfy human beings but also in everything which serves to test them. When one will once again be able to test the laboratory sacramentally, at a higher level, and make the clinic an altar and not a mere slaughterhouse and wood workshop in a crude sense, the time will have come which divine evolution demands for the soul of today. No wonder then that much can be misunderstood in such a time— misunderstood above all because remnants still remain of the Academy of Gondishapur, wanting to take natural science without wishing to develop a connection with the Mystery on Golgotha. That makes natural science entirely ahrimanic, meeting all ahrimanic needs of humanity, in accord with the attitude of wanting to order the world purely according to external criteria. We may say: 'We must take up the impulse of the Mystery on Golgotha over and over again. We must take the words "I am with you always, to the end of the world",[96] until the earth's cycles are fulfilled, seriously.' These words must be taken seriously. Wanting to connect with the Mystery on Golgotha we must keep our souls fresh so that we may take up more and more new impulses flowing from the spiritual world in cycles, wanting to come to humanity not all the time but from time to time.

On the other hand there is a natural science where one does not want to know of such influences, simply putting the scientists into the laboratory or clinic and so on, and everything continues in treadmill fashion. People investigate the actions of invisible rays and do not wish to know what reveals itself to the world in those rays. They investigate aspirin, acetin or phenacetin and so on, giving them to patients; giving one after the other. One only has to look and record what one has seen, using the external senses; no need to make the soul stir itself. That is the attitude which has largely resulted from the Gondishapur impulse. For if that academy had won through with its impulses, people could rest at ease and have nothing more to do. They would in that case have been given as a grace everything which they would have wanted to do to further the spiritual soul. This attitude exists, applied to the sense-perceptible, in natural science.

The other attitude has been poured out into the world from Rome. It lives on in all kinds of different forms of something which has not come from Palestine, nor from the Mystery on Golgotha, but from Rome. This has gradually developed in two directions. Scatter incense to develop a ritual which does not call for intelligence but only sentient soul, and a rhetoric which seeks merely to formulate the words or to figure human actions in a way which in its legislation really is sheer rhetoric itself. Both sides have survived. Both sides can only be helped if one understands that on the other hand there must not be a natural science without the spirit in future. We will have to know where natural science has its limits, though we do not fight it. There is no need to fight; if you look at it in a positive spirit you find it provides tremendous, mighty things and no one has the right to speak derogatively about natural science unless they are fully cognisant of its findings. Anyone not cognisant is doing wrong to criticize natural science. Only those who believe in natural science, have really studied it and adopted its methods for themselves have gained the right to judge it by stating its limits and showing how natural science itself should lead to our grasping the world spiritually.

People with a hostile attitude have among other things discovered that in my books I expressed appreciation of Haeckel[97] and modern natural science. I would never dare to say anything derogatory about natural science unless I had first done everything possible for its appreciation. Basing oneself on a positive approach one only has the right to offer negative criticism if one is also able to show that one fully recognizes the object of one's criticism within the limits where recognition is due. I believe that I have fully gained the right to speak of a spiritual evolution of humanity, and within this I have shown the things which the senses do not teach, also having shown the significance of Darwinism and Haeckelianism in the life of science.

Basing oneself on the science of the spirit one is entitled to ask that one's words are taken in a slightly different way than they usually are. I therefore do not wish for things I am going to say from such a point of view as the one taken today—about Roman Catholicism or other endeavours in the present age—to be taken from the usual philistine point of view and confused with things which any liberalizing society may say in criticism of Roman Catholicism or similar endeavours. Nothing is meant in any other way than said here, and nothing else is meant but what can indeed also be justified from the point of view of spiritual-scientific investigation. Natural-scientific research needs deepening so that it may gradually take us into spiritual life. Something which has survived from ancient times, partly worn out in the course of human life, is now coming up again for the reasons I have just given—people's need for sacramentalism, for form. Seeing the divine alive in the world as we perceive forms, but understanding the forms; not to speak of Lucifer, Ahriman and the Christ as if it were dogma but to have this trinity before us also in works of art. That is what we need.

For this reason the central creation of Christ-Lucifer-Ahriman will be the wood carving which has arisen from the idea of creating figures that form a whole and reflect the challenge which lies in human evolution[98] but in such a way that we penetrate through to the spirit as we look at the forms. The creation of such forms had to be the basis for our building. One also does not have the right to consider this building in a commonplace way but must consider it according to the fundamental intentions for what are the great challenges of our time. It is needed at a time when we must once again approach the Mystery on Golgotha, this time in a new way.

In our time, I would like to say, the necessary point in time is given to find the Christ again, finding him at a higher standpoint. This means that there will also be resistance to the Christ. Such resistance existed also in the past. We know that the principles that were to come from Gondishapur were meant to prevent Christianity from developing altogether. The principles established by Augustus in Rome were intended to establish something which has nothing to do with the Christ impulse. It later developed into Catholicism because the Christian impulse erupted into Romanism. The persecution of Christians, the age of Nero, the Great or Diocletian persecution, everything that happened, including the rejection of Apollonius of Tyana,[99] happened because in Rome there was the greatest resistance to any acceptance of Christianity. It was to be eliminated but did not allow itself to be eliminated. Because of this, Romanism, having taken in as much of Christianity as possible, became the Roman Catholic Church, and the Roman Catholic Church continued to develop in that spirit—the moment a new revelation comes to humanity which takes it forward in understanding the Mystery on Golgotha the Roman Catholic Church turns not towards but away from it.

Do consider—we must again and again stress the fact that when Copernicus,[100] himself a canon, established his theory, the Roman Catholic Church declared it to be heresy. Until 1827 it was forbidden for true believers in the Roman Catholic Church to believe in the teaching of Copernicus. Since then it has been permitted to believe in it. It then became possible for a university professor of Roman

Catholic philosophy to say, 'Yes, the Roman Catholic Church banned the teaching of Copernicus, treated Galileo[101] the way it did. But', said Professor Muellner[102] in his vice-chancellor's address at Vienna University, 'today it is no longer appropriate to think so, today it is appropriate to say that the discoveries made by Copernicus and Galileo concerning the overt secrets of the universe have made the wonders of God's great powers so much more apparent.' It certainly was a Christian way of putting it, but it definitely was not a Roman Catholic way, for in that case censorship would apply. So it took some time until pressure from outside made the Roman Catholic Church acknowledge that insight into the universe does not suppress but promote Christianity. How long the Church will need to acknowledge the spiritual-scientific and anthroposophical findings—well, let us wait and see. As we wait we will probably have to depend on it that we will not arrive at a result whilst incarnated in this earthly body. That is one aspect of the matter.

Confusion and misunderstandings can easily happen, however. The confusion and misunderstandings are that there definitely is a subconscious urge in human souls to feel sacramental. The whole of humanity is today seeking to gain a sacramental feeling or sentience. Naturally the Roman Catholic Church uses this urge for its own purposes. What one would so much wish for is that in the present day, when people are, alas, deeply asleep, they will wake up to the important things that are happening (even if in many areas they cannot, as individuals, change things), at least wake up to what is going on. We do not, of course, need to say to ourselves: 'How do I, all on my own, change this?' With some things we have to let time pass, with others it will be necessary to act when conditions are right. There is no need to ask for everything all at once, according to one and the same recipe, but we do need a clear mind to observe things, so that when something is asked of us at a particular point we do really know what needs to be done. Above all it is necessary to see that wherever possible human beings, thinking that they do a lot of thinking, are actually asleep; people are asleep, and one would wish for them to come to true insight into the impulses which exist in human evolution. This is difficult, however. But others are on the alert. Jesuits are on the alert, Rome is wide awake. And these powers use every opportunity, every channel, to prevent the inherent faculties from developing in the direction of the spiritual soul and make them develop to suit Rome. If people would only wake up and see what Rome intends, if people were to judge things, which sometimes are perfectly evident, and which they judge according to quite different criteria, if they were to perceive the hand of Rome, of Jesuitism, this would be of enormous significance for solving the problems which will need to be solved in the near future, problems arising from the confused chaos of the present time.

It is therefore also of tremendous importance that we accept a fact like the one which we have been considering yesterday and today. We should not wish to judge the world according to abstract principles today. For the things that will have to happen over the next few years can only come from people who take their principles, the impulses for their actions and activities from spiritual insight into the world's progress. And I have to say that it is wrong, on the one hand, to take the sound, genuine, delightfully refreshing inclination which human souls have towards sacramentalism and use it to renew ancient rites. They do not use it to gain insight into the Mystery on Golgotha but to continue the mindless symbolism of Rome that was inaugurated in Augustus' day and is currently aimed at in Rome to meet their own purposes. That is the one way in which human souls can be exposed to misunderstandings, misunderstandings when it comes to sacramentalism, rites and also rhetoric, life in concepts, in words which people formulate but which clearly have not come from the efforts which Demosthenes made in Greece when he put stones on his tongue because he stammered but still wanted to convey the warmth and love that lived in his soul to the Greeks. Those other words are blandishments which captivate and enmesh people when they are not able to come fully awake in the impulses of human evolution.

This, too, is known among those who want to serve their own purposes. You can see how something which humanity, having sound impulses, had already been leaving behind in recent times is being brought back again! Read the writings and treatises published today about the aims of the Roman Catholic Church to renew the *corpus juris canonici* which is to rise again from its grave. The *corpus juris canonici* is to be the law again for Roman Catholic Christians. It is a made-up system. You will then be aware of the channels through which everything is meant to flow which comes from that Rome and the rhetoric, the clever, brilliantly clever thoughts, also so brilliantly initiated in the secrets of human evolution. They can never be effectively combated with the powers which governments have but only with the means available for cultural and spiritual battle. Let the Jesuits enter into everything but also give people everywhere the means of informing themselves at the same deep cultural and spiritual level as the Jesuits. In that case the Jesuits will no longer be a danger. It is only when one protects oneself and not the other thing but rather fights that other thing that Jesuitism will be a danger. Jesuitism can be allowed to enter into everything if we let the war we must wage against it unfold in exactly the same freedom and with the same lack of bias as anything coming from that side. The way we live today is still far, far removed from this.

But the things that are meant to spread do not just spread from this side. The spirit which lives in Roman sacramentalism, in Roman rhetoric, seeing its greatest triumphs today especially in the preaching of sermons, is only one side of it all.

The other side is the thinking of people who swear on crude natural science, not wanting to grow spiritual, wanting natural science to have validity only in so far as it becomes a technology which wants to reject everything which the tremendous, great phenomena of nature can tell about the spiritual in the world. I did once say, truly not from rhetoric but from deeper insight gained in the soul, 'Our physics, our mechanics, the whole of our ordinary science will not have reached its goal until the spirit of the Christ has entered into it.' The Mystery on Golgotha should not only be known as history. We should know that following the Mystery of Golgotha the phenomena of nature must also be seen in such a way that we know: 'The Christ is on earth. Before, he was not on earth.' A truly Christian science will not look for atoms and their laws, nor for the conservation of matter and energy, but for the revelation of the Christ in all natural phenomena which in consequence are a sacramentalism for humanity.

Looking at nature like this will also mean looking at moral, social, political and religious principles in human life in a way that is truly commensurate with this life. If we absorb the divine quality of nature, if we absorb the power of the Christ from insight into nature, we bring the Christology into everything we do, into the way we take the laws we prescribe for humanity, into all the external social care we want to provide for humanity, be it in looking after the poor, be it in any other sphere. If, however, we are unable to see the Christ in all of nature around us, if we cannot discover the Christ at work in all human actions, even if they are testing activities, we will also not be able to enter into our social, moral and political life with the powers which our age truly calls for. We would stop on the side of crude natural science, which is nothing but a failure to perceive the supersensible, or we would stop at mere rhetoric, a legacy of Romanism, the spectre of Romanism. On the one hand we have to refer to Rome when speaking of the misunderstood sacramentalism and ritual, to present-day Rome, a Rome grown strong particularly thanks to Leo XIII, the intellectual pope. And we must also find the name which points to the empty phrases in rhetoric which anyone who truly imbues himself with anthroposophical insight into spiritual life must perceive in rhetoric today. I have referred to this rhetoric here on a number of occasions. I have to speak of current events at this point, something I generally do only when the other subject matter has been given the time it needs.

Where do we find the rhetoric which, just like Roman pulpit rhetoric in Jesuitism, is the counterpart to a ritualism that has grown invalid? Where do we find the rhetoric which is the counterpart to a present-day natural science which cries out for spirituality, a science which threatens our human race because people are asleep as they take in things which for external reasons may perhaps be necessary but should remain completely alien to them in areas where there is need to gain insight? In Wilsonism! Woodrow Wilson is the name to use for living in sheer rhetoric, in sheer combining of words without substance, be they League of Nations or whatever; that is sheer indulgence in mere rhetoric. It is something humanity should not sleep through. Present-day humanity needs to understand what I have been stressing here: that true Wilsonism is the opposition to true progress for humanity. It has to be seen as rhetoric on feet of clay. On the one hand a state of the human soul which is no longer valid today is aiming for Rome, on the other a soul which misunderstands itself, eaten into by the natural-scientific, crude philosophy of life, tends towards something which today wafts through the world as mere rhetoric and is hostile to everything connected with true, beneficent progress for the human race.

One cannot put this in just a few bourgeois, philistine thoughts. The threat to our age coming from this direction has to be calmly considered as we study the day's events. On the other hand, however, we have to know its full significance. It will not do for the whole of humanity to stay asleep, letting the world be Wilsonized. There may be Wilsonians in America, in Europe, in one place or another, but there must also be people who know that there is a profound connection between Jesuitism on the one hand and Wilsonism on the other. There have to be such people. They need to grow beyond the philistinism of the present time and not base their opinion on what the day or perhaps also the year brings. They must be able to form an opinion according to what lies in the centuries and what the centuries reveal if we are really and truly able to look with inmost, active powers of soul to that hill where the cross stood, the cross on Golgotha which is the symbol for everything that has flowed into humanity as the revelation of the most ancient secrets and yet always will be young, bringing ever new revelations for humanity if human beings do not close their eyes and ears to it, letting themselves be lulled to sleep by Rome, or by the brilliant rhetoric towards which they are so much inclined today.

NOTES

1. *Human Evolution. A Spiritual Quest*, CW 347, Rudolf Steiner Press 2014. Lectures given in Dornach from 17 August to 2 September 1918.
2. Aurelius Augustinus, Doctor of the Church. Principal works: *Confessiones, De civitate dei*.
3. See Note 1, lecture of 26 August 1918.
4. René Descartes (1596–1650), mathematician, physicist and philosopher. His *Cogito ergo sum*, self-awareness, is the guarantee for all existence. See his work *Principiorum Philosophiae*, Amsterdam 1644.
5. *The Riddle of Man*, CW 20, tr. W. Lindeman, Mercury Press, Spring Valley 1990.
6. *Occult Science. An Outline*, CW 13, tr. G. & M. Adams, Rudolf Steiner Press, London 1962/3. See also *An Outline of Esoteric Science*.
7. See lectures 4, 5 and 6 in *Human Evolution* (Note 1).
8. Claude-Henri de Rouvroy Comte de Saint-Simon (1760–1825), French social philosopher. Mainly concerned with the consequences of industrialization for human development in modern forms of society. Considered the main problem to be the contradistinction between the 'idle' human being (nobility, landed gentry, priests and civil servants) and those working in production (entrepreneurs, workers). He considered a kind of moralistic and religious reflection on basic religious values was the way to solve the social question.
9. Auguste Comte (1798–1857), philosopher, founder of positivism and sociology. *Cours de Philosophie Positive* (1830–42), Paris, vol. III, ch. 7, vol. IV, ch. 1, 4 and 5. See also Rudolf Steiner, *The Riddles of Philosophy*, CW 18, Anthroposophic Press, New York 1973.
10. Friedrich Wilhelm Joseph Schelling (1775–1854), German natural and religious philosopher. Close friend of Hegel and Hoelderlin. Professor of Philosophy in Jena (with Hegel and Fichte), later taught at other German universities. Rudolf Steiner considered Schelling's philosophy to be extraordinarily significant. See his *Riddles of Philosophy* (as in Note 9) and *The Riddle of Man*, chapter on Schelling.
11. Johann Gottlieb Fichte (1762–1814), Professor of Philosophy in Jena and at other German universities. Rudolf Steiner had studied Fichte from his young days.
12. The works of Schelling translated into English include: *Treatise on The Deities of Samothrace* (1977), a translation and introduction by R.F. Brown; *Of Human Freedom* (1936), a translation with critical introduction and notes by J. Gutmann.

13. Jakob Boehme (1575–1624). During his travels as a journeyman shoemaker he came in touch with the thinking of Schwenckfeldt and got involved in the battles between Protestants and Catholics. Wrote his *Die Morgenroete im Aufgang* (aurora at dawn) in 1610, much to the displeasure of Church and magistrate. See Rudolf Steiner's lecture of 9 January 1913 entitled *Jacob Boehme*, tr. M.W. Barnetson, New York & London 1942, and the chapter on Valentin Weigel and Jacob Boehme in *Mystics after Modernism*, tr. K. Zimmer, Hudson 2000.
14. In Acts 17:34, Dionysius the Areopagite is mentioned as a follower of Paul who converted him to Christianity; first Bishop of Athens. At the end of the fifth century works appeared under his name, written in Greek, which are now considered to be those of the Pseudo-Areopagite.
15. Jeremy Bentham (1748–1832), philosopher, pacifist and protagonist of free trade. Developed social ethics based on ethical individualism aiming for the greatest happiness for the greatest number, and was a major influence especially in England. A major work of his was *Introduction to the Principles of Morals and Legislation* (1780).
16. Rudolf Steiner was probably referring to C.G. Harrison's *The Transcendental Universe*.
17. Ludwig Feuerbach (1804–72), German philosopher. Works include *The Essence of Christianity*, tr. Marian Evans, Oxford, and *Grundsaetze der Philosophie der Zukunft* (principles of future philosophy).
18. See Rudolf Steiner's lecture of 18 October 1915 in *The Occult Movement in the Nineteenth Century*, CW 254, tr. D.S. Osmond, Rudolf Steiner Press, London 1973.
19. Karl Marx (1818–83), founder of scientific socialism and historical materialism.
20. See lecture of 2 September in *Human Evolution. A Spiritual Quest* (details in Note 1).
21. See lecture given in Berlin on 12 October 1905 on War and Peace and the Science of the Spirit, *Anthroposophical Review*, 1985:3.
22. Woodrow Wilson (1856–1924), US political scientist, President of the USA 1912–21. Stood for national right of self-determination. Rudolf Steiner was highly critical of Wilson's views, e.g. in *Ideas for a New Europe* and *Social Future*.
23. Leopold von Ranke (1795–1886), German historian.
24. Rudolf Eucken (1846–1929), German philosopher, awarded the Nobel Prize for Literature in 1908. Works include: *The Truth of Religion* (1901); *Main Currents of Modern Thought* (1878, tr. M. Stuart Phelps, New York 1880).
25. Otto Liebmann (1840–1912), German philosopher, taught in Strasbourg and Jena. Works include: *Zur Analyse der Wirklichkeit* (1880, on analysis of actuality); *Gedanken und Tatsachen* (1882–1904, thoughts and facts).
26. Arthur Schopenhauer (1788–1860), German philosopher. See Rudolf Steiner's essay on Schopenhauer (in German, GA 33).
27. Wilhelm Wundt (1832–1920), German physician, philosopher and psychologist, taught in Heidelberg, Zurich and Leipzig. Published lectures on

the human and animal soul (1863), basic principles of physiological psychology (1873–4). See Rudolf Steiner, *The Riddles of Philosophy*, CW 18.
28. See Rudolf Steiner, *Inner Development Impulses of Humanity, Goethe and the Crisis of the 19th Century*. Cosmic and Human History Vol. 2. CW 171.
29. At the end of the lecture Rudolf Steiner added the following comments relating to disagreements among some of the members. See also the volume now in preparation on anthroposophy and its opponents (*Die Anthroposophie und ihre Gegner*, CW 255b). These were not included in earlier editions of this volume.

'In addition I wish to say the following: I am under no illusion. You know—or at least some who do truly understand some of the things I put forward should know—I am not inclined towards persecution mania nor to any kind of illusions in life. Genuine spiritual science does thoroughly rid one of such things. In spite of this I do sometimes have to comment on one thing or another. It is sometimes necessary to make such a comment so that members who call themselves anthroposophic do not completely go to sleep. I do not want people to be under any illusion.

'Well, there are a number of things that need to be said. However, because of a particular recent incident I want to say the following. It is true that in the immediate future this movement which I call anthroposophic will be exposed to major attacks from various angles, and particularly from one side which is already very evident. Individual attacks are of very little account, for whatever people say individually is usually as amateurish as can be. But the fact remains that it has been an attack, especially when coming from the clerical side as of now. There is an intention behind this and that is more important than what is said in individual instances and must be taken very seriously.

'With regard to something which happened just the other day I therefore wish to say the following. The kind of thing I mean here must, of course, be taken as such in human life that one does not pay further attention to it the way it comes to me. Those concerned will know what this is about. Anyone who wishes to tell me something, or discuss something with me, should do so quite openly, nor should they imagine that they have something to bring that is essential if they are not speaking openly. As I said, I am under no illusion and anyone who thinks that I am under some illusion is very much in error. Even if it should be the case that there are people here on the building site who bear things on two shoulders, as the saying goes, given up to some ambiguity, there is no need to try and inform me about this in some covert way. I know more about people, including those who walk around on our building site, than I am able to tell, things I must have in mind. No one should think that it is necessary to draw my attention to it in a covert way that harmful things may perhaps be happening here. For in the way in which social life has to be when one is having an eye on something as real as this building project, it is not always possible to act according to genuine insight gained from deeper background knowledge. Anyone who does after all want to tell me something should do so openly. Otherwise people will be

under the illusion that I am deluded and had illusions about the people with whom I have to deal. I do not do so; I know that people can also be two-faced.'
30. Jean Paul (Friedrich Richter, 1763–1825), the passage appears in *Levana oder Erziehlehre*, 3. Aufl., Stuttgart 1845, Seite XXVII.
31. *The Spiritual Guidance of the Individual and Humanity* (CW 15), tr. R. Desch, Anthroposophic Press, New York 1992.
32. See lectures of 13 and 19 May 1917 in *Die geistigen Hintergruende des Ersten Weltkrieges* (CW 174b, not translated), and *Mitteleuropa zwischen Ost und West* ('Laws of Human Evolution', typescript at Rudolf Steiner House Library in London).
33. Ulrich von Wilamowitz-Moellendorff (1848–1931), philologist and translator of *Griechische Tragoedien* (Greek tragedies), 3 vols.
34. *Internationale Rundschau*, Zurich, 4. Jahrg., Heft 5, of 25 April 1918.
35. Karl Johann Kautsky (1854–1938), social democrat theoretician and historian.
36. The actual words given are: 'Philosophers have merely interpreted the world in different ways, what matters is to change it.' In *Thesen ueber Feuerbach*, 1845/46, 11.
37. Wilhelm Traugott Krug (1770–1842), philosopher (following Kant). *Allgemeines Handwoerterbuch der philosophischen Wissenschaften*, fuenf Baende, Leipzig 1827–9, and *Fundamentalphilosophie* (1803).
38. Meister Eckhart (*c.* 1260–1327), mystic. See Rudolf Steiner in *Mystics after Modernism* (CW 7), tr. K. Zimmer. Rudolf Steiner Publications, Hudson 2000.
39. Johannes Tauler (*c.* 1300–61), mystic. See ref. 38.
40. Rudolf Steiner's correspondence with Marie Steiner-von Sivers (CW 262) shows that this was in Colmar. Rudolf Steiner gave lectures there on 19 and 20 November 1905.
41. Written by Rudolf Steiner and performed in Munich with him as director. *The Portal of Initiation*, Scene 4.
42. *Truth and Science*, CW 3, tr. W. Lindeman, Mercury Press, Spring Valley 1993.
43. *The Philosophy of Spiritual Activity. A Philosophy of Freedom*, CW 4, tr. R. Stebbing, Rudolf Steiner Press, Bristol 1992.
44. Plato (427–347 BC), philosopher. See Rudolf Steiner, *The Riddles of Philosophy*, Anthroposophic Press, New York 1973.
45. Aristotle (384–322 BC), philosopher. See also Note 44.
46. Friedrich Hebbel (1813–63) wrote in his diary: 'According to the migration of souls it is possible that Plato is now a schoolboy getting the cane because he does not understand Plato.' Diaries vol. 1 Nr. 1745. German edition R.M. Werner, Berlin 1901.
47. Name often given to God in the cabbala. The term 'the Ancient of days' comes from the Old Testament, Daniel 7:9 and 13. In the German Bible the term is simply *der Alte* (the old one).
48. See lecture of 14 September 1918 in this volume.
49. The Goetheanum designed by Rudolf Steiner was a monumental two-domed building in Dornach, nr Basel (1913–21). See Rudolf Steiner/various translators, *Architecture as a Synthesis of the Arts* (CW 286).

50. Michel Eyquem de Montaigne (1533–92), French writer on philosophy, most famous for his *Essais* (1580–8). Rudolf Steiner spoke of him on 2 December 1915 (CW 65, not available in English).
51. *The Inner Nature of Man*, tr. A. Meuss (CW 153), lecture of 14 April 1914.
52. *Anthroposophy and the Social Question*, tr. E. Bowen-Wedgwood, Mercury Press, Spring Valley 1982. Also included in *Reincarnation and Immortality*.
53. C.H. Meray, *Weltmutation. Schoepfungsgesetze ueber Krieg und Frieden und die Geburt einer neuen Zivilisation*. Zurich 1918, S. 124ff.
54. *The Apocalypse of St John*, tr. J. Collis, lecture of 24 June 1908 (CW 104).
55. Rudolf Steiner, tr. *The Fall of the Spirits of Darkness*, A.R. Meuss, lectures given in September/October 1917 (CW 177).
56. See 'The Problem of Faust', typescript translation of lectures given on 27, 28 and 29 September 1918 in Basel (CW 273). The Library, Rudolf Steiner House, London.
57. Gottfried Wilhelm Leibniz (1646–1716), German polymath and philosopher. According to his *Monadology*, tr. Nicholas Rescher 1991 (*The Monadology: An Edition for Students*, University of Pittsburgh Press), 'no two entities exist in the natural world who are completely the same'. Two princesses attempted to refute this in Herrenhausen Park, Hanover. An engraving by Schubert (1796) shows this.
58. Friedrich Nietzsche (1844–1900), German philologist, poet and philosopher. See also Rudolf Steiner, *Friedrich Nietzsche*, tr. M. Ingram deRis (CW 5).
59. Anaxagoras (500–428 BC), philosopher, mathematician and astronomer. See Rudolf Steiner, *The Riddles of Philosophy* (CW 5), Anthroposophic Press, New York 1973.
60. Heraclitus (c. 544–483 BC), Greek philosopher.
61. Thales of Miletus (625–545 BC), Greek philosopher.
62. Julian the Apostate, Roman emperor AD 361–3.
63. Publius Cornelius Tacitus (c. AD 55–120), Roman historian.
64. *Christianity as Mystical Fact*, tr. A. Welburn (CW 8).
65. Gaius Julius Caesar Octavianus, Augustus (63 BC–AD 14), first Roman emperor, his title being Caesar Augustus.
66. *Goethe's Standard of the Soul*, tr. D.S. Osmond (CW 22).
67. Titus Flavius Clemens, known as Clement of Alexandria (c. AD 150–c. AD 217), philosopher and Church Father. See Rudolf Steiner, *Christianity as Mystical Fact*, tr. A. Welburn (CW 8).
68. Origen or Origen Adamantus (AD 185–254), Greek philosopher, founder of Christian gnosticism and theology.
69. Quintus Septimus Florens Tertullian (c. AD 150–230), in *Apologeticum*.
70. Rudolf Steiner, *The Fifth Gospel*, tr. A.R. Meuss (CW 148).
71. Reform movement within the Roman Catholic Church with the intention of making epistemological and historical criticism and also the idea of evolution bear fruit for the Church. Was absolutely rejected by the Vatican, so much so that from 1910 onwards professors and clerics had to swear an 'Oath against Modernism'.
72. Richard Wahle (1857–1935). Works included *Das Ganze der Philosophie und*

ihr Ende, Vienna and Leipzig 1894, and *Ueber den Mechanismus des geistigen Lebens*, Vienna and Leipzig 1906.
73. Loc. cit. 1. Buch, 4. Kap., S. 92.
74. Richard Wahle, *Die Tragikomoedie der Weisheit*, Vienna and Leipzig 1905, S. 132.
75. Earlier editions had 'a certain letter'. Corrected acc. to shorthand record. 'General letters' were originally (acc. to Clement of Alexandria and Origen) letters addressed not to individual congregations but 'encyclic', addressed to all. The authors of these epistles, seven in all, were James, Peter, John and Judas. They were included in the New Testment together with Paul's epistles.
76. The passages given by Rudolf Steiner ('beast bound in fetters' and 'kept in balance') could not be found in the New Testament nor in the apocryphal Protevangelium of James. They can, however, be found in the Book of Revelation 20:2 and 6:5. The text of the Protevangelium appears in *Apokryphen zum alten und neuen Testament* (Menesse-Bibliothek der Weltliteratur).
77. John, Book of Revelation 13:8.
78. There followed a short example of cleverness on the part of the authorities. This had not been included in earlier editions since the stenographer had clearly found it difficult to follow the meaning and take it down accurately. Below is the actual text.

'With some things which are today considered rather clever, my friends, one is reminded of an announcement I read the other day. A local or government authority made it known that they were about to issue 500 g coupons for I do not know what kind of food. The statement said that they would shortly issue 500 g coupons for butter or whatever. That is exactly what they said. Well, you'll find it difficult to put such a coupon in your pocket, with every coupon weighing 500 g! Now if the matter is as crude as that you'll certainly notice it. But whoever wrote it cannot have noticed. But behold, such judgements are frequently made, and many such things are said. If we were to examine some of the things said or written today even where the problem is not so obvious, we would find that it was just the same as with these 500 g bread or fat or cheese coupons.'
79. Justinian I, Roman emperor, reigned from 527 to 565.
80. Socrates (469–399 BC), Greek philosopher.
81. Aristotle (384–322 BC), Greek philosopher.
82. Zeno the Isaurian (*c.* 440–91), Byzantine emperor 474–91, ordered the closure of the School of Edessa in 489.
83. Gondishapur or Gundeshapur, est. by Shapur I, Sassanid emperor. City in Mesopotamia, between the ruins of Susa and the city of Shushtar, was for a long time the cultural metropolis of the Sassanid Empire. Works of Aristotle were translated into Persian at Gondishapur. Khosrau I (also known as Chosroes I and Kasra in classical sources, 501–79, most commonly known in Persian as Anushiruwān 'the immortal soul' and Anushiruwan the Just, was the great sponsor of these translations. In Ferdinand Justi's *Geschichte des alten Persiens* (history of ancient Persia) it says on p. 213: 'Khosrau ordered the translation of Aristotle and Plato. The works on medicine and logic were translated from Persian to Arabic under the Caliphate.'

84. Muhammad (c. 570–632), founder of Islam.
85. Roger Bacon (1214–94), Franciscan, taught at Oxford University. Was called 'doctor mirabilis' because of his vast knowledge. He applied natural-scientific thinking also to theological thinking.
86. Showing Thomas Aquinas with Averroes under his feet. One of these paintings is in the Louvre in Paris.
87. Moshe ben Maimon or Mūsā ibn Maymūn, acronymed RaMBaM for *Rabbeinu Moshe Ben Maimon*, 'Our Rabbi/Teacher Moses Son of Maimon' (1135–1204), Jewish philosopher.
88. Avicenna (980–1037), Arab philosopher.
89. Averroes (1126–98), Arab philosopher and physician.
90. *The Riddle of Man*, tr. W. Lindeman, Preface and Introduction, Mercury Press, Spring Valley 1990.
91. Descartes, see Note 4.
92. Demosthenes (384–22 BC), prominent Greek orator.
93. Hermann Bahr (1863–1934), Austrian writer and poet.
94. Max Scheler (1874–1928), German philosopher.
95. Borries von Muenchhausen (1874–1945), German poet.
96. End of the Gospel of Matthew.
97. Ernst Haeckel (1834–1919), zoologist. See R. Steiner, *Three Essays on Haeckel and Karma*, essay from CW 30, Theosophical Publishing Co., London 1914.
98. See R. Steiner/varous translators, *Architecture as a Synthesis of the Arts* (CW 286), Rudolf Steiner Press, London 1999.
99. Apollonius of Tyana lived in the first century; neopythagorean itinerant preacher.
100. Nicolaus Copernicus (1473–1543), philosopher, humanist, astronomer.
101. Galileo Galilei (1564–1642), mathematician.
102. Laurenz Muellner (1848–1911), *Die Bedeutung Galileis fuer die Philosophie*, inaugural address of 8 November 1894 at Vienna University. Reprinted in *Die Drei*, 16, 1933/34, S. 29ff. See also R. Steiner, *Autobiography*, tr. R. Stebbing (CW 28), chapter 7.

RUDOLF STEINER'S COLLECTED WORKS

The German Edition of Rudolf Steiner's Collected Works (the *Gesamtausgabe* [GA] published by Rudolf Steiner Verlag, Dornach, Switzerland) presently runs to 354 titles, organized either by type of work (written or spoken), chronology, audience (public or other), or subject (education, art, etc.). For ease of comparison, the Collected Works in English [CW] follows the German organization exactly. A complete listing of the CWs follows with literal translations of the German titles. Other than in the case of the books published in his lifetime, titles were rarely given by Rudolf Steiner himself, and were often provided by the editors of the German editions. The titles in English are not necessarily the same as the German; and, indeed, over the past seventy-five years have frequently been different, with the same book sometimes appearing under different titles.

For ease of identification and to avoid confusion, we suggest that readers looking for a title should do so by CW number. Because the work of creating the Collected Works of Rudolf Steiner is an ongoing process, with new titles being published every year, we have not indicated in this listing which books are presently available. To find out what titles in the Collected Works are currently in print, please check our website at www.rudolfsteinerpress.com (or www.steinerbooks.org for US readers).

Written Work

CW 1	Goethe: Natural-Scientific Writings, Introduction, with Footnotes and Explanations in the text by Rudolf Steiner
CW 2	Outlines of an Epistemology of the Goethean World View, with Special Consideration of Schiller
CW 3	Truth and Science
CW 4	The Philosophy of Freedom
CW 4a	Documents to 'The Philosophy of Freedom'
CW 5	Friedrich Nietzsche, A Fighter against His Time
CW 6	Goethe's Worldview
CW 6a	Now in CW 30
CW 7	Mysticism at the Dawn of Modern Spiritual Life and Its Relationship with Modern Worldviews
CW 8	Christianity as Mystical Fact and the Mysteries of Antiquity
CW 9	Theosophy: An Introduction into Supersensible World Knowledge and Human Purpose
CW 10	How Does One Attain Knowledge of Higher Worlds?
CW 11	From the Akasha-Chronicle

CW 12	Levels of Higher Knowledge
CW 13	Occult Science in Outline
CW 14	Four Mystery Dramas
CW 15	The Spiritual Guidance of the Individual and Humanity
CW 16	A Way to Human Self-Knowledge: Eight Meditations
CW 17	The Threshold of the Spiritual World. Aphoristic Comments
CW 18	The Riddles of Philosophy in Their History, Presented as an Outline
CW 19	Contained in CW 24
CW 20	The Riddles of the Human Being: Articulated and Unarticulated in the Thinking, Views and Opinions of a Series of German and Austrian Personalities
CW 21	The Riddles of the Soul
CW 22	Goethe's Spiritual Nature And Its Revelation In 'Faust' and through the 'Fairy Tale of the Snake and the Lily'
CW 23	The Central Points of the Social Question in the Necessities of Life in the Present and the Future
CW 24	Essays Concerning the Threefold Division of the Social Organism and the Period 1915–1921
CW 25	Cosmology, Religion and Philosophy
CW 26	Anthroposophical Leading Thoughts
CW 27	Fundamentals for Expansion of the Art of Healing according to Spiritual-Scientific Insights
CW 28	The Course of My Life
CW 29	Collected Essays on Dramaturgy, 1889–1900
CW 30	Methodical Foundations of Anthroposophy: Collected Essays on Philosophy, Natural Science, Aesthetics and Psychology, 1884–1901
CW 31	Collected Essays on Culture and Current Events, 1887–1901
CW 32	Collected Essays on Literature, 1884–1902
CW 33	Biographies and Biographical Sketches, 1894–1905
CW 34	Lucifer-Gnosis: Foundational Essays on Anthroposophy and Reports from the Periodicals 'Lucifer' and 'Lucifer-Gnosis,' 1903–1908
CW 35	Philosophy and Anthroposophy: Collected Essays, 1904–1923
CW 36	The Goetheanum-Idea in the Middle of the Cultural Crisis of the Present: Collected Essays from the Periodical 'Das Goetheanum,' 1921–1925
CW 37	Now in CWs 260a and 251
CW 38	Letters, Vol. 1: 1881–1890
CW 39	Letters, Vol. 2: 1890–1925
CW 40	Truth-Wrought Words
CW 40a	Sayings, Poems and Mantras; Supplementary Volume
CW 42	Now in CWs 264–266
CW 43	Stage Adaptations
CW 44	On the Four Mystery Dramas. Sketches, Fragments and Paralipomena on the Four Mystery Dramas
CW 45	Anthroposophy: A Fragment from the Year 1910

Rudolf Steiner's Collected Works * 281

Public Lectures

CW 51	On Philosophy, History and Literature
CW 52	Spiritual Teachings Concerning the Soul and Observation of the World
CW 53	The Origin and Goal of the Human Being
CW 54	The Riddles of the World and Anthroposophy
CW 55	Knowledge of the Supersensible in Our Times and Its Meaning for Life Today
CW 56	Knowledge of the Soul and of the Spirit
CW 57	Where and How Does One Find the Spirit?
CW 58	The Metamorphoses of the Soul Life. Paths of Soul Experiences: Part One
CW 59	The Metamorphoses of the Soul Life. Paths of Soul Experiences: Part Two
CW 60	The Answers of Spiritual Science to the Biggest Questions of Existence
CW 61	Human History in the Light of Spiritual Research
CW 62	Results of Spiritual Research
CW 63	Spiritual Science as a Treasure for Life
CW 64	Out of Destiny-Burdened Times
CW 65	Out of Central European Spiritual Life
CW 66	Spirit and Matter, Life and Death
CW 67	The Eternal in the Human Soul. Immortality and Freedom
CW 68	Public lectures in various cities, 1906–1918
CW 69	Public lectures in various cities, 1906–1918
CW 70	Public lectures in various cities, 1906–1918
CW 71	Public lectures in various cities, 1906–1918
CW 72	Freedom—Immortality—Social Life
CW 73	The Supplementing of the Modern Sciences through Anthroposophy
CW 73a	Specialized Fields of Knowledge and Anthroposophy
CW 74	The Philosophy of Thomas Aquinas
CW 75	Public lectures in various cities, 1906–1918
CW 76	The Fructifying Effect of Anthroposophy on Specialized Fields
CW 77a	The Task of Anthroposophy in Relation to Science and Life: The Darmstadt College Course
CW 77b	Art and Anthroposophy. The Goetheanum-Impulse
CW 78	Anthroposophy, Its Roots of Knowledge and Fruits for Life
CW 79	The Reality of the Higher Worlds
CW 80	Public lectures in various cities, 1922
CW 81	Renewal-Impulses for Culture and Science—Berlin College Course
CW 82	So that the Human Being Can Become a Complete Human Being
CW 83	Western and Eastern World-Contrast. Paths to Understanding It through Anthroposophy
CW 84	What Did the Goetheanum Intend and What Should Anthroposophy Do?

Lectures to the Members of the Anthroposophical Society

CW 88	Concerning the Astral World and Devachan
CW 89	Consciousness—Life—Form. Fundamental Principles of a Spiritual-Scientific Cosmology
CW 90	Participant Notes from the Lectures during the Years 1903–1905
CW 91	Participant Notes from the Lectures during the Years 1903–1905
CW 92	The Occult Truths of Ancient Myths and Sagas
CW 93	The Temple Legend and the Golden Legend
CW 93a	Fundamentals of Esotericism
CW 94	Cosmogony. Popular Occultism. The Gospel of John. The Theosophy in the Gospel of John
CW 95	At the Gates of Theosophy
CW 96	Origin-Impulses of Spiritual Science. Christian Esotericism in the Light of New Spirit-Knowledge
CW 97	The Christian Mystery
CW 98	Nature Beings and Spirit Beings—Their Effects in Our Visible World
CW 99	The Theosophy of the Rosicrucians
CW 100	Human Development and Christ-Knowledge
CW 101	Myths and Legends. Occult Signs and Symbols
CW 102	The Working into Human Beings by Spiritual Beings
CW 103	The Gospel of John
CW 104	The Apocalypse of John
CW 104a	From the Picture-Script of the Apocalypse of John
CW 105	Universe, Earth, the Human Being: Their Being and Development, as well as Their Reflection in the Connection between Egyptian Mythology and Modern Culture
CW 106	Egyptian Myths and Mysteries in Relation to the Active Spiritual Forces of the Present
CW 107	Spiritual-Scientific Knowledge of the Human Being
CW 108	Answering the Questions of Life and the World through Anthroposophy
CW 109	The Principle of Spiritual Economy in Connection with the Question of Reincarnation. An Aspect of the Spiritual Guidance of Humanity
CW 110	The Spiritual Hierarchies and Their Reflection in the Physical World. Zodiac, Planets and Cosmos
CW 111	Contained in CW 109
CW 112	The Gospel of John in Relation to the Three Other Gospels, Especially the Gospel of Luke
CW 113	The Orient in the Light of the Occident. The Children of Lucifer and the Brothers of Christ
CW 114	The Gospel of Luke
CW 115	Anthroposophy—Psychosophy—Pneumatosophy
CW 116	The Christ-Impulse and the Development of 'I'-Consciousness
CW 117	The Deeper Secrets of the Development of Humanity in Light of the Gospels

Rudolf Steiner's Collected Works * 283

CW 118	The Event of the Christ-Appearance in the Etheric World
CW 119	Macrocosm and Microcosm. The Large World and the Small World. Soul-Questions, Life-Questions, Spirit-Questions
CW 120	The Revelation of Karma
CW 121	The Mission of Individual Folk-Souls in Connection with Germanic-Nordic Mythology
CW 122	The Secrets of the Biblical Creation-Story. The Six-Day Work in the First Book of Moses
CW 123	The Gospel of Matthew
CW 124	Excursus in the Area of the Gospel of Mark
CW 125	Paths and Goals of the Spiritual Human Being. Life Questions in the Light of Spiritual Science
CW 126	Occult History. Esoteric Observations of the Karmic Relationships of Personalities and Events of World History
CW 127	The Mission of the New Spiritual Revelation. The Christ-Event as the Middle-Point of Earth Evolution
CW 128	An Occult Physiology
CW 129	Wonders of the World, Trials of the Soul, and Revelations of the Spirit
CW 130	Esoteric Christianity and the Spiritual Guidance of Humanity
CW 131	From Jesus to Christ
CW 132	Evolution from the View Point of the Truth
CW 133	The Earthly and the Cosmic Human Being
CW 134	The World of the Senses and the World of the Spirit
CW 135	Reincarnation and Karma and their Meaning for the Culture of the Present
CW 136	The Spiritual Beings in Celestial Bodies and the Realms of Nature
CW 137	The Human Being in the Light of Occultism, Theosophy and Philosophy
CW 138	On Initiation. On Eternity and the Passing Moment. On the Light of the Spirit and the Darkness of Life
CW 139	The Gospel of Mark
CW 140	Occult Investigation into the Life between Death and New Birth. The Living Interaction between Life and Death
CW 141	Life between Death and New Birth in Relationship to Cosmic Facts
CW 142	The Bhagavad Gita and the Letters of Paul
CW 143	Experiences of the Supersensible. Three Paths of the Soul to Christ
CW 144	The Mysteries of the East and of Christianity
CW 145	What Significance Does Occult Development of the Human Being Have for the Sheaths—Physical Body, Etheric Body, Astral Body, and Self?
CW 146	The Occult Foundations of the Bhagavad Gita
CW 147	The Secrets of the Threshold
CW 148	Out of Research in the Akasha: The Fifth Gospel
CW 149	Christ and the Spiritual World. Concerning the Search for the Holy Grail

CW 150	The World of the Spirit and Its Extension into Physical Existence; The Influence of the Dead in the World of the Living
CW 151	Human Thought and Cosmic Thought
CW 152	Preliminary Stages to the Mystery of Golgotha
CW 153	The Inner Being of the Human Being and Life Between Death and New Birth
CW 154	How does One Gain an Understanding of the Spiritual World? The Flowing in of Spiritual Impulses from out of the World of the Deceased
CW 155	Christ and the Human Soul. Concerning the Meaning of Life. Theosophical Morality. Anthroposophy and Christianity
CW 156	Occult Reading and Occult Hearing
CW 157	Human Destinies and the Destiny of Peoples
CW 157a	The Formation of Destiny and the Life after Death
CW 158	The Connection Between the Human Being and the Elemental World. Kalevala—Olaf Åsteson—The Russian People—The World as the Result of the Influences of Equilibrium
CW 159	The Mystery of Death. The Nature and Significance of Middle Europe and the European Folk Spirits
CW 160	In CW 159
CW 161	Paths of Spiritual Knowledge and the Renewal of the Artistic Worldview
CW 162	Questions of Art and Life in Light of Spiritual Science
CW 163	Coincidence, Necessity and Providence. Imaginative Knowledge and the Processes after Death
CW 164	The Value of Thinking for a Knowledge That Satisfies the Human Being. The Relationship of Spiritual Science to Natural Science
CW 165	The Spiritual Unification of Humanity through the Christ-Impulse
CW 166	Necessity and Freedom in the Events of the World and in Human Action
CW 167	The Present and the Past in the Human Spirit
CW 168	The Connection between the Living and the Dead
CW 169	World-being and Selfhood
CW 170	The Riddle of the Human Being. The Spiritual Background of Human History. Cosmic and Human History, Vol. 1
CW 171	Inner Development-Impulses of Humanity. Goethe and the Crisis of the 19th Century. Cosmic and Human History, Vol. 2
CW 172	The Karma of the Vocation of the Human Being in Connection with Goethe's Life. Cosmic and Human History, Vol. 3
CW 173	Contemporary-Historical Considerations: The Karma of Untruthfulness, Part One. Cosmic and Human History, Vol. 4
CW 174	Contemporary-Historical Considerations: The Karma of Untruthfulness, Part Two. Cosmic and Human History, Vol. 5
CW 174a	Middle Europe between East and West. Cosmic and Human History, Vol. 6
CW 174b	The Spiritual Background of the First World War. Cosmic and Human History, Vol. 7

CW 175	Building Stones for an Understanding of the Mystery of Golgotha. Cosmic and Human Metamorphoses
CW 176	Truths of Evolution of the Individual and Humanity. The Karma of Materialism
CW 177	The Spiritual Background of the Outer World. The Fall of the Spirits of Darkness. Spiritual Beings and Their Effects, Vol. 1
CW 178	Individual Spiritual Beings and their Influence in the Soul of the Human Being. Spiritual Beings and their Effects, Vol. 2
CW 179	Spiritual Beings and Their Effects. Historical Necessity and Freedom. The Influences on Destiny from out of the World of the Dead. Spiritual Beings and Their Effects, Vol. 3
CW 180	Mystery Truths and Christmas Impulses. Ancient Myths and their Meaning. Spiritual Beings and Their Effects, Vol. 4
CW 181	Earthly Death and Cosmic Life. Anthroposophical Gifts for Life. Necessities of Consciousness for the Present and the Future.
CW 182	Death as Transformation of Life
CW 183	The Science of the Development of the Human Being
CW 184	The Polarity of Duration and Development in Human Life. The Cosmic Pre-History of Humanity
CW 185	Historical Symptomology
CW 185a	Historical-Developmental Foundations for Forming a Social Judgement
CW 186	The Fundamental Social Demands of Our Time—In Changed Situations
CW 187	How Can Humanity Find the Christ Again? The Threefold Shadow-Existence of our Time and the New Christ-Light
CW 188	Goetheanism, a Transformation-Impulse and Resurrection-Thought. Science of the Human Being and Science of Sociology
CW 189	The Social Question as a Question of Consciousness. The Spiritual Background of the Social Question, Vol. 1
CW 190	Impulses of the Past and the Future in Social Occurrences. The Spiritual Background of the Social Question, Vol. 2
CW 191	Social Understanding from Spiritual-Scientific Cognition. The Spiritual Background of the Social Question, Vol. 3
CW 192	Spiritual-Scientific Treatment of Social and Pedagogical Questions
CW 193	The Inner Aspect of the Social Riddle. Luciferic Past and Ahrimanic Future
CW 194	The Mission of Michael. The Revelation of the Actual Mysteries of the Human Being
CW 195	Cosmic New Year and the New Year Idea
CW 196	Spiritual and Social Transformations in the Development of Humanity
CW 197	Polarities in the Development of Humanity: West and East Materialism and Mysticism Knowledge and Belief
CW 198	Healing Factors for the Social Organism
CW 199	Spiritual Science as Knowledge of the Foundational Impulses of Social Formation

CW 200	The New Spirituality and the Christ-Experience of the 20th Century
CW 201	The Correspondences Between Microcosm and Macrocosm. The Human Being—A Hieroglyph of the Universe. The Human Being in Relationship with the Cosmos: 1
CW 202	The Bridge between the World-Spirituality and the Physical Aspect of the Human Being. The Search for the New Isis, the Divine Sophia. The Human Being in Relationship with the Cosmos: 2
CW 203	The Responsibility of Human Beings for the Development of the World through their Spiritual Connection with the Planet Earth and the World of the Stars. The Human Being in Relationship with the Cosmos: 3
CW 204	Perspectives of the Development of Humanity. The Materialistic Knowledge-Impulse and the Task of Anthroposophy. The Human Being in Relationship with the Cosmos: 4
CW 205	Human Development, World-Soul, and World-Spirit. Part One: The Human Being as a Being of Body and Soul in Relationship to the World. The Human Being in Relationship with the Cosmos: 5
CW 206	Human Development, World-Soul, and World-Spirit. Part Two: The Human Being as a Spiritual Being in the Process of Historical Development. The Human Being in Relationship with the Cosmos: 6
CW 207	Anthroposophy as Cosmosophy. Part One: Characteristic Features of the Human Being in the Earthly and the Cosmic Realms. The Human Being in Relationship with the Cosmos: 7
CW 208	Anthroposophy as Cosmosophy. Part Two: The Forming of the Human Being as the Result of Cosmic Influence. The Human Being in Relationship with the Cosmos: 8
CW 209	Nordic and Central European Spiritual Impulses. The Festival of the Appearance of Christ. The Human Being in Relationship with the Cosmos: 9
CW 210	Old and New Methods of Initiation. Drama and Poetry in the Change of Consciousness in the Modern Age
CW 211	The Sun Mystery and the Mystery of Death and Resurrection. Exoteric and Esoteric Christianity
CW 212	Human Soul Life and Spiritual Striving in Connection with World and Earth Development
CW 213	Human Questions and World Answers
CW 214	The Mystery of the Trinity: The Human Being in Relationship with the Spiritual World in the Course of Time
CW 215	Philosophy, Cosmology, and Religion in Anthroposophy
CW 216	The Fundamental Impulses of the World-Historical Development of Humanity
CW 217	Spiritually Active Forces in the Coexistence of the Older and Younger Generations. Pedagogical Course for Youth

CW 217a	Youth's Cognitive Task
CW 218	Spiritual Connections in the Forming of the Human Organism
CW 219	The Relationship of the World of the Stars to the Human Being, and of the Human Being to the World of the Stars. The Spiritual Communion of Humanity
CW 220	Living Knowledge of Nature. Intellectual Fall and Spiritual Redemption
CW 221	Earth-Knowing and Heaven-Insight
CW 222	The Imparting of Impulses to World-Historical Events through Spiritual Powers
CW 223	The Cycle of the Year as Breathing Process of the Earth and the Four Great Festival-Seasons. Anthroposophy and the Human Heart (Gemüt)
CW 224	The Human Soul and its Connection with Divine-Spiritual Individualities. The Internalization of the Festivals of the Year
CW 225	Three Perspectives of Anthroposophy. Cultural Phenomena observed from a Spiritual-Scientific Perspective
CW 226	Human Being, Human Destiny, and World Development
CW 227	Initiation-Knowledge
CW 228	Science of Initiation and Knowledge of the Stars. The Human Being in the Past, the Present, and the Future from the Viewpoint of the Development of Consciousness
CW 229	The Experiencing of the Course of the Year in Four Cosmic Imaginations
CW 230	The Human Being as Harmony of the Creative, Building, and Formative World-Word
CW 231	The Supersensible Human Being, Understood Anthroposophically
CW 232	The Forming of the Mysteries
CW 233	World History Illuminated by Anthroposophy and as the Foundation for Knowledge of the Human Spirit
CW 233a	Mystery Sites of the Middle Ages: Rosicrucianism and the Modern Initiation-Principle. The Festival of Easter as Part of the History of the Mysteries of Humanity
CW 234	Anthroposophy. A Summary after 21 Years
CW 235	Esoteric Observations of Karmic Relationships in 6 Volumes, Vol. 1
CW 236	Esoteric Observations of Karmic Relationships in 6 Volumes, Vol. 2
CW 237	Esoteric Observations of Karmic Relationships in 6 Volumes, Vol. 3: The Karmic Relationships of the Anthroposophical Movement
CW 238	Esoteric Observations of Karmic Relationships in 6 Volumes, Vol. 4: The Spiritual Life of the Present in Relationship to the Anthroposophical Movement
CW 239	Esoteric Observations of Karmic Relationships in 6 Volumes, Vol. 5

CW 240	Esoteric Observations of Karmic Relationships in 6 Volumes, Vol. 6
CW 243	The Consciousness of the Initiate
CW 245	Instructions for an Esoteric Schooling
CW 250	The Building-Up of the Anthroposophical Society. From the Beginning to the Outbreak of the First World War
CW 251	The History of the Goetheanum Building-Association
CW 252	Life in the Anthroposophical Society from the First World War to the Burning of the First Goetheanum
CW 253	The Problems of Living Together in the Anthroposophical Society. On the Dornach Crisis of 1915. With Highlights on Swedenborg's Clairvoyance, the Views of Freudian Psychoanalysts, and the Concept of Love in Relation to Mysticism
CW 254	The Occult Movement in the 19th Century and Its Relationship to World Culture. Significant Points from the Exoteric Cultural Life around the Middle of the 19th Century
CW 255	Rudolf Steiner during the First World War
CW 255a	Anthroposophy and the Reformation of Society. On the History of the Threefold Movement
CW 255b	Anthroposophy and Its Opponents, 1919–1921
CW 256	How Can the Anthroposophical Movement Be Financed?
CW 256a	Futurum, Inc. / International Laboratories, Inc.
CW 256b	The Coming Day, Inc.
CW 257	Anthroposophical Community-Building
CW 258	The History of and Conditions for the Anthroposophical Movement in Relationship to the Anthroposophical Society. A Stimulus to Self-Contemplation
CW 259	The Year of Destiny 1923 in the History of the Anthroposophical Society. From the Burning of the Goetheanum to the Christmas Conference
CW 260	The Christmas Conference for the Founding of the General Anthroposophical Society
CW 260a	The Constitution of the General Anthroposophical Society and the School for Spiritual Science. The Rebuilding of the Goetheanum
CW 261	Our Dead. Addresses, Words of Remembrance, and Meditative Verses, 1906–1924
CW 262	Rudolf Steiner and Marie Steiner-von Sivers: Correspondence and Documents, 1901–1925
CW 263/1	Rudolf Steiner and Edith Maryon: Correspondence: Letters, Verses, Sketches, 1912–1924
CW 264	On the History and the Contents of the First Section of the Esoteric School from 1904 to 1914. Letters, Newsletters, Documents, Lectures
CW 265	On the History and from the Contents of the Ritual-Knowledge Section of the Esoteric School from 1904 to 1914. Documents, and Lectures from the Years 1906 to 1914, as well as on New Approaches to Ritual-Knowledge Work in the Years 1921–1924

CW 266/1	From the Contents of the Esoteric Lessons. Volume 1: 1904–1909. Notes from Memory of Participants. Meditation texts from the notes of Rudolf Steiner
CW 266/2	From the Contents of the Esoteric Lessons. Volume 2: 1910–1912. Notes from Memory of Participants
CW 266/3	From the Contents of the Esoteric Lessons. Volume 3: 1913, 1914 and 1920–1923. Notes from Memory of Participants. Meditation texts from the notes of Rudolf Steiner
CW 267	Soul-Exercises: Vol. 1: Exercises with Word and Image Meditations for the Methodological Development of Higher Powers of Knowledge, 1904–1924
CW 268	Soul-Exercises: Vol. 2: Mantric Verses, 1903–1925
CW 269	Ritual Texts for the Celebration of the Free Christian Religious Instruction. The Collected Verses for Teachers and Students of the Waldorf School
CW 270	Esoteric Instructions for the First Class of the School for Spiritual Science at the Goetheanum 1924, 4 Volumes
CW 271	Art and Knowledge of Art. Foundations of a New Aesthetic
CW 272	Spiritual-Scientific Commentary on Goethe's 'Faust' in Two Volumes. Vol. 1: Faust, the Striving Human Being
CW 273	Spiritual-Scientific Commentary on Goethe's 'Faust' in Two Volumes. Vol. 2: The Faust-Problem
CW 274	Addresses for the Christmas Plays from the Old Folk Traditions
CW 275	Art in the Light of Mystery-Wisdom
CW 276	The Artistic in Its Mission in the World. The Genius of Language. The World of Self-Revealing Radiant Appearances—Anthroposophy and Art. Anthroposophy and Poetry
CW 277	Eurythmy. The Revelation of the Speaking Soul
CW 277a	The Origin and Development of Eurythmy
CW 278	Eurythmy as Visible Song
CW 279	Eurythmy as Visible Speech
CW 280	The Method and Nature of Speech Formation
CW 281	The Art of Recitation and Declamation
CW 282	Speech Formation and Dramatic Art
CW 283	The Nature of Things Musical and the Experience of Tone in the Human Being
CW 284/285	Images of Occult Seals and Pillars. The Munich Congress of Whitsun 1907 and Its Consequences
CW 286	Paths to a New Style of Architecture. 'And the Building Becomes Human'
CW 287	The Building at Dornach as a Symbol of Historical Becoming and an Artistic Transformation Impulse
CW 288	Style-Forms in the Living Organic
CW 289	The Building-Idea of the Goetheanum: Lectures with Slides from the Years 1920–1921
CW 290	The Building-Idea of the Goetheanum: Lectures with Slides from the Years 1920–1921

CW 291	The Nature of Colours
CW 291a	Knowledge of Colours. Supplementary Volume to 'The Nature of Colours'
CW 292	Art History as Image of Inner Spiritual Impulses
CW 293	General Knowledge of the Human Being as the Foundation of Pedagogy
CW 294	The Art of Education, Methodology and Didactics
CW 295	The Art of Education: Seminar Discussions and Lectures on Lesson Planning
CW 296	The Question of Education as a Social Question
CW 297	The Idea and Practice of the Waldorf School
CW 297a	Education for Life: Self-Education and the Practice of Pedagogy
CW 298	Rudolf Steiner in the Waldorf School
CW 299	Spiritual-Scientific Observations on Speech
CW 300a	Conferences with the Teachers of the Free Waldorf School in Stuttgart, 1919 to 1924, in 3 Volumes, Vol. 1
CW 300b	Conferences with the Teachers of the Free Waldorf School in Stuttgart, 1919 to 1924, in 3 Volumes, Vol. 2
CW 300c	Conferences with the Teachers of the Free Waldorf School in Stuttgart, 1919 to 1924, in 3 Volumes, Vol. 3
CW 301	The Renewal of Pedagogical-Didactical Art through Spiritual Science
CW 302	Knowledge of the Human Being and the Forming of Class Lessons
CW 302a	Education and Teaching from a Knowledge of the Human Being
CW 303	The Healthy Development of the Human Being
CW 304	Methods of Education and Teaching Based on Anthroposophy
CW 304a	Anthroposophical Knowledge of the Human Being and Pedagogy
CW 305	The Soul-Spiritual Foundational Forces of the Art of Education. Spiritual Values in Education and Social Life
CW 306	Pedagogical Praxis from the Viewpoint of a Spiritual-Scientific Knowledge of the Human Being. The Education of the Child and Young Human Beings
CW 307	The Spiritual Life of the Present and Education
CW 308	The Method of Teaching and the Life-Requirements for Teaching
CW 309	Anthroposophical Pedagogy and Its Prerequisites
CW 310	The Pedagogical Value of a Knowledge of the Human Being and the Cultural Value of Pedagogy
CW 311	The Art of Education from an Understanding of the Being of Humanity
CW 312	Spiritual Science and Medicine
CW 313	Spiritual-Scientific Viewpoints on Therapy
CW 314	Physiology and Therapy Based on Spiritual Science
CW 315	Curative Eurythmy
CW 316	Meditative Observations and Instructions for a Deepening of the Art of Healing
CW 317	The Curative Education Course

CW 318	The Working Together of Doctors and Pastors
CW 319	Anthroposophical Knowledge of the Human Being and Medicine
CW 320	Spiritual-Scientific Impulses for the Development of Physics 1: The First Natural-Scientific Course: Light, Colour, Tone, Mass, Electricity, Magnetism
CW 321	Spiritual-Scientific Impulses for the Development of Physics 2: The Second Natural-Scientific Course: Warmth at the Border of Positive and Negative Materiality
CW 322	The Borders of the Knowledge of Nature
CW 323	The Relationship of the various Natural-Scientific Fields to Astronomy
CW 324	Nature Observation, Mathematics, and Scientific Experimentation and Results from the Viewpoint of Anthroposophy
CW 324a	The Fourth Dimension in Mathematics and Reality
CW 325	Natural Science and the World-Historical Development of Humanity since Ancient Times
CW 326	The Moment of the Coming Into Being of Natural Science in World History and Its Development Since Then
CW 327	Spiritual-Scientific Foundations for Success in Farming. The Agricultural Course
CW 328	The Social Question
CW 329	The Liberation of the Human Being as the Foundation for a New Social Form
CW 330	The Renewal of the Social Organism
CW 331	Work-Council and Socialization
CW 332	The Alliance for Threefolding and the Total Reform of Society. The Council on Culture and the Liberation of the Spiritual Life
CW 332a	The Social Future
CW 333	Freedom of Thought and Social Forces
CW 334	From the Unified State to the Threefold Social Organism
CW 335	The Crisis of the Present and the Path to Healthy Thinking
CW 336	The Great Questions of the Times and Anthroposophical Spiritual Knowledge
CW 337a	Social Ideas, Social Reality, Social Practice, Vol. 1: Question-and-Answer Evenings and Study Evenings of the Alliance for the Threefold Social Organism in Stuttgart, 1919–1920
CW 337b	Social Ideas, Social Realities, Social Practice, Vol. 2: Discussion Evenings of the Swiss Alliance for the Threefold Social Organism
CW 338	How Does One Work on Behalf of the Impulse for the Threefold Social Organism?
CW 339	Anthroposophy, Threefold Social Organism, and the Art of Public Speaking
CW 340	The National-Economics Course. The Tasks of a New Science of Economics, Volume 1
CW 341	The National-Economics Seminar. The Tasks of a New Science of Economics, Volume 2

CW 342	Lectures and Courses on Christian Religious Work, Vol. 1: Anthroposophical Foundations for a Renewed Christian Religious Working
CW 343	Lectures and Courses on Christian Religious Work, Vol. 2: Spiritual Knowledge—Religious Feeling—Cultic Doing
CW 344	Lectures and Courses on Christian Religious Work, Vol. 3: Lectures at the Founding of the Christian Community
CW 345	Lectures and Courses on Christian Religious Work, Vol. 4: Concerning the Nature of the Working Word
CW 346	Lectures and Courses on Christian Religious Work, Vol. 5: The Apocalypse and the Work of the Priest
CW 347	The Knowledge of the Nature of the Human Being According to Body, Soul and Spirit. On Earlier Conditions of the Earth
CW 348	On Health and Illness. Foundations of a Spiritual-Scientific Doctrine of the Senses
CW 349	On the Life of the Human Being and of the Earth. On the Nature of Christianity
CW 350	Rhythms in the Cosmos and in the Human Being. How Does One Come To See the Spiritual World?
CW 351	The Human Being and the World. The Influence of the Spirit in Nature. On the Nature of Bees
CW 352	Nature and the Human Being Observed Spiritual-Scientifically
CW 353	The History of Humanity and the World-Views of the Folk Cultures
CW 354	The Creation of the World and the Human Being. Life on Earth and the Influence of the Stars

SIGNIFICANT EVENTS IN THE LIFE OF RUDOLF STEINER

1829: June 23: birth of Johann Steiner (1829–1910)—Rudolf Steiner's father—in Geras, Lower Austria.
1834: May 8: birth of Franciska Blie (1834–1918)—Rudolf Steiner's mother—in Horn, Lower Austria. 'My father and mother were both children of the glorious Lower Austrian forest district north of the Danube.'
1860: May 16: marriage of Johann Steiner and Franciska Blie.
1861: February 25: birth of *Rudolf Joseph Lorenz Steiner* in Kraljevec, Croatia, near the border with Hungary, where Johann Steiner works as a telegrapher for the South Austria Railroad. Rudolf Steiner is baptized two days later, February 27, the date usually given as his birthday.
1862: Summer: the family moves to Mödling, Lower Austria.
1863: The family moves to Pottschach, Lower Austria, near the Styrian border, where Johann Steiner becomes stationmaster. 'The view stretched to the mountains ... majestic peaks in the distance and the sweet charm of nature in the immediate surroundings.'
1864: November 15: birth of Rudolf Steiner's sister, Leopoldine (d. November 1, 1927). She will become a seamstress and live with her parents for the rest of her life.
1866: July 28: birth of Rudolf Steiner's deaf-mute brother, Gustav (d. May 1, 1941).
1867: Rudolf Steiner enters the village school. Following a disagreement between his father and the schoolmaster, whose wife falsely accused the boy of causing a commotion, Rudolf Steiner is taken out of school and taught at home.
1868: A critical experience. Unknown to the family, an aunt dies in a distant town. Sitting in the station waiting room, Rudolf Steiner sees her 'form,' which speaks to him, asking for help. 'Beginning with this experience, a new soul life began in the boy, one in which not only the outer trees and mountains spoke to him, but also the worlds that lay behind them. From this moment on, the boy began to live with the spirits of nature...'
1869: The family moves to the peaceful, rural village of Neudörfl, near Wiener-Neustadt in present-day Austria. Rudolf Steiner attends the village school. Because of the 'unorthodoxy' of his writing and spelling, he has to do 'extra lessons.'
1870: Through a book lent to him by his tutor, he discovers geometry: 'To grasp something purely in the spirit brought me inner happiness. I know that I first learned happiness through geometry.' The same tutor allows

him to draw, while other students still struggle with their reading and writing. 'An artistic element' thus enters his education.

1871: Though his parents are not religious, Rudolf Steiner becomes a 'church child,' a favourite of the priest, who was 'an exceptional character.' 'Up to the age of ten or eleven, among those I came to know, he was far and away the most significant.' Among other things, he introduces Steiner to Copernican, heliocentric cosmology. As an altar boy, Rudolf Steiner serves at Masses, funerals, and Corpus Christi processions. At year's end, after an incident in which he escapes a thrashing, his father forbids him to go to church.

1872: Rudolf Steiner transfers to grammar school in Wiener-Neustadt, a five-mile walk from home, which must be done in all weathers.

1873–75: Through his teachers and on his own, Rudolf Steiner has many wonderful experiences with science and mathematics. Outside school, he teaches himself analytic geometry, trigonometry, differential equations, and calculus.

1876: Rudolf Steiner begins tutoring other students. He learns bookbinding from his father. He also teaches himself stenography.

1877: Rudolf Steiner discovers Kant's *Critique of Pure Reason*, which he reads and rereads. He also discovers and reads von Rotteck's *World History*.

1878: He studies extensively in contemporary psychology and philosophy.

1879: Rudolf Steiner graduates from high school with honours. His father is transferred to Inzersdorf, near Vienna. He uses his first visit to Vienna 'to purchase a great number of philosophy books'—Kant, Fichte, Schelling, and Hegel, as well as numerous histories of philosophy. His aim: to find a path from the 'I' to nature.

October 1879–1883: Rudolf Steiner attends the Technical College in Vienna—to study mathematics, chemistry, physics, mineralogy, botany, zoology, biology, geology, and mechanics—with a scholarship. He also attends lectures in history and literature, while avidly reading philosophy on his own. His two favourite professors are Karl Julius Schröer (German language and literature) and Edmund Reitlinger (physics). He also audits lectures by Robert Zimmermann on aesthetics and Franz Brentano on philosophy. During this year he begins his friendship with Moritz Zitter (1861–1921), who will help support him financially when he is in Berlin.

1880: Rudolf Steiner attends lectures on Schiller and Goethe by Karl Julius Schröer, who becomes his mentor. Also 'through a remarkable combination of circumstances,' he meets Felix Koguzki, a 'herb gatherer' and healer, who could 'see deeply into the secrets of nature.' Rudolf Steiner will meet and study with this 'emissary of the Master' throughout his time in Vienna.

1881: January: '... I didn't sleep a wink. I was busy with philosophical problems until about 12:30 a.m. Then, finally, I threw myself down on my couch. All my striving during the previous year had been to research whether the following statement by Schelling was true or not: *Within everyone dwells a secret, marvelous capacity to draw back from the stream of time—out of the self clothed in all that comes to us from outside—into our innermost being and there, in the immutable form of the Eternal, to look into ourselves.* I believe, and I am still quite certain of it, that I discovered this capacity in myself; I had long had an inkling of it. Now the whole of idealist philosophy stood before me in modified form. What's a sleepless night compared to that!'

Rudolf Steiner begins communicating with leading thinkers of the day, who send him books in return, which he reads eagerly.

July: 'I am not one of those who dives into the day like an animal in human form. I pursue a quite specific goal, an idealistic aim—knowledge of the truth! This cannot be done offhandedly. It requires the greatest striving in the world, free of all egotism, and equally of all resignation.'

August: Steiner puts down on paper for the first time thoughts for a 'Philosophy of Freedom.' 'The striving for the absolute: this human yearning is freedom.' He also seeks to outline a 'peasant philosophy,' describing what the worldview of a 'peasant'—one who lives close to the earth and the old ways—really is.

1881–1882: Felix Koguzki, the herb gatherer, reveals himself to be the envoy of another, higher initiatory personality, who instructs Rudolf Steiner to penetrate Fichte's philosophy and to master modern scientific thinking as a preparation for right entry into the spirit. This 'Master' also teaches him the double (evolutionary and involutionary) nature of time.

1882: Through the offices of Karl Julius Schröer, Rudolf Steiner is asked by Joseph Kürschner to edit Goethe's scientific works for the *Deutschen National-Literatur* edition. He writes 'A Possible Critique of Atomistic Concepts' and sends it to Friedrich Theodor Vischer.

1883: Rudolf Steiner completes his college studies and begins work on the Goethe project.

1884: First volume of Goethe's *Scientific Writings* (CW 1) appears (March). He lectures on Goethe and Lessing, and Goethe's approach to science. In July, he enters the household of Ladislaus and Pauline Specht as tutor to the four Specht boys. He will live there until 1890. At this time, he meets Josef Breuer (1842–1925), the co-author with Sigmund Freud of *Studies in Hysteria*, who is the Specht family doctor.

1885: While continuing to edit Goethe's writings, Rudolf Steiner reads deeply in contemporary philosophy (Eduard von Hartmann, Johannes Volkelt, and Richard Wahle, among others).

1886: May: Rudolf Steiner sends Kürschner the manuscript of *Outlines of Goethe's Theory of Knowledge* (CW 2), which appears in October, and which he sends out widely. He also meets the poet Marie Eugenie Delle Grazie and writes 'Nature and Our Ideals' for her. He attends her salon, where he meets many priests, theologians, and philosophers, who will become his friends. Meanwhile, the director of the Goethe Archive in Weimar requests his collaboration with the *Sophien* edition of Goethe's works, particularly the writings on colour.

1887: At the beginning of the year, Rudolf Steiner is very sick. As the year progresses and his health improves, he becomes increasingly 'a man of letters,' lecturing, writing essays, and taking part in Austrian cultural life. In August–September, the second volume of Goethe's *Scientific Writings* appears.

1888: January–July: Rudolf Steiner assumes editorship of the 'German Weekly' (*Deutsche Wochenschrift*). He begins lecturing more intensively, giving, for example, a lecture titled 'Goethe as Father of a New Aesthetics.' He meets and becomes soul friends with Friedrich Eckstein (1861–1939), a vegetarian, philosopher of symbolism, alchemist, and musician, who will introduce him to various spiritual currents (including Theosophy) and with whom he will meditate and interpret esoteric and alchemical texts.

1889: Rudolf Steiner first reads Nietzsche (*Beyond Good and Evil*). He encounters Theosophy again and learns of Madame Blavatsky in the Theosophical circle around Marie Lang (1858–1934). Here he also meets well-known figures of Austrian life, as well as esoteric figures like the occultist Franz Hartmann and Karl Leinigen-Billigen (translator of C.G. Harrison's *The Transcendental Universe*). During this period, Steiner first reads A.P. Sinnett's *Esoteric Buddhism* and Mabel Collins's *Light on the Path*. He also begins travelling, visiting Budapest, Weimar, and Berlin (where he meets philosopher Eduard von Hartmann).

1890: Rudolf Steiner finishes volume 3 of Goethe's scientific writings. He begins his doctoral dissertation, which will become *Truth and Science* (CW 3). He also meets the poet and feminist Rosa Mayreder (1858–1938), with whom he can exchange his most intimate thoughts. In September, Rudolf Steiner moves to Weimar to work in the Goethe-Schiller Archive.

1891: Volume 3 of the Kürschner edition of Goethe appears. Meanwhile, Rudolf Steiner edits Goethe's studies in mineralogy and scientific writings for the *Sophien* edition. He meets Ludwig Laistner of the Cotta Publishing Company, who asks for a book on the basic question of metaphysics. From this will result, ultimately, *The Philosophy of Freedom* (CW 4), which will be published not by Cotta but by Emil Felber. In October, Rudolf Steiner takes the oral exam for a doctorate in philosophy, mathematics, and mechanics at Rostock University, receiving his doctorate on the twenty-sixth. In November, he gives his first lecture on Goethe's 'Fairy Tale' in Vienna.

1892: Rudolf Steiner continues work at the Goethe-Schiller Archive and on his *Philosophy of Freedom*. *Truth and Science*, his doctoral dissertation, is published. Steiner undertakes to write introductions to books on Schopenhauer and Jean Paul for Cotta. At year's end, he finds lodging with Anna Eunike, née Schulz (1853–1911), a widow with four daughters and a son. He also develops a friendship with Otto Erich Hartleben (1864–1905) with whom he shares literary interests.

1893: Rudolf Steiner begins his habit of producing many reviews and articles. In March, he gives a lecture titled 'Hypnotism, with Reference to Spiritism.' In September, volume 4 of the Kürschner edition is completed. In November, *The Philosophy of Freedom* appears. This year, too, he meets John Henry Mackay (1864–1933), the anarchist, and Max Stirner, a scholar and biographer.

1894: Rudolf Steiner meets Elisabeth Förster Nietzsche, the philosopher's sister, and begins to read Nietzsche in earnest, beginning with the as yet unpublished *Antichrist*. He also meets Ernst Haeckel (1834–1919). In the fall, he begins to write *Nietzsche, A Fighter against His Time* (CW 5).

1895: May, *Nietzsche, A Fighter against His Time* appears.

1896: January 22: Rudolf Steiner sees Friedrich Nietzsche for the first and only time. Moves between the Nietzsche and the Goethe-Schiller Archives, where he completes his work before year's end. He falls out with Elisabeth Förster Nietzsche, thus ending his association with the Nietzsche Archive.

1897: Rudolf Steiner finishes the manuscript of *Goethe's Worldview* (CW 6). He moves to Berlin with Anna Eunike and begins editorship of the *Magazin für Literatur*. From now on, Steiner will write countless reviews, literary and philosophical articles, and so on. He begins lecturing at the 'Free Literary Society.' In September, he attends the Zionist Congress in Basel. He sides with Dreyfus in the Dreyfus affair.

1898: Rudolf Steiner is very active as an editor in the political, artistic, and theatrical life of Berlin. He becomes friendly with John Henry Mackay and poet Ludwig Jacobowski (1868–1900). He joins Jacobowski's circle of writers, artists, and scientists—'The Coming Ones' (*Die Kommenden*)— and contributes lectures to the group until 1903. He also lectures at the 'League for College Pedagogy.' He writes an article for Goethe's sesquicentennial, 'Goethe's Secret Revelation,' on the 'Fairy Tale of the Green Snake and the Beautiful Lily.'

1898–99: 'This was a trying time for my soul as I looked at Christianity. . . . I was able to progress only by contemplating, by means of spiritual perception, the evolution of Christianity. . . . Conscious knowledge of real Christianity began to dawn in me around the turn of the century. This seed continued to develop. My soul trial occurred shortly before the beginning of the twentieth century. It was decisive for my soul's development that I stood spiritually before the Mystery of Golgotha in a deep and solemn celebration of knowledge.'

1899: Rudolf Steiner begins teaching and giving lectures and lecture cycles at the Workers' College, founded by Wilhelm Liebknecht (1826–1900). He will continue to do so until 1904. Writes: *Literature and Spiritual Life in the Nineteenth Century; Individualism in Philosophy*; *Haeckel and His Opponents; Poetry in the Present;* and begins what will become (fifteen years later) *The Riddles of Philosophy* (CW 18). He also meets many artists and writers, including Käthe Kollwitz, Stefan Zweig, and Rainer Maria Rilke. On October 31, he marries Anna Eunike.

1900: 'I thought that the turn of the century must bring humanity a new light. It seemed to me that the separation of human thinking and willing from the spirit had peaked. A turn or reversal of direction in human evolution seemed to me a necessity.' Rudolf Steiner finishes *World and Life Views in the Nineteenth Century* (the second part of what will become *The Riddles of Philosophy*) and dedicates it to Ernst Haeckel. It is published in March. He continues lecturing at *Die Kommenden*, whose leadership he assumes after the death of Jacobowski. Also, he gives the Gutenberg Jubilee lecture before 7,000 typesetters and printers. In September, Rudolf Steiner is invited by Count and Countess Brockdorff to lecture in the Theosophical Library. His first lecture is on Nietzsche. His second lecture is titled 'Goethe's Secret Revelation.' October 6, he begins a lecture cycle on the mystics that will become *Mystics after Modernism* (CW 7). November–December: 'Marie von Sivers appears in the audience....' Also in November, Steiner gives his first lecture at the Giordano Bruno Bund (where he will continue to lecture until May, 1905). He speaks on Bruno and modern Rome, focusing on the importance of the philosophy of Thomas Aquinas as monism.

1901: In continual financial straits, Rudolf Steiner's early friends Moritz Zitter and Rosa Mayreder help support him. In October, he begins the lecture cycle *Christianity as Mystical Fact* (CW 8) at the Theosophical Library. In November, he gives his first 'Theosophical lecture' on Goethe's 'Fairy Tale' in Hamburg at the invitation of Wilhelm Hubbe-Schleiden. He also attends a gathering to celebrate the founding of the Theosophical Society at Count and Countess Brockdorff's. He gives a lecture cycle, 'From Buddha to Christ,' for the circle of the *Kommenden*. November 17, Marie von Sivers asks Rudolf Steiner if Theosophy needs a Western-Christian spiritual movement (to complement Theosophy's Eastern emphasis). 'The question was posed. Now, following spiritual laws, I could begin to give an answer....' In December, Rudolf Steiner writes his first article for a Theosophical publication. At year's end, the Brockdorffs and possibly Wilhelm Hubbe-Schleiden ask Rudolf Steiner to join the Theosophical Society and undertake the leadership of the German section. Rudolf Steiner agrees, on the condition that Marie von Sivers (then in Italy) work with him.

1902: Beginning in January, Rudolf Steiner attends the opening of the Workers' School in Spandau with Rosa Luxemberg (1870–1919). January 17, Rudolf Steiner joins the Theosophical Society. In April, he is asked to become general secretary of the German Section of the Theosophical Society, and works on preparations for its founding. In July, he visits London for a Theosophical congress. He meets Bertram Keightly, G.R.S. Mead, A.P. Sinnett, and Annie Besant, among others. In September, *Christianity as Mystical Fact* appears. In October, Rudolf Steiner gives his first public lecture on Theosophy ('Monism and Theosophy') to about three hundred people at the Giordano Bruno Bund. On October 19–21, the German Section of the Theosophical Society has its first meeting; Rudolf Steiner is the general secretary, and Annie Besant attends. Steiner lectures on practical karma studies. On October 23, Annie Besant inducts Rudolf Steiner into the Esoteric School of the Theosophical Society. On October 25, Steiner begins a weekly series of lectures: 'The Field of Theosophy.' During this year, Rudolf Steiner also first meets Ita Wegman (1876–1943), who will become his close collaborator in his final years.

1903: Rudolf Steiner holds about 300 lectures and seminars. In May, the first issue of the periodical *Luzifer* appears. In June, Rudolf Steiner visits

London for the first meeting of the Federation of the European Sections of the Theosophical Society, where he meets Colonel Olcott. He begins to write *Theosophy* (CW 9).

1904: Rudolf Steiner continues lecturing at the Workers' College and elsewhere (about 90 lectures), while lecturing intensively all over Germany among Theosophists (about 140 lectures). In February, he meets Carl Unger (1878–1929), who will become a member of the board of the Anthroposophical Society (1913). In March, he meets Michael Bauer (1871–1929), a Christian mystic, who will also be on the board. In May, *Theosophy* appears, with the dedication: 'To the spirit of Giordano Bruno.' Rudolf Steiner and Marie von Sivers visit London for meetings with Annie Besant. June: Rudolf Steiner and Marie von Sivers attend the meeting of the Federation of European Sections of the Theosophical Society in Amsterdam. In July, Steiner begins the articles in *Luzifer-Gnosis* that will become *How to Know Higher Worlds* (CW 10) and *Cosmic Memory* (CW 11). In September, Annie Besant visits Germany. In December, Steiner lectures on Freemasonry. He mentions the High Grade Masonry derived from John Yarker and represented by Theodore Reuss and Karl Kellner as a blank slate 'into which a good image could be placed.'

1905: This year, Steiner ends his non-Theosophical lecturing activity. Supported by Marie von Sivers, his Theosophical lecturing—both in public and in the Theosophical Society—increases significantly: 'The German Theosophical Movement is of exceptional importance.' Steiner recommends reading, among others, Fichte, Jacob Boehme, and Angelus Silesius. He begins to introduce Christian themes into Theosophy. He also begins to work with doctors (Felix Peipers and Ludwig Noll). In July, he is in London for the Federation of European Sections, where he attends a lecture by Annie Besant: 'I have seldom seen Mrs. Besant speak in so inward and heartfelt a manner....' 'Through Mrs. Besant I have found the way to H.P. Blavatsky.' September to October, he gives a course of thirty-one lectures for a small group of esoteric students. In October, the annual meeting of the German Section of the Theosophical Society, which still remains very small, takes place. Rudolf Steiner reports membership has risen from 121 to 377 members. In November, seeking to establish esoteric 'continuity,' Rudolf Steiner and Marie von Sivers participate in a 'Memphis-Misraim' Masonic ceremony. They pay forty-five marks for membership. 'Yesterday, you saw how little remains of former esoteric institutions.' 'We are dealing only with a "framework"... for the present, nothing lies behind it. The occult powers have completely withdrawn.'

1906: Expansion of Theosophical work. Rudolf Steiner gives about 245 lectures, only 44 of which take place in Berlin. Cycles are given in Paris, Leipzig, Stuttgart, and Munich. Esoteric work also intensifies. Rudolf Steiner begins writing *An Outline of Esoteric Science* (CW 13). In January, Rudolf Steiner receives permission (a patent) from the Great Orient of the Scottish A & A Thirty-Three Degree Rite of the Order of the Ancient

Freemasons of the Memphis-Misraim Rite to direct a chapter under the name 'Mystica Aeterna.' This will become the 'Cognitive-Ritual Section' (also called 'Misraim Service') of the Esoteric School. (See: *Freemasonry and Ritual Work: The Misraim Service*, CW 265). During this time, Steiner also meets Albert Schweitzer. In May, he is in Paris, where he visits Edouard Schuré. Many Russians attend his lectures (including Konstantin Balmont, Dimitri Mereszkovski, Zinaida Hippius, and Maximilian Woloshin). He attends the General Meeting of the European Federation of the Theosophical Society, at which Col. Olcott is present for the last time. He spends the year's end in Venice and Rome, where he writes and works on his translation of H.P. Blavatsky's *Key to Theosophy*.

1907: Further expansion of the German Theosophical Movement according to the Rosicrucian directive to 'introduce spirit into the world'—in education, in social questions, in art, and in science. In February, Col. Olcott dies in Adyar. Before he dies, Olcott indicates that 'the Masters' wish Annie Besant to succeed him: much politicking ensues. Rudolf Steiner supports Besant's candidacy. April-May: preparations for the Congress of the Federation of European Sections of the Theosophical Society—the great, watershed Whitsun 'Munich Congress,' attended by Annie Besant and others. Steiner decides to separate Eastern and Western (Christian-Rosicrucian) esoteric schools. He takes his esoteric school out of the Theosophical Society (Besant and Rudolf Steiner are 'in harmony' on this). Steiner makes his first lecture tours to Austria and Hungary. That summer, he is in Italy. In September, he visits Edouard Schuré, who will write the introduction to the French edition of *Christianity as Mystical Fact* in Barr, Alsace. Rudolf Steiner writes the autobiographical statement known as the 'Barr Document.' In *Luzifer-Gnosis*, 'The Education of the Child' appears.

1908: The movement grows (membership: 1,150). Lecturing expands. Steiner makes his first extended lecture tour to Holland and Scandinavia, as well as visits to Naples and Sicily. Themes: St. John's Gospel, the Apocalypse, Egypt, science, philosophy, and logic. *Luzifer-Gnosis* ceases publication. In Berlin, Marie von Sivers (with Johanna Mücke (1864–1949) forms the *Philosophisch-Theosophisch* (after 1915 *Philosophisch-Anthroposophisch*) *Verlag* to publish Steiner's work. Steiner gives lecture cycles titled *The Gospel of St. John* (CW 103) and *The Apocalypse* (104).

1909: *An Outline of Esoteric Science* appears. Lecturing and travel continues. Rudolf Steiner's spiritual research expands to include the polarity of Lucifer and Ahriman; the work of great individualities in history; the Maitreya Buddha and the Bodhisattvas; spiritual economy (CW 109); the work of the spiritual hierarchies in heaven and on earth (CW 110). He also deepens and intensifies his research into the Gospels, giving lectures on the Gospel of St. Luke (CW 114) with the first mention of two Jesus children. Meets and becomes friends with Christian Morgenstern (1871–1914). In April, he lays the foundation stone for the Malsch model—the building that will lead to the first Goetheanum. In May, the International Congress of the Federation of European Sections of the

Theosophical Society takes place in Budapest. Rudolf Steiner receives the Subba Row medal for *How to Know Higher Worlds*. During this time, Charles W. Leadbeater discovers Jiddu Krishnamurti (1895–1986) and proclaims him the future 'world teacher,' the bearer of the Maitreya Buddha and the 'reappearing Christ.' In October, Steiner delivers seminal lectures on 'anthroposophy,' which he will try, unsuccessfully, to rework over the next years into the unfinished work, *Anthroposophy (A Fragment)* (CW 45).

1910: New themes: *The Reappearance of Christ in the Etheric* (CW 118); *The Fifth Gospel; The Mission of Folk Souls* (CW 121); *Occult History* (CW 126); the evolving development of etheric cognitive capacities. Rudolf Steiner continues his Gospel research with *The Gospel of St. Matthew* (CW 123). In January, his father dies. In April, he takes a month-long trip to Italy, including Rome, Monte Cassino, and Sicily. He also visits Scandinavia again. July–August, he writes the first mystery drama, *The Portal of Initiation* (CW 14). In November, he gives 'psychosophy' lectures. In December, he submits 'On the Psychological Foundations and Epistemological Framework of Theosophy' to the International Philosophical Congress in Bologna.

1911: The crisis in the Theosophical Society deepens. In January, 'The Order of the Rising Sun,' which will soon become 'The Order of the Star in the East,' is founded for the coming world teacher, Krishnamurti. At the same time, Marie von Sivers, Rudolf Steiner's co-worker, falls ill. Fewer lectures are given, but important new ground is broken. In Prague, in March, Steiner meets Franz Kafka (1883–1924) and Hugo Bergmann (1883-1975). In April, he delivers his paper to the Philosophical Congress. He writes the second mystery drama, *The Soul's Probation* (CW 14). Also, while Marie von Sivers is convalescing, Rudolf Steiner begins work on *Calendar 1912/1913*, which will contain the 'Calendar of the Soul' meditations. On March 19, Anna (Eunike) Steiner dies. In September, Rudolf Steiner visits Einsiedeln, birthplace of Paracelsus. In December, Friedrich Rittelmeyer, future founder of the Christian Community, meets Rudolf Steiner. The *Johannes-Bauverein*, the 'building committee,' which would lead to the first Goetheanum (first planned for Munich), is also founded, and a preliminary committee for the founding of an independent association is created that, in the following year, will become the Anthroposophical Society. Important lecture cycles include *Occult Physiology* (CW 128); *Wonders of the World* (CW 129); *From Jesus to Christ* (CW 131). Other themes: esoteric Christianity; Christian Rosenkreutz; the spiritual guidance of humanity; the sense world and the world of the spirit.

1912: Despite the ongoing, now increasing crisis in the Theosophical Society, much is accomplished: *Calendar 1912/1913* is published; eurythmy is created; both the third mystery drama, *The Guardian of the Threshold* (CW 14) and *A Way of Self-Knowledge* (CW 16) are written. New (or renewed) themes included life between death and rebirth and karma and reincarnation. Other lecture cycles: *Spiritual Beings in the Heavenly Bodies and in the Kingdoms of Nature* (CW 136); *The Human Being in the Light of Occultism, Theosophy, and Philosophy* (CW 137); *The Gospel of St. Mark* (CW 139); and *The Bhagavad Gita and the Epistles of Paul* (CW 142). On May 8, Rudolf Steiner celebrates White Lotus Day, H.P. Blavatsky's death day, which he had faithfully observed for the past decade, for the last time. In August, Rudolf Steiner suggests the 'independent association' be called the 'Anthroposophical Society.' In September, the first eurythmy course takes place. In October, Rudolf Steiner declines recognition of a Theosophical Society lodge dedicated to the Star of the East and decides to expel all Theosophical Society members belonging to the order. Also, with Marie von Sivers, he first visits Dornach, near Basel, Switzerland, and they stand on the hill where the Goetheanum will be built. In November, a Theosophical Society lodge is opened by direct mandate from Adyar (Annie Besant). In December, a meeting of the German section occurs at which it is decided that belonging to the Order of the Star of the East is incompatible with membership in the Theosophical Society. December 28: informal founding of the Anthroposophical Society in Berlin.

1913: Expulsion of the German section from the Theosophical Society. February 2–3: Foundation meeting of the Anthroposophical Society. Board members include: Marie von Sivers, Michael Bauer, and Carl Unger. September 20: Laying of the foundation stone for the *Johannes Bau* (Goetheanum) in Dornach. Building begins immediately. The third mystery drama, *The Soul's Awakening* (CW 14), is completed. Also: *The Threshold of the Spiritual World* (CW 147). Lecture cycles include: *The Bhagavad Gita and the Epistles of Paul* and *The Esoteric Meaning of the Bhagavad Gita* (CW 146), which the Russian philosopher Nikolai Berdyaev attends; *The Mysteries of the East and of Christianity* (CW 144); *The Effects of Esoteric Development* (CW 145); and *The Fifth Gospel* (CW 148). In May, Rudolf Steiner is in London and Paris, where anthroposophical work continues.

1914: Building continues on the *Johannes Bau* (Goetheanum) in Dornach, with artists and co-workers from seventeen nations. The general assembly of the Anthroposophical Society takes place. In May, Rudolf Steiner visits Paris, as well as Chartres Cathedral. June 28: assassination in Sarajevo ('Now the catastrophe has happened!'). August 1: War is declared. Rudolf Steiner returns to Germany from Dornach—he will travel back and forth. He writes the last chapter of *The Riddles of Philosophy*. Lecture cycles include: *Human and Cosmic Thought* (CW 151); *Inner Being of Humanity between Death and a New Birth* (CW 153); *Occult Reading and Occult Hearing* (CW 156). December 24: marriage of Rudolf Steiner and Marie von Sivers.

1915: Building continues. Life after death becomes a major theme, also art. Writes: *Thoughts during a Time of War* (CW 24). Lectures include: *The Secret of Death* (CW 159); *The Uniting of Humanity through the Christ Impulse* (CW 165).

1916: Rudolf Steiner begins work with Edith Maryon (1872–1924) on the sculpture 'The Representative of Humanity' ('The Group'—Christ, Lucifer, and Ahriman). He also works with the alchemist Alexander von Bernus on the quarterly *Das Reich*. He writes *The Riddle of Humanity* (CW 20). Lectures include: *Necessity and Freedom in World History and Human Action* (CW 166); *Past and Present in the Human Spirit* (CW 167); *The Karma of Vocation* (CW 172); *The Karma of Untruthfulness* (CW 173).

1917: Russian Revolution. The U.S. enters the war. Building continues. Rudolf Steiner delineates the idea of the 'threefold nature of the human being' (in a public lecture March 15) and the 'threefold nature of the social organism' (hammered out in May-June with the help of Otto von Lerchenfeld and Ludwig Polzer-Hoditz in the form of two documents titled *Memoranda*, which were distributed in high places). August–September: Rudolf Steiner writes *The Riddles of the Soul* (CW 20). Also: commentary on 'The Chymical Wedding of Christian Rosenkreutz' for Alexander Bernus (*Das Reich*). Lectures include: *The Karma of Materialism* (CW 176); *The Spiritual Background of the Outer World: The Fall of the Spirits of Darkness* (CW 177).

1918: March 18: peace treaty of Brest-Litovsk—'Now everything will truly enter chaos! What is needed is cultural renewal.' June: Rudolf Steiner visits Karlstein (Grail) Castle outside Prague. Lecture cycle: *From Symptom to Reality in Modern History* (CW 185). In mid-November, Emil Molt, of the Waldorf-Astoria Cigarette Company, has the idea of founding a school for his workers' children.

1919: Focus on the threefold social organism: tireless travel, countless lectures, meetings, and publications. At the same time, a new public stage of Anthroposophy emerges as cultural renewal begins. The coming years will see initiatives in pedagogy, medicine, pharmacology, and agriculture. January 27: threefold meeting: ' We must first of all, with the money we have, found free schools that can bring people what they need.' February: first public eurythmy performance in Zurich. Also: 'Appeal to the German People' (CW 24), circulated March 6 as a newspaper insert. In April, *Towards Social Renewal* (CW 23) appears— 'perhaps the most widely read of all books on politics appearing since the war.' Rudolf Steiner is asked to undertake the 'direction and leadership' of the school founded by the Waldorf-Astoria Company. Rudolf Steiner begins to talk about the 'renewal' of education. May 30: a building is selected and purchased for the future Waldorf School. August–September, Rudolf Steiner gives a lecture course for Waldorf teachers, *The Foundations of Human Experience (Study of Man)* (CW 293). September 7: Opening of the first Waldorf School. December (into January): first science course, the *Light Course* (CW 320).

1920: The Waldorf School flourishes. New threefold initiatives. Founding of limited companies *Der Kommende Tag* and *Futurum A.G.* to infuse spiritual values into the economic realm. Rudolf Steiner also focuses on the sciences. Lectures: *Introducing Anthroposophical Medicine* (CW 312); *The Warmth Course* (CW 321); *The Boundaries of Natural Science* (CW 322); *The Redemption of Thinking* (CW 74). February: Johannes Werner

Klein—later a co-founder of the Christian Community—asks Rudolf Steiner about the possibility of a 'religious renewal,' a 'Johannine church.' In March, Rudolf Steiner gives the first course for doctors and medical students. In April, a divinity student asks Rudolf Steiner a second time about the possibility of religious renewal. September 27–October 16: anthroposophical 'university course.' December: lectures titled *The Search for the New Isis* (CW 202).

1921: Rudolf Steiner continues his intensive work on cultural renewal, including the uphill battle for the threefold social order. 'University' arts, scientific, theological, and medical courses include: *The Astronomy Course* (CW 323); *Observation, Mathematics, and Scientific Experiment* (CW 324); the *Second Medical Course* (CW 313); *Colour*. In June and September–October, Rudolf Steiner also gives the first two 'priests' courses' (CW 342 and 343). The 'youth movement' gains momentum. Magazines are founded: *Die Drei* (January), and—under the editorship of Albert Steffen (1884–1963)—the weekly, *Das Goetheanum* (August). In February–March, Rudolf Steiner takes his first trip outside Germany since the war (Holland). On April 7, Steiner receives a letter regarding 'religious renewal,' and May 22–23, he agrees to address the question in a practical way. In June, the Klinical-Therapeutic Institute opens in Arlesheim under the direction of Dr. Ita Wegman. In August, the Chemical-Pharmaceutical Laboratory opens in Arlesheim (Oskar Schmiedel and Ita Wegman are directors). The Clinical Therapeutic Institute is inaugurated in Stuttgart (Dr. Ludwig Noll is director); also the Research Laboratory in Dornach (Ehrenfried Pfeiffer and Günther Wachsmuth are directors). In November–December, Rudolf Steiner visits Norway.

1922: The first half of the year involves very active public lecturing (thousands attend); in the second half, Rudolf Steiner begins to withdraw and turn toward the Society—'The Society is asleep.' It is 'too weak' to do what is asked of it. The businesses—*Der Kommende Tag* and *Futurum A.G.*—fail. In January, with the help of an agent, Steiner undertakes a twelve-city German lecture tour, accompanied by eurythmy performances. In two weeks he speaks to more than 2,000 people. In April, he gives a 'university course' in The Hague. He also visits England. In June, he is in Vienna for the East–West Congress. In August–September, he is back in England for the Oxford Conference on Education. Returning to Dornach, he gives the lectures *Philosophy, Cosmology, and Religion* (CW 215), and gives the third priests' course (CW 344). On September 16, The Christian Community is founded. In October–November, Steiner is in Holland and England. He also speaks to the youth: *The Youth Course* (CW 217). In December, Steiner gives lectures titled *The Origins of Natural Science* (CW 326), and *Humanity and the World of Stars: The Spiritual Communion of Humanity* (CW 219). December 31: Fire at the Goetheanum, which is destroyed.

1923: Despite the fire, Rudolf Steiner continues his work unabated. A very hard year. Internal dispersion, dissension, and apathy abound. There is conflict—between old and new visions—within the Society. A wake-up call is needed, and Rudolf Steiner responds with renewed lecturing vitality. His focus: the spiritual context of human life; initiation science; the course of the year; and community building. As a foundation for an artistic school, he creates a series of pastel sketches. Lecture cycles: *The Anthroposophical Movement; Initiation Science* (CW 227) (in England at the Penmaenmawr Summer School); *The Four Seasons and the Archangels* (CW 229); *Harmony of the Creative Word* (CW 230); *The Supersensible Human* (CW 231), given in Holland for the founding of the Dutch society. On November 10, in response to the failed Hitler-Ludendorff putsch in Munich, Steiner closes his Berlin residence and moves the *Philosophisch-Anthroposophisch Verlag* (Press) to Dornach. On December 9, Steiner begins the serialization of his *Autobiography: The Course of My Life* (CW 28) in *Das Goetheanum*. It will continue to appear weekly, without a break, until his death. Late December–early January: Rudolf Steiner refounds the Anthroposophical Society (about 12,000 members internationally) and takes over its leadership. The new board members are: Marie Steiner, Ita Wegman, Albert Steffen, Elisabeth Vreede, and Günther Wachsmuth. (See *The Christmas Meeting for the Founding of the General Anthroposophical Society*, CW 260). Accompanying lectures: *Mystery Knowledge and Mystery Centres* (CW 232); *World History in the Light of Anthroposophy* (CW 233). December 25: the Foundation Stone is laid (in the hearts of members) in the form of the 'Foundation Stone Meditation.'

1924: January 1: having founded the Anthroposophical Society and taken over its leadership, Rudolf Steiner has the task of 'reforming' it. The process begins with a weekly newssheet ('What's Happening in the Anthroposophical Society') in which Rudolf Steiner's 'Letters to Members' and 'Anthroposophical Leading Thoughts' appear (CW 26). The next step is the creation of a new esoteric class, the 'first class' of the 'University of Spiritual Science' (which was to have been followed, had Rudolf Steiner lived longer, by two more advanced classes). Then comes a new language for Anthroposophy—practical, phenomenological, and direct; and Rudolf Steiner creates the model for the second Goetheanum. He begins the series of extensive 'karma' lectures (CW 235–40); and finally, responding to needs, he creates two new initiatives: biodynamic agriculture and curative education. After the middle of the year, rumours begin to circulate regarding Steiner's health. Lectures: January–February, *Anthroposophy* (CW 234); February: *Tone Eurythmy* (CW 278); June: *The Agriculture Course* (CW 327); June–July: *Speech Eurythmy* (CW 279); *Curative Education* (CW 317); August: (England, 'Second International Summer School'), *Initiation Consciousness: True and False Paths in Spiritual Investigation* (CW 243); September: *Pastoral Medicine* (CW 318). On September 26, for the first time, Rudolf Steiner cancels a lecture. On September 28, he gives his last lecture. On September 29, he withdraws to his studio in the carpenter's shop; now he is definitively ill. Cared for by Ita Wegman, he continues working, however, and writing the weekly installments of his *Autobiography* and *Letters to the Members/Leading Thoughts* (CW 26).

1925: Rudolf Steiner, while continuing to work, continues to weaken. He finishes *Extending Practical Medicine* (CW 27) with Ita Wegman.
On March 30, around ten in the morning, Rudolf Steiner dies

INDEX

Abraham, 203
Academy of Gondishapur, 237–240, 242–243, 249, 251, 254, 256, 258, 261, 263, 266
  gnostic movement, wisdom of, 239, 241
  Gondishapur impulse, 264
Adam, 76
Aeschylus, 90
Africa, 239
'age of science', 218
Ahriman, 54, 70, 74, 133, 136–138, 140–144, 160, 172–173, 175, 178, 180, 184, 188–189, 191, 193–194, 243, 249–251, 265
ahrimanic, xiv, 23, 28, 34–35, 52–54, 58, 70–71, 74–76, 79, 100, 102–103, 108–109, 122, 129, 136–138, 140–141, 143, 146, 148, 152, 155, 158, 162, 164, 167–168, 171–176, 178, 180–186, 190, 202, 204, 208, 225, 228, 234, 239, 241, 248, 251, 256, 263
  ahrimanic-science, 34
  lawful ahrimanic areas, 109
ambition, 204
America/American, 69, 156, 160, 271
anachronism/anachronistic, 33–34, 59, 62
anatomist/anatomy, 41, 77, 93, 165
Anaxagoras, 186, 237

Ancient of Days, 128
animal world, 37, 40, 43–44, 46, 70, 150, 153, 165–166, 179, 202, 212, 222–223, 229
angel. *See Hierarchies (beings), 9th, Angeloi*
anthropomorphizing, 50
anthropologist/anthropology, 69, 207, 218
anthroposophical/anthroposophy, xiv–xv, 4, 10, 22, 26, 28, 32–34, 39, 48, 53, 55, 62, 64, 68, 72–74, 77, 79–80, 82, 84, 89, 91–93, 97, 106, 110–111, 113, 119–120, 126, 151–155, 158–159, 162–165, 168, 172, 193, 204, 207, 216, 218, 231, 241, 248, 261, 265, 267
  anthroposophical movement, 118–119, 156
  Anthroposophical Society, xiv
  Christology, 270
antipathy, 59, 67
aperçu, 18
aphorism/aphoristic, 62, 66, 69, 81
Apollo, 29, 49
Apollonius of Tyana, 266
Arab/Arabic, 237–238, 240–241, 243
  philosophers, 240
archai. *See Hierarchies (beings), 7th, Archai*
arche spirit, 39
as Powers, 173

as Prime Origins, 173–174
as spirits of age, 21–22, 38
archangel. *See Hierarchies (beings), 8th, Archangeloi*
Aristotle, 126–127, 237–238
arrogance/arrogant, 110, 218–219, 228
art/artistic, 120, 236
　Greek, 168
　paintings, 240
astral body, xiv, 20-21, 23–24, 26, 37-38, 41-43, 46, 49, 92–93, 164-165, 167, 208
atavistic. *See clairvoyant, atavistic*
Atlantean/Atlantis, 88, 122, 183–184, 225
Augustine of Hippo, 2–6, 11–12, 15, 17, 20, 33, 37, 72, 142, 192, 244–245, 255
Augustinian era, 260–261
Augustus, Emperor, 190, 256–259, 262, 266
Averroes, 241
awareness, conscious, 6, 9–10, 20, 22–26, 30, 32, 37–40, 53, 59, 73, 82–83, 85, 107, 110, 122, 123, 126, 135, 165, 167, 176, 179, 217, 223–224, 232–233, 250, 256
　awareness of the gods, 258
　Christian awareness, 198
　hyperconscious awareness, 169, 171, 177
　self-awareness, 224

Bacon, Francis, 240
　as Baron of Verulam, 240
Bacon, Roger, 240
Bahr, Hermann, 262–263
balance, 74, 88–89, 100, 102, 131, 138, 141–143, 159, 171, 176, 179–180, 183–186, 190, 194, 204, 210, 228, 230, 233, 253–254
　balancing beam, 102–104, 171, 228, 253
　pivoting point, 253–254
　beast kept in balance, 231
　counterbalance, 60, 180, 228, 233
Bentham/Benthamism, 35–36, 45–46, 53
　his thesis as 'devilish', 35, 45
bias, 142
　lack of, 269
Bible, Holy, 96, 214
biography, 113, 246
biology, 14
blandishments, 268
blasphemous/blasphemy, 198, 204, 212
blessedness, 112
blood
　flesh and blood, 24–27
　related by blood, 175
body, soul, spirit, 65
Boehme, Jakob, 16
　Philosophy of Mythology, 16
　Philosophy of Revelation, 16
botanist/botany, 218
brain, 85, 137, 260
Buddha, 7–8
　his turning away from the corpse, 7–8

Cabeiri, 16
calculus, 57
cancer/cancerous, 155–157
　social cancer, 155–156
Capesius (mystery plays), 104
capital, 158
Catholic, 114, 262, 265–267
　Catholicism, 17, 261–263, 266
　Church, Roman Catholic, 14–15, 17, 74, 113, 159–160, 218, 260–261, 266–267, 269

as the Church, 14, 30, 160
  Fathers, 192, 197, 205, 214
  priests, 96
  Sacrifice of the Mass, 260–261
chaos/chaotic, 214, 225, 235, 240, 268
chemist/chemistry, 14, 168
children, 84–85, 149, 181
Christ, 7–8, 10, 14–15, 17, 25, 62, 127, 162, 188, 191–193, 196–197, 199, 205, 210, 212–214, 230–231, 234–236, 239–241, 243, 254–255, 265–266, 269–270
  Christ impulse, 17, 187, 191–192, 194, 239, 244, 266
  'Christ in me', 26
  Christ mystery, 183, 193
  contemporaries of, 191–193, 196, 212–213
  His crucifixion, 199, 213
  His ether body, 262
  as healer, 212
  as physician of humanity, 212
  His sacrificed death; resurrection, 197
    as saviour, 212
  His second coming, 261
  as Son (of God), 125, 199–200, 213
  as Son of Sun, 10
  His world destiny, 188, 191
Christ-Lucifer-Ahriman (wood carving), 265–266. *See also Representative of Man*
Christ-Yahweh impulse, 182
Christian/Christianity, 12, 14–15, 17–18, 30–32, 48, 55, 162, 192, 196–199, 213, 237, 239–240, 249, 254–255, 257–258, 266–267, 269–270

Christian era, 2, 24, 95, 237
  post-Christian, 2, 9–10, 24
  pre-Christian, 2, 7, 9–10, 25, 33–34, 49, 62, 121
clairvoyance/clairvoyant, 30
  atavistic, 2, 6–7, 10, 28, 109, 196, 209, 224, 257
clarity, 125
Clement of Alexandria, 196
clinic, as an altar, 263
'come to know yourself', 186
common sense, objective, 69, 197, 200, 210–211, 213
  cosmic, 74
community, human, 110
Comte, Auguste/Comteanism, 12–19, 32–36, 38, 64, 79
  his trinity, 36
confusion, 267
conscience, 250
conscientiousness, 250
consciousness, 165
conservation (of matter and energy), 71
contemplate, 60–61
Copernicus, 266–267
courage/courageous, 5, 112, 198, 242–243, 246, 251, 263
cosmic/cosmos, 10, 42, 53, 68–71, 73–74, 77–78, 82, 84–86, 89, 93, 101–104, 112–113, 124, 132–133, 135–139, 143–144, 148–150, 172–173, 230
  intelligence, 124
  movement, 167
  principle, 69–71
  rationality, 69
  sentience, 138–140
  will, 167
  wisdom, 167
cosmologically/cosmology, 8–10, 59, 101, 103

cowardice, 242
creationism, uncorrupted, 115
cross, 8, 255, 271
crystalline/crystallize, 149–151
cube, 149

Darwin/Darwinism, 63, 265
   his theory of evolution, 223
dead human bodies, 150–151
deception/deceptive, 58
delusion, 3, 23–26, 29, 33, 54–56, 130
   life-delusion, 26, 29
demon/devil, 159, 193, 198–199, 208, 213–214, 219
   demonic/demonology, 12, 14–15, 28, 200
Demosthenes, 259, 268
dentition, second (teeth), 84–85, 105, 130–131
Descartes, 4–6, 244–245
destiny, 188, 191, 234, 236
devotion, 88, 212
dialectics, 67, 94
dichotomy, 66
differentiated/differentiation, 80
Diocletian (Great) persecution, 266
Dionysius the Areopagite, 30
disciples, 10, 236
discordant creatures, as, 107
diseases, 247
dogma, 4, 18, 66, 160, 193, 197
dream/dreamer, 27–28, 135, 172
dualism/dualistic, 1–2, 62–63, 66–67, 75–76, 79, 97, 107, 115–117, 128
duality, 26, 97

ears, 3, 28, 139, 249
Eckhart, Meister, 95
economic, 156–157
   economy, world, 151
egotistical, 140, 230, 250

Egypt/Egyptian, 30, 50, 52, 56, 257
   ancient, 30, 51
Egypto-Chaldean, 39, 48–51, 56, 59, 256
   ancient, 208
Eighth Ecumenical Council, Constantinople (869), 65–66, 193, 229
eighth sphere (stage), 47, 52, 58
electricity, 26, 70, 150–152, 164
elemental
   realms (3), 43
   spirits, 13, 63
emanation/emanationism, 114–115
embryology, 77
English (British), 31, 35–36, 45, 57, 160, 201, 239
enthusiasm, xiv, 155
epistemology, 116
equilibrium, 179–180, 182, 194, 230, 253
eternal/eternity, 106–108, 110, 112–116, 121, 129, 132–137, 142, 175–177, 180
etheric body, 20, 23–24, 26, 38–39, 41–43, 46–48, 92–93, 164–165, 167, 208
   as body of creative powers, 164, 167
ethnology, 201
Eucken, 64
Europe, Southern, 254, 256
eurythmy, xiii–xiv
evil, 2, 35–36, 45–46, 67, 76, 171, 204, 212
ex cathedra, 160
eyes, 3, 28, 249

faith, 89
   Christian faith, 198
Fall (from Paradise), 76
fantasies/fantasist, 11, 78, 139,

169–171, 176, 188, 207, 227, 233, 238
fatalism/fatalistic, 1, 62–63, 66–67
Father Rhine, 246–247
feel/feeling, 3–4, 6, 11, 17, 22, 24, 27, 38, 45, 54, 72, 99–100, 105, 119, 123–124, 127, 130–132, 139, 144, 154, 165, 188, 203, 219, 243, 250, 257, 261
Feuerbach, 38
Fichte, Johann Gottlieb, 16
fixed point, 12, 15
form, creating, 209
foundation, 64
free/freedom, 11, 22, 26, 67, 97, 269
Freemasonry. See *Masonry*
French, 36, 239

Galileo, 14, 267
genius, 227–228, 234, 241
geology, 43
geometry, 121, 149
　three-dimensions, 121–122
German/Germany, xv, 31–32, 36, 201, 204
ghosts, 219–225, 229, 241–243, 248–249, 251
gnosis/gnostic, 114, 127, 239
God, 76, 94, 126, 198–199, 204, 208, 267
　as deity, 208
　as Father, 125
　as godhead, 257, 263
　godliness, 142
　as 'space', 126
Goethe, 112–113, 122, 203
　Faust, 122, 193
　Faust II
　　Classical Walpurgis Night, xiv
　his philosophy of life, xiv, 165, 167, 202–203
　his theory of evolution, 223

Goethean/Goetheanism, 36, 77–78, 151, 169, 173
Goetheanum, 1st, xiii, 118–119, 214
　foundation stone laying, xiv, 118, 120
Golgotha, 7, 30
　cross on, 271
　event on, 217–218, 233–235, 238
Gondishapur. See *Academy of Gondishapur*
good will, 111
Gospels, 159, 189, 192, 196, 199, 230
gravity, 173–174
'greatest happiness principle', 35
Greco-Roman, 47, 50, 217, 226, 236, 253
Greek, 29, 50, 185–186, 190, 197, 203, 236–237, 257, 259, 268
　ancient, 121
　art, 185
　philosopher/philosophy, 62, 186, 203, 237, 254
　plays, 90
　wisdom, 185, 254
Greenland, 69
group sculpture. See *Representative of Man*
Guardian of the Threshold, 138

Haeckel, 243, 265
hallucination, 65–66, 75–76, 78–79, 95, 104
harmonious/harmony, 14, 112, 116, 123, 152, 232, 249, 257
Harnack, 211
hate/hatred, 68–71, 75, 144, 162
　cosmic hatred, 68, 70–71, 75
head (human), 77–78, 81, 84, 86, 101, 140, 146–148, 161
healed/healing, 157
　healing power, 80, 250
heart, 77

Hebbel, 127
Hebrew, 9, 79
Hegel/Hegelian, 94
Heraclitus, 186, 237
hereditary/heredity, 180, 201–205, 209–212
heresy, 65
Hierarchies (beings), 28–30, 38, 40–41, 43, 47, 51, 70, 105–116, 127, 133, 166, 176, 183, 208
  as creators, 43
  as gods, 28–32, 122, 132, 178, 186–187, 190, 220, 226–227, 257
  as spirits, 29, 38, 47, 49, 51, 55, 60, 100, 102–103, 105, 109, 113–114, 135–137, 160, 165, 176, 185, 208–209, 230, 233, 235, 241, 261
  as powers, 238
  I (Spirits of Strength), 40, 42, 47
  II (Spirits of Light), 39–42, 47
  III (Spirits of Soul), 21–22, 25–26, 29–30, 39–42, 46, 49, 60
  1st, Seraphim (Spirits of Universal Love), 39
  2nd, Cherubim (Spirits of Harmony), 39
  3rd, Thrones (Spirits of Will), 39, 167
  4th, Kyriotetes (Spirits of Wisdom), 39, 41, 167, 176
  5th, Dynameis (Spirits of Movement), 39, 41, 167
  6th, Exusiai (Spirits of Form), 39, 41, 166, 173–176, 209
  7th, Archai (Spirits of Personality), 21–22, 30, 37–38, 40, 49–51, 56, 173–174
  8th, Archangeloi (Spirits of Fire), 21–22, 25, 30–31, 37–38, 40, 49–52, 55–56, 173

  9th, Angeloi (Spirits of Life), xiv, 21–22, 25, 30–31, 37–38, 40, 49–52, 56, 137, 173
historical life (of humanity), 40–42, 49–51, 60, 169, 172
Holy Spirit, 125
Homer, 90–91
homunculi/homunculus, 224, 242
human social order. *See threefold social order (human)*
hyperconscious awareness, 169, 171, 177
hypnotic state, 257

I (ego), 20–24, 26, 37–38, 41, 43, 46, 49, 92–93, 149, 165–166, 209
  abstract I, 21
'I am with you always, to the end of the world', 263
ideal, 26–28, 37, 131, 147
  idealism/ideality, 1, 17, 34, 36, 62, 93, 145, 147–148
  idealistic, 160
ignominious, 199
illusion, 24–25, 28, 33, 45, 54–55, 58, 64–66, 68–70, 74, 78–80, 103–104, 108, 167, 177–178, 247, 251
  illusionary, 66, 79
  illusory, 66–67, 76–78, 83, 107, 112
  life-illusion, 25, 33
  as non-truth, 251
image, 20, 22–24, 26, 30, 63, 73, 78–79, 93, 101, 106, 123, 125, 128, 133–134, 144, 159, 165, 174, 177, 180, 223, 243, 245–246, 251
  man as absolute image of the Deity, 108
  mirror-image, 20, 22, 26, 178
  nature image, 161

shadow image, 79
imagination/imaginative, 77, 92, 220, 223, 239
Imagination (stage), 78
immaculate conception, 210–211
immortality, 205–206, 212, 251
impressions, 2
India/Indian philosophy, 64
individual, 1, 11–12, 21–22, 24, 38, 40, 44, 46–47, 49, 73, 80, 83–84, 89, 187–188, 190, 241, 255
   individuality, 187, 241
   individualization, 68–70
infallibility, 161
   papal infallibility, 161
infinity to infinity, 123
initiate/initiation, 1, 7, 10, 101, 107–111, 113, 130, 133, 138–140, 148, 160, 186, 190, 214, 257–258
   Anglo-American, 161
   Christian, 10
   Hebrew, 9
   initiation knowledge, 112
   initiation science, 113, 130, 138–139, 195–196, 206, 211
inspiration/inspire, 21, 73, 92, 192–193, 196, 212–213, 229
Inspiration (stage), 78
intellect, modern, 69, 72–76, 90, 92, 205–206
   as a blinding light, 79
   as a powerful light, 74
intellectual/intellectuality, 74, 78, 85, 91–92, 94, 104, 169, 215
intelligence/intelligent, xiv, 57, 94, 124, 137, 140, 175, 191, 200, 219, 259–260
   cosmic intelligence, 86
intuiting/intuition, 21, 73, 92, 222

Intuition (stage), 78
Isaac, 203
Islam, 239, 254
isolated individual, after death, 109
Italian/Italy, 69, 113

Jacob, 203
James, 192
James, epistle of, 230
   said to be apocryphal, 230
Jesuit, 159, 162, 193, 213–214, 268–271
Jesus of Nazareth, 10
Job, Book of, 75–76
joy, 168
judgement, 165, 172, 200
Julian the Apostate, 14, 187–188, 254
Julio-Claudian Dynasty, 190
Jupiter (stage), 44, 143, 150, 191, 230
   as plant realm, 44
justice, 97
justification, 6
Justinian, Emperor, 237, 254, 260

Kant/Kantianism, 55, 116, 207
Kant-Laplace theory, 92–93, 207
karma, 154
Kautsky, 90
knowledge, 4, 53, 72, 80, 107–111, 114, 116, 138–139, 142, 159, 170–171, 187, 196, 201, 213, 216, 222, 230, 235, 237–238, 240, 242–243, 246, 251, 256
   ancient, 237
   ghostly knowledge of nature, 242, 248, 250–251
   immature knowledge, 235
   mystery knowledge, 8
   'self-knowledge', 76, 131, 168, 175, 191

Krug, Wilhelm Traugott, 94

labour, 57–58
language, 69–70, 86, 101
  Arabic, 237–238
  Greek, 238
  Latin, 197
  Syrian, 237–238
larynx, 139
League of Nations, 271
Leibniz, 57, 142, 175
Lemurian, 150, 183, 225
Leo XIII, Pope, 270
Leonardo da Vinci, 236
  Last Supper, 236
Liebmann, 64
Life Spirit, 230, 235, 238, 241, 258
light, 2–3, 8–9, 106, 116, 150, 188, 233, 260
  light side, 80
  light signals, 55
  light of sun, 9
logic/logical, 69, 84, 142, 207
love, 89, 111–112, 144, 159, 170, 268
  loving, 75, 112
Lucifer, 70, 95, 138, 140–144, 172, 177–178, 184, 186, 188–189, 191, 193–194, 206, 212, 214, 243, 246, 250–251, 265
  as God, 178
luciferic, xiv, 53, 70–71, 74–76, 79, 103, 129, 133, 136–137, 140–141, 143, 146–148, 152, 155, 161–162, 164, 167–173, 175–186, 189–191, 202, 204, 206, 208, 225, 234

macrocosm, 7–8, 40, 149
magnetism, 26, 70, 78, 151–152, 164

Manichaeism, 2, 255
manifoldness, 142
Marx, Karl/Marxism, 53–54, 56–58, 94
Masonry, 260
  occult type, 161
materialism/materialistic, 1–2, 5, 16, 38–39, 58, 60, 64, 116, 132–133, 138, 145–148, 155, 160–162, 223, 228, 249
  mathematical, 14
maximation of happiness, 45
maya, 45, 55–56, 64, 103, 108, 116–117, 128, 132–135, 138–139, 141, 145, 153, 230, 241, 247, 251
medicine, spiritual, 247
meditation, 54
mediums, 160
memory, 29–30, 73, 75, 177
  of cosmic past, 73, 93
Meray, C. H.
  World Mutation, 156
metamorphosis. *See transformation*
metaphysical/metaphysics, 13–15, 18–19, 31–32, 60
Michaelic order, 160
microcosm, 40, 149
mineral/mineralization, 139, 150
mineral world, 37, 40, 43–44, 46, 70, 139, 148–149, 165
  as fourth realm, 43
Minerva, 49
misfortune, coming from sin, 76
misunderstanding, 267–268
monads, 141–142
monism/monistic, 116, 141–142, 145, 148, 156, 241
monotheism, 128
monster, being born as one, 109
Montaigne, 142
Moon (old), 8, 10, 41, 43, 135–136, 143, 148, 173, 230

Moon, sphere, 8–10, 188
moral/morally, 26, 62, 67–68, 89, 162, 172, 180–181, 204–205, 212, 224, 270
Moses, 75–76
Moses, (Jewish) book of, 76
Muellner, Prof., 267
Muenchhausen, von, Boerries, 262–263
Muhammed, 239
mysteries, 1, 7–9
　mystery truths, 1, 7
　old mysteries, 8–10
Mystery of Death, 12
Mystery on Golgotha, 7–8, 10, 12, 16, 24–25, 28–30, 47, 50, 109, 159, 183, 185–192, 195–196, 199–200, 203, 205, 207, 209–212, 218–219, 225–226, 228–230, 241, 252–257, 261–264, 266, 268–269
mystic/mysticism, 34, 36, 48, 82–83, 95–97, 120, 142, 164, 178
mythological/mythology, 49–50

Napoleon, 14
native Americans, 69
nature, 8–9, 63–66, 68, 77–79, 151–153, 155, 178, 187, 202–203, 207, 215, 220, 222, 225, 241–243, 248–249, 251
　natural order, 37, 64, 71, 77, 206, 211
　rhythms of nature, 249
Neo-Persian Empire, 254
Nero, 266
New Testament, 230
Newton, 14, 57
Nietzsche, 186
non-spatial-sphere, 174–176
'Not I but Christ in me', 26, 231

nothingness, 28
Novalis, 262

observation, 18, 84, 91, 120, 123, 126, 149, 180
Occident, 114, 225
octahedron, 149
Old Testament, 75
orders
　bodily, 29
　divine, 28–29, 33–34
　humanity's, 29, 33
　ideal, 26–28
　natural, 26–28, 34–35
　social, 32, 34
　theocratic, 32
oriental populations, 95
Origen, 196
'original sin', 204, 212
　as 'hereditary sin' (in German), 204
Osiris, 59
Ostwald, 243

pacifism, 59
pain, 32, 168
Palestine, 255, 264
papal infallibility, 161
paradise, 204
passion, 197
passionate, 222, 240
Paul, Jean, 85
Paul (St), 26
Pentateuch (5 books of Moses), 75
perceive/perceptible, 99–100, 110, 134, 155, 163, 188, 202, 213, 225, 250
Persia
　age, 127
　ancient, 257
personality, 256
perspective, 54, 56, 77, 105–106, 114
Peter (St), 172, 192

philologists, 69
philosophical/philosophy, 1–2, 12,
    15, 35–36, 53, 55, 60,
    64–66, 72, 78–79, 83, 94,
    114–116, 121, 126, 190,
    206, 216, 220–222, 237,
    242–243, 245, 248
  creationistic, 114
  Greek, 62
  Indian, 64
  philosophers of paganism, 206
  positive, 14
  Roman Catholic, 267
  utilitarian, 35
philosophy of life, 2–5, 7–9, 12, 14,
    16–18, 28, 34, 36, 52–55,
    59–60, 62, 67, 75, 80, 83,
    89, 112–116, 145, 160,
    187, 204–206, 211, 238,
    255, 271
  a corrupted one, 206, 208, 212
  Karl Marx's, 53
  philosophy of emanation, 114
  western, 2–3
physicist/physics, 14, 27, 55, 77
physiologist/physiology, 41, 77, 165
piety/pious, 219
plant (vegetable) world, 37, 40,
    43–46, 70, 165, 179, 202
  plant set, 74
Plato, 126–127, 237
  his Dialogues, 127
  his philosophy, 186
pneumatological/pneumatology,
    80–81
poetry, 188
polarity, xiv, 2
  eternal, 2
  false, 193
  polar opposite, 149–152, 159,
    185, 194, 204, 224
politics (threefold), 81, 110, 216
positivism/positivist, 36, 64

positivist church, 14
positivist science, 13–15, 18–19,
    32
Post-Atlantean Cultural Eras (7),
    120, 183
  1st Ancient Indian, 220
  2nd Ancient Persian, 6, 126, 220
  3rd Egypto-Babylonian-Chaldean,
    6, 22, 25, 39, 48–51, 56
  4th Graeco-Roman, 1–2, 6-7, 12,
    15, 22, 47, 50–51, 226, 228,
    230, 253, 261
  5th Present, 2, 4, 6, 10, 12, 15, 22,
    47, 50, 183–185, 217, 233
  6th Slavic, 230
precipitate movement, 143
prejudice, 17, 65–66, 112, 163–164,
    181, 220
Protestant/Protestantism, 210, 262
Psalms, 90
psyche, 251
psychoanalysis/psychoanalyst, 225
psychological/psychology, 68

rabbinical theology, 205
rainbow, 248–249
Ranke, 60
Rascher, Max, 156
rational (intellectual/mind) soul, 217,
    226–227, 229–230,
    256–259
  age of, 226
rationality, 85
  cosmic rationality, 85
  cosmic sense as rationality, 85
realism, 17, 36, 145
reality, 5–6, 10–11, 18, 20, 28, 32,
    34, 40, 46, 51–56, 58,
    65–68, 70, 75, 77, 82–83,
    93, 96, 99–100, 103, 104,
    107–109, 115–116,
    129–130, 133–134, 139,
    145, 147–148, 155–156,

158–159, 162, 167,
169–170, 180, 182,
188–189, 205, 208, 214,
223–224, 226, 234, 239,
242–245, 248–249, 251,
257
  psychological, 68
  realization, xiv, 28, 68, 174
  sense perception, 12
  spiritual, 55, 59
  unreality, 6, 11, 60
reason, 6, 57, 66, 118, 214
reflection, 134
  reflective state, 102, 105
relationship, human, 110
religious community (threefold), 81, 110
Representative of Mankind, xiii, 143–144, 243
resignation, 94
resurrection, 210–211
retrograde movement, 143
Revelation, Book of, 231, 235
rhetoric, 259–260, 264, 268–271
rhythm/rhythmic, 249–250
rites/rituals, 262–264, 270
  ancient, 258–260, 268
  ritualism grown invalid, 270
Rome/Roman, 31, 47, 160–162, 186, 189–190, 193, 197–199, 236, 253, 255–259, 262, 264, 266, 268–271
  ancient rites, 258-260
  Romanism, 15, 266, 270
  toga, 259
Romantics, 262–263
Russian, 201

sacramental/sacramentally, 262–263, 267–268
  Roman, 269
  sacramentalism, 265, 270
Saint Gotthard Tunnel, 57

Saint-Simon, de, Henri, 12–13, 15, 18, 32, 34–36
salt, 149
Samothrace, gods of, 16
Saturn (old), 41, 43, 93, 106, 135–136, 143, 148, 173, 230
Scheler, 262–263
Schelling, 15–17
Schopenhauer, 64
sculptured group. *See Representative of Mankind*
seed, 11, 71–72, 78–79, 115, 153–154
  seed-like, 75
selfless, 250
Semitic, 185, 203
senses/sensory perception, 2–3, 5, 12–13, 25, 27–28, 31–32, 34, 49–50, 60, 99, 101, 103–104, 106, 108, 121, 123, 130, 147, 153, 165, 168, 178, 188–189, 194, 201–208, 210–211, 215, 232, 234, 239, 244–245, 247, 249, 264
sentience/sentient, 32, 88–89, 121–126, 128–29, 138–140, 143, 163, 187–188, 190, 197–198, 255, 257, 259, 262, 267
sentient soul, 256–259, 261
sentiment, 219
seven-year periods, 86–87, 113, 130
sexual maturity, 84–87, 105, 128, 131
shooting, sprouting, life forms, 7, 9
similarity, 180–181
sin, 76
  sinning against life, 109
skeleton, 140
skepticism, 2–3
sleep, 5–6, 10, 20–23, 37–40, 46,

72, 108, 134, 165, 267, 270–271
social, moral, political, 270
socialism/socialist, 33, 57, 80–81, 90, 205, 209
Socrates, 237
Sorat, 226, 230
  as beast, 226
    as beast of 666, 229, 231
  as dragon, 226
  as serpent, 226
sorrow, 168
sovereign, 201
space, concept of, 121, 125–126, 128, 133, 174, 178
  divine in space, 125
  God is 'space', 126
  threefold (trinity), 123–125
Spain/Spanish, 69, 239
spectral/spectres, 136, 220, 242, 248–249, 251
  Romanism, 270
speech, 74
Spirit. *See Holy Spirit*
Spirit Man, 230, 235, 238, 241, 258
Spirit Self, 158, 230, 235, 238, 241, 258
Spirits of the Age, 215
Spirits of Form. *See Hierarchies (beings), 6th, Exusiai*
  sometimes disguises as Prime Origins, 174
Spirits of Wisdom. *See Hierarchies (beings), 4th, Kyriotetes*
spiritual (consciousness) soul, 217–219, 224, 226–227, 229–231, 233, 238, 241, 244, 251, 256, 258–260, 263–264, 268
  age, 217–218, 220, 222–224, 229–232, 253
spiritual science. *See anthroposophical/anthroposophy*

spiritualism/spiritualist, 36, 45, 159
spirituality/spiritualized, 7, 35–36, 45–46, 116, 143, 147–148, 162, 188, 241, 262, 270
Strader (mystery play), 104
Steiner, Rudolf
  Anthroposophy and the Social Question, 155
  The Case for Anthroposophy, 244
  Christianity as Mystical Fact, 189, 196
  The Education of the Child, 84, 131
  'Fifth Gospel', 211
  Goethe's Conception, xiii
  Goethe's Philosophy of Life, xiii
  Goethe's Standard of the Soul, 144
  Human Evolution, xiii
  The Inner Nature of Man and Our Life, 152
  Knowledge of the Higher Worlds, xiii, 78
  his Mystery Plays, 104
  Occult Science, An Outline, 8–9, 41, 43, 70, 92, 106, 135, 148, 165, 204, 246
  Philosophy of Spiritual Activity, xiii, 117
  The Portal of Initiation (mystery play), 133, 261
  Riddles of Man, 5, 16
  Riddles of Philosophy, xiii
  Road to Self-Knowledge, xiii
  The Spiritual Guidance of the Individual and Humanity, 85
  Theosophy, xiii, 92
  Threshold of the Spiritual World, xiii
  Truth and Science, 117
  Twelve Moods, xiv
subconscious, 83–84, 91, 93, 111, 132, 165, 167, 171–173, 184–185, 201, 267
subjective principle, 7
suffering, 7, 45

Sun (old), 41, 43, 106, 135–136, 143, 148, 173, 230
Sun, sphere, 9–10, 188
superconscious, 138
supersensible, 2–3, 43, 49, 53, 60, 104, 109–110, 114, 159, 180, 189, 193, 195–196, 198, 200, 205–207, 209–215, 223, 229, 232, 236, 239, 244–246, 251, 262, 270
superstition, 70–71
sympathies/sympathy, 59, 67, 146, 159
Syria/Syrian, 237–238, 254

Tacitus, 189
Tauler, 95
temperament, 197, 231
temptation, 239
Tertullian, 196–200, 212–214, 219
De carne Christi, 200
Thales, 186
theocratic/theocracy, 30–32, 60
theoretician, 64
theosophical/theosophy, 2, 16
thinking, 3, 5, 11–12, 14, 17, 30, 33, 35, 37, 45–46, 55, 64, 70, 72–75, 80, 83, 88, 93–94, 96, 99–100, 102–104, 111, 120, 128, 131–132, 137, 148, 156, 162, 165, 169, 177, 197, 202, 204, 219, 232, 237, 239–240, 242, 244, 248, 250, 253–254, 267, 269
 ahrimanic-free, 26
 Augustinian, 3
 'I think, therefore I am', 4
 inner, 244
 Oriental, 39
 spiritual, 1
 thinkable, 22

thinking, feeling, doing, 99–100, 104–105, 108, 131–134, 136, 170
thoughts, 1–2, 21–22, 24, 45–46, 53, 58, 66, 71, 80, 88, 94, 96, 99–100, 103, 111, 118, 120, 130, 133–134, 172, 215, 238, 241, 251, 269, 271
 counter, 111
 intellectual, 75
 unrealistic, 59
threefold (human social organism), xiv, 18, 80, 110
threefold god (Father, Son, Spirit), 125
 oneness of, 126
threshold, 138
time (concept of), 54–56, 58, 77, 106–108, 110, 128, 131–136, 144, 175–177
torture, 197–198
transience, region of, 115–116
transformation (metamorphosis), 77–78, 120, 146, 156, 173, 202, 211
transition-science, 71, 105–106, 110, 112–113, 128
trichotomy (body, soul, spirit), 65
trinity, 36, 79–80, 97, 125–126, 128, 144
truth, 3–7, 10–12, 14, 24, 32–34, 53–55, 58, 66, 83–84, 86, 88–89, 94–98, 100, 104, 110–111, 115–116, 134, 139, 147, 153–155, 159, 162–163, 189, 194, 196–199, 202, 210, 213–215, 232, 236, 244–247, 251
 absolute, 95
 cosmological, 10
 half-truth, 219
 mystery, 7

spiritual, 54, 159–161
supersensible, 245
truth for life, 89
untruth, 251

unconscious, 5-6, 83–84, 86–87, 91, 93, 126, 146, 179
unreality, 6
utilitarian, 35–36, 45

value to humanity, 56–58
   economic value, 57–58
velocity, 55
Venus (stage), 28, 44, 143, 191, 230
   as animal realm, 44
vision, 6, 238, 262
   apocalyptic, 79
   prophetic, 79
   volatilize, 141
Vulcan (stage), 44, 143, 191, 230
   as human realm, 44

Wahle, Richard, 221–222, 248
   On the Mechanism of Intellectual Life, 221
warmth, 188, 268
   of heart, xiv, 260
wealth, 158
Wilamowitz, 90
will, 72–73, 93–94, 100, 103–105, 111, 123–124, 133, 137, 204, 215, 217, 234, 260
   acting out of the will, 72, 93, 99, 133–134
   cosmic will, 167
   free will, 137–138
   God-willing, 198
   self-willed, 140
   will to act, 53, 73–75, 103–104, 146, 165
   will-based, 12–13
   will of the gods, 137

world will, 124
Wilson, Woodrow (US President), 59, 271
Wilsonism/Wilsonized, 271
wisdom, 2, 85, 89, 93, 96, 123–124, 153, 171, 186–187, 192–193, 196, 212, 222, 234–235, 241, 243–244, 258
   ancient, 237
   Christian wisdom, 198
   cosmic wisdom, 86, 167
   divine wisdom, 186
   gnostic wisdom of Gondishapur, 238–239, 241
   sham wisdom, 214
   Venus wisdom, 192
   wisdom of the beast, 228
   wisdom-filled, 2
   wisdom of life, 93
   wisdom of world history, 239
world order, ideal, 35
Wundt, 65

Yahweh, 9, 203
   as Moon god, 9
   as Semitic god, 203
Year 333, 51, 109–110, 192, 226, 228, 253–254, 256, 261
   as mid-point of 4th post-Atlantean cultural era, 226, 253
Year 666, 225–230, 233–234, 253–254, 256

Zarathustra, 127
Zeno the Isaurian, 237
Zeus, 29, 49
zodiac, 101
   signs of constellation positions, 102, 104, 225
zoologist/zoology, 218